THE
CULTURAL
POLITICS OF
TEL QUEL

PENN STATE STUDIES
in ROMANCE LITERATURES

Editors
Frederick A. de Armas
Alan E. Knight

Danielle Marx-Scouras

The
Cultural
Politics of
Tel Quel

Literature and the
Left in the Wake
of Engagement

The Pennsylvania State University Press
University Park, Pennsylvania

Library of Congress Cataloging-in-Publication Data

Marx-Scouras, Danielle
    The cultural politics of Tel quel / Danielle Marx-Scouras.
        p.   cm. — (Penn State studies in Romance literatures)
    Includes bibliographical references and index.
    ISBN 0-271-01574-8 (cloth : alk. paper)
    ISBN 0-271-01575-6 (paper : alk. paper)
    1. Tel quel. 2. Avant-garde (Aesthetics)—France. 3. France—
Intellectual life—20th century. I. Title. II. Series.
PN5190.T44M37   1996
054′.1—dc20   95-41285
                                                                          CIP

It is the policy of The Pennsylvania State University Press to use acid-free paper for
the first printing of all clothbound books. Publications on uncoated stock satisfy the
minimum requirements of American National Standard for Information Sciences—
Permanence of Paper for Printed Library Materials, ANSI Z39.48–1992.

For Tana and Salah

CONTENTS

Without Tel Quel, *literature and the Left would not be what they are today in France.*
—Jean-Jacques Brochier

ACKNOWLEDGMENTS

This book has been many years in the making. Too many, my family and friends would say; for them the "book" has become—as my sister Tana claims—a four-letter word! My interest in *Tel Quel* stems from an earlier study on cultural renewal and the review-form in France and Italy. I am most grateful to Leon Roudiez of Columbia University for introducing me to *Tel Quel* and for his sustained interest and encouragement over the years.

I had the pleasure of interviewing a number of Telquelians from 1978 to 1987: Philippe Sollers, Julia Kristeva, Marcelin Pleynet, Jean-Pierre Faye, Jean Thibaudeau, Tzvetan Todorov, Gérard Genette, Jean-Louis Houdebine, Guy Scarpetta, and Jacques Henric. I thank them for giving generously of their time and for being so open with me. I also thank Jacques Leenhardt for insightful conversations on the avant-garde and the Services de Presse at the Seuil publishing house for letting me consult their archives.

A number of institutions funded my travel and research. I thank the American Council of Learned Societies for a travel grant that enabled me to present a paper on *Tel Quel* at an international conference in Budapest in 1984. I was also the recipient of Mazer and Sachar faculty research grants while at Brandeis University. I am grateful to the Mazer and Sachar families for their generosity. The College of Humanities at Ohio State University was instrumental in bringing this project to a happy close. I thank former deans Michael Riley, David Frantz, and Isaac Mowoe for supporting my project by giving me time off from teaching and funds for editorial assistance.

Very special thanks go to my colleagues and graduate students in the Department of French and Italian at Ohio State University for making the last stage of this book a pleasurable one. I thank the graduate students in my *Tel Quel* seminars for their interest in the subject and for being my first *Tel Quel* audience. I am most grateful to my former graduate research assistants for their hard work, enduring patience, and continual good humor: Medha Karmarkar, Lois Niedzwiedski, and Steven Baldauf. Warm thanks go to Ruthmarie Mitsch for copyediting my manuscript with her never-flagging skill and conscientiousness. I thank Robert Cottrell for his valuable reading of an earlier draft of this manuscript. I am also deeply indebted to the late Richard Bjornson for his sustained advice and support. But above all, I wish to thank my former chair, Charles Williams, for always being there for me.

I am deeply grateful to Penn State University Press for making the realization of this book such a positive experience. Heartfelt thanks go to my editor, Philip Winsor, for his patience and kindness. I also thank Betty Waterhouse for meticulously copyediting my manuscript. I was most fortunate to have David Schalk and Alan Stoekl as readers. Their encouragement and criticism were pivotal in bringing my writing to a positive close.

A number of colleagues and friends generously gave intellectual and moral support over the years. I thank, in particular, Eric Sellin, John Erickson, Ronnie Scharfman, Evelyne Accad, Elisabeth Mudimbe-Boyi, Susan Suleiman, Dante Della Terza, Alice Jardine, Judith Mayne, and Kathleen Perry Long. For the emotional support that only lifelong friends can give, my warmest appreciation goes to Ann Sheperdson-Price and Pilar Arrizabalaga-Borda.

This book could never have been brought to fruition without the exceptional love and support of my family who certainly never want to hear of *Tel Quel* again. Words cannot begin to convey the profound gratitude I owe my parents Marie-Thérèse Jansen-Marx and Charles Nicholas Scouras, my sister Tana Scouras, my husband Salah Khellaf and my son Kyle. I am deeply indebted to Tana and Salah for listening to the never-ending saga of *Tel Quel*, reading endless versions of this manuscript, and bearing with me in my worst moments!

INTRODUCTION

In the spring of 1960—at the height of the Algerian War—an apparently insignificant event took place: a small literary magazine (*petite revue*) was launched by a group of relatively unknown writers in their mid-twenties. These included Philippe Sollers, Jean-Edern Hallier, Jean-René Huguenin, Renaud Matignon, Jacques Coudol, and Fernand de Jacquelot du Boisrouvray. What importance could the founding of a belletristic review assume at a time when the energy and resources of the French intelligentsia were engaged, for the most part, in opposing the war? Who could foresee that a modest literary venture would become "one of the most challenging and controversial enterprises in recent French intellectual history,"[1] leaving its mark on more than a quarter-century of French intellectual thought and writing? For more than two decades, *Tel Quel* succeeded in gathering under its aegis an impressive constellation of names that stand for what is most noteworthy and provocative in French intellectual thought and writing at this time:

1. Leon Roudiez, *French Fiction Today* (New Brunswick: Rutgers University Press, 1972), 341.

Roland Barthes, Georges Bataille, Hubert Damisch, Jacques Derrida, Jean-Pierre Faye, Michel Foucault, Gérard Genette, Jean-Joseph Goux, Pierre Guyotat, Jacques Henric, Jean-Louis Houdebine, Julia Kristeva, Bernard-Henri Lévy, Marcelin Pleynet, Francis Ponge, Jean Ricardou, Jacqueline Risset, Denis Roche, Maurice Roche, Guy Scarpetta, Daniel Sibony, Philippe Sollers, Jean Thibaudeau, Tzvetan Todorov.

The birth of *Tel Quel* in March 1960 should have been a negligible event for a society torn asunder by the sociopolitical chaos occasioned by war. Nonetheless, a seemingly unimportant review developed overnight into a vast and powerful intellectual enterprise that terrorized the French intellectual scene for over two decades. What diabolical powers did *Tel Quel's* founding team possess to mastermind such a powerful intellectual coup? What led to the alliance of six upper-middle-class students and compelled them to stage such an intellectual onslaught? Although they had a common outlook—the insouciance and impertinence that comes from an upper-middle-class upbringing—and a shared aspiration to achieve fame, their association would be tempestuous from the onset. After trying to agree on the direction of *Tel Quel* with Hallier and Sollers in December 1958, Huguenin confessed: "I'm now convinced that I'll never get along with Sollers. I greatly esteem and respect him; nevertheless, he is the continuation of a race that I hate, the race of the intellectual haunted by language."[2] With hostilities like these preceding the actual founding of the journal, it is a wonder that *Tel Quel* was ever launched. But nothing was going to get in the way of the *Tel Quel* conquest, least of all their mutual dislike. In a letter addressed to Sollers in June 1959, Huguenin wrote: "From the beginning, we were aware of all that separated us, but it was the privilege of our age that allowed us to get along even if we didn't agree."[3] Indeed, the arrogance of youth was their major asset. These rebellious *fils à papa* had nothing to lose and everything to gain. Sons of generals and industrialists, educated at home in prestigious *grandes écoles* and abroad at Oxford, they had acquired their haughtiness through an upper-class upbringing, elitist education, and entrepreneurial training.

Huguenin clearly viewed Sollers as an obstacle to the successful realization of their literary venture. However, were it not for Sollers, *Tel Quel* would not even have existed, for the story of *Tel Quel* actually begins with Sollers. With

---

2. Jean-René Huguenin, *Journal* (Paris: Seuil, 1964), 72. All translations in this book are my own, unless otherwise noted.

3. Huguenin, *Le Feu à sa vie* (Paris: Seuil, 1987), 170.

the exception of Sollers, *Tel Quel*'s founders were extras on the French literary stage of 1960. Unknown to literary France, these six musketeers, nevertheless, knew one another. They were childhood friends. As the best-known writer of the group, Sollers would be the catalyst that brought them all together under the Seuil roof. If the story of *Tel Quel* begins with Sollers's literary career, it also ends with him: he would be the only original founding member to survive the vicissitudes and schisms of the *Tel Quel* enterprise. Although he was behind *Tel Quel* from the first to last issue—ninety-three in all—ironically, he became the symbol of the writer who has nothing definitive about him.[4]

Launched in 1957 by another writer from Bordeaux, the progressive Catholic novelist François Mauriac, Sollers (b. Joyaux in 1936) was already a rising star at the age of twenty-one. He received the Fénéon Prize for his novelette *Le Défi* [The challenge] published in *Ecrire* 3. Under the direction of Jean Cayrol, this Seuil collection was aimed at promoting promising new writers, bringing them under the banner of the Seuil publishing house. In 1958, his novel *Une curieuse solitude* [A strange solitude] was highly praised by the Communist writer Louis Aragon and by the Academician Emile Henriot. Despite their apparent ideological divergences, Mauriac, Aragon, and Henriot converged on one point: all three were convinced that Sollers was embarking on a brilliant literary career. Their prophecy would in fact be fulfilled by Sollers, who was never to be eclipsed at the forefront of the Parisian literary scene.

The Sollersian mystique captivated Coudol and Boisrouvray, two cohorts from the *grande école* Hautes Etudes Commerciales (HEC). Like Sollers, who had attended the Ecole Supérieure des Sciences Economiques et Commerciales (ESSEC), they would abandon their careers as business executives for *Tel Quel*. Following in Sollers's footsteps, Coudol and Boisrouvray published their first literary texts in *Ecrire*. Boisrouvray's *Autre Chose* [Something else] and Coudol's *Le Paradis* were published in *Ecrire* 6 and 7 (1959) respectively. Both texts were dedicated to Sollers.

Sollers's literary success did not spare three former classmates from the Lycée Claude-Bernard in Paris: Hallier, Huguenin, and Matignon. Perennial foes, Hallier and Huguenin continued to play out their archrivalry in the *Tel Quel* venture, where their hostilities were further fueled by Sollers. Destined

4. See Roland Barthes's defense of Sollers in "Oscillation." In *Writer Sollers*, trans. Philip Thody (Minneapolis: University of Minnesota Press, 1987). Originally published as *Sollers Ecrivain* (Paris: Seuil, 1979).

to be an *énarque*, Huguenin abandoned a career in administration for the literary politics of *Tel Quel*. A former student and disciple of the surrealist Julien Gracq, Huguenin's first novel, *La Côte sauvage* [The other side of summer] (Seuil 1960), was also hailed by Mauriac and Aragon. Mauriac also contributed a preface to Huguenin's *Journal*, which was published posthumously in 1964.

Although brought together by the common cause of the launching of *Tel Quel*, the association of these enfants terribles was anything but serene. From the onset, their alliance manifested schisms inherent in intellectual rivalry. The first split among *Tel Quel*'s founding team was triggered by Huguenin's ardent support for a new romanticism. Huguenin reproached Sollers for lacking "the sense of the tragic, the taste for risk, wild extravagances, despair"; for already being, at the age of twenty-two, "a man of letters."[5] He accused his *Tel Quel* partners of being mere "technicians, specialists, as polarized at twenty-five, as definitively closed off as engineers or surgeons" (180). Huguenin was disenchanted with *Tel Quel*'s literary orientation at the hands of Sollers, whom he respected and despised at the same time. Too temperate for his tastes, Huguenin's fellow Telquelians only roused his disdain and hate. How could a new romanticism ever emerge from a group of "technicians" obsessed by language? In the preface to Huguenin's *Journal* (1964), published two years after his death (Huguenin was killed in an automobile accident at the age of twenty-six), Mauriac wrote: "In his [Huguenin's] eyes, language did not have that absolute value conferred upon it by his *Tel Quel* friends" (10).

Perpetually at odds with Sollers and Hallier, Huguenin also had no use for Coudol, whose work was esteemed by Sollers and Boisrouvray. Huguenin's continual castigations were not easily tolerated by the *Tel Quel* team, which ousted him in July 1960, only a few months after the founding of the review. A few years later, the same fate would befall Hallier, the other member of the triumvirate caught in the *Tel Quel* power struggle. Hallier, the review's managing editor, was deposed in 1963.[6] His dramatic account of his *Tel Quel* experience, which appeared in his autobiographical novel *La Cause des peuples* [The peoples' cause] (1972), is an excellent testament to the inimical association that founded *Tel Quel*. Hallier would write acrimoni-

---

5. Huguenin, *Journal*, 77.

6. A brief note ("Mise au point") in the sixteenth issue (Winter 1964) of *Tel Quel* read: "The Committee, which proceeded to the exclusion of Jean-Edern Hallier, had accepted that it be presented as a resignation" (95).

ously: "After a bitter struggle among Sollers, Huguenin, and myself, I had conquered the editorship of the literary review *Tel Quel*. We would soon reciprocally exclude one another; I too would go to the guillotine of this ingenuous Convention, happy to have been the most Montagnard of all, for it was not with a dead hand that I activated the blade."[7]

Coudol left *Tel Quel* in 1963, only subsequently to abandon the literary domain. Matignon also departed in 1963. Boisrouvray followed suit in 1966. Except for Sollers, no one from the original founding team remained after 1966. He would be the main driving force behind *Tel Quel* until 1982, when it became *L'Infini*. Although upon being excluded from *Tel Quel*, Huguenin proclaimed it "was on the road to ruin," the breakup of the founding team did not lead to the demise of *Tel Quel*. Quite the contrary. As the founding numbers left, new names appeared on the editorial committee: Jean Thibaudeau, who replaced Huguenin after two issues (1960–71), Michel Maxence (1961–63), Jean Ricardou (1962–71), Marcelin Pleynet, who became assistant managing editor (1963–82), Denis Roche (1963–73), Jean-Louis Baudry (1963–75), Jean-Pierre Faye (1963–67), Jacqueline Risset (1967–82), Pierre Rottenberg (1967–79), Julia Kristeva (1970–82), Marc Devade (1971–82). More important, *Tel Quel* did not merely outlast the exodus of its original members; it sustained its sure ascent to the apex of French letters and intellectual thought.

In *Le Pouvoir Intellectuel en France* [Teachers, writers, celebrities], Régis Debray contends that intellectual power in contemporary France has been characterized by three major cycles: the university cycle (1880–1930), the publishing cycle (1920–1960), and the media cycle (1968–).[8] Viewed within this paradigm, *Tel Quel* represents the end of a literary age initiated by *La Nouvelle Revue Française* in 1909, a period bordering on, but still this side of, the current mass-media rift (Debray 73). If we concur with Debray that the great publishing cycle has in fact been replaced by the power of the media, we can only marvel at *Tel Quel*'s endurance over the years, and, in particular, since the 1970s. Unlike other small literary magazines, ephemeral for the most part, *Tel Quel* (now *L'Infini*) has indeed endured the test of time. It has been in existence for more than a quarter of a century. Although *Tel Quel*'s success can be attributed to the brilliant enterprising spirit of

7. Jean-Edern Hallier, *La Cause des peuples* (Paris: Seuil, 1972), 126.

8. Régis Debray, *Teachers, Writers, Celebrities*, trans. David Macey (London: NLB and Verso, 1981). Originally published as *Le Pouvoir intellectuel en France* (Paris: Editions Ramsay, 1979).

Sollers and the Editions du Seuil, behind them looms the powerful force of historical circumstances. Sollers and the Seuil publishing house were successful to the degree that they were able to weather an ever-changing and often unpredictable cultural and intellectual climate, turning it to their advantage.

In 1980, Sollers declared that *Tel Quel* was on the eve of an extraordinary explosion: "I think that *Tel Quel* is now beginning. We needed a little experience of twenty-odd years. That's very little for a fundamental experience. And now we can get started."[9] The problem with *Tel Quel* was that it was always just beginning, "dangerously establishing itself in a continual relaunching."[10] In 1982, the opening editorial of a new review read: "*Tel Quel* is over. *L'Infini* is beginning."[11] For twenty-two years, *Tel Quel* created an uproar because no one could anticipate what it was going to publish; no one knew where it was going.[12] Even worse, no one could read it. In a *New Yorker* article of 30 June 1980 on intellectual life in France ("A Reporter in Europe"), Jane Kramer wrote:

> In fact, in Paris it is often considered a mark of intellect to be *illisible*. Philippe Sollers's *Tel Quel*—which is subsidized by Editions du Seuil, sells about six thousand copies, and has taken up Marx, Mao, structuralism, psycholinguistics, Freud, Saint Augustine, Solzhenitsyn, and the Free World, roughly in that order, over the past ten years—is considered the last word in Paris *discours*, the Yves Saint Laurent of thought, and not really because of the brilliant piece it will sometimes run but because so few people can understand a word in the magazine. *Tel Quel* sets a standard for obscurity. (50)

Kramer was not alone in her appraisal. On behalf of *Tel Quel*'s leading spokesperson, even the French master of obscurity, Jacques Lacan, wrote, "I won't tell you to read Philippe Sollers. He's unreadable (like me, I might add)."[13] Although Lacan and Kramer do not share the same ideological perspective on readability, as friend and foe respectively of *Tel Quel*, they

---

9. Philippe Sollers, "On n'a encore rien vu," *Tel Quel* 85 (Autumn 1980): 24.

10. Hubert Juin, "L'étonnante aventure de la revue *Tel Quel*," *Le Monde* (30 January 1981): 19.

11. Sollers, editorial, *L'Infini* 1 (Winter 1983): 3.

12. Sollers, "Le G.S.I.," *Tel Quel* 86 (Winter 1980): 10.

13. Jacques Lacan, *Le Séminaire* 20 (in *Encore*), ed. Jacques-Alain Miller (Paris: Seuil, 1975), 37.

nevertheless agree on one thing: we only read what suits us. If for so many years *Tel Quel* was merely the latest in Parisian fashion, why then did so many journalists and academics trouble their heads about a cultural enterprise apparently devoid of coherence or seriousness? They even found it necessary to add to their vocabulary the term "Parisianism"—which is used to dismiss any cultural venture or intellectual current that is "too French!" (Sollers, *Théorie des exceptions* 303).

Tel Quel's cryptic and chameleonic nature did not deter followers: just the opposite! The inability to read the journal did not prevent intellectuals the world over from talking about it unrelentingly. I recall a heated debate over *Tel Quel* that took place in the early 1970s among North American, Latin American, and European city planners, architects, and art historians in New York. At the time a naive graduate student, I asked, "But how can you understand, let alone read *Tel Quel*?" To which several people momentarily cut short the dispute to respond, with embarrassed laughter, "We can't!" And as mercurial as *Tel Quel* may have been—especially with respect to its political trajectory—the group's infidelities never discouraged journalists from *Le Monde*, Communist militants, and other politicians from incessantly criticizing *Tel Quel*'s erratic journey from its so-called apolitical beginnings to its apparently overnight affiliation with the French Communist Party or its deviation from Maoism to the United States. Even if no one admits to taking *Tel Quel*'s politics seriously, how ironic that all discussions on *Tel Quel* inevitably revert to its politics—or lack thereof.

For more than a quarter of a century, journalists, academics, and politicians carefully shrouded their obsessive interest in *Tel Quel* in virulent and relentless attacks. The polemical climate surrounding *Tel Quel* may have contributed to its success and notoriety in France and abroad, but it also prevented any serious examination of the *Tel Quel* enterprise. Only a comprehensive examination of *Tel Quel* will permit us to surmount the mystique of obscurantism and volatility that beclouds this cultural endeavor. We shall never understand *Tel Quel* if we continue to separate *Tel Quel*'s poetics from its politics, as journalists, academics, politicians, and even former Telquelians have done. Journalists and politicians have preferred to comment on *Tel Quel*'s curious political trajectory, emphasizing the review's political moments to the detriment of its cultural evolution. Literary critics, on the other hand, dismiss *Tel Quel*'s politics as a French *maladie* and concentrate instead on the great names associated with the review or on questions of aesthetic and philosophical interest. But one cannot argue for aesthetic coherence without considering the review's fluctuating political sympathies. Nor is it plausible to view *Tel Quel*'s changing political stances without regard for its cultural positions. *Tel Quel*'s poetics and politics must necessarily be viewed in relation to one another, and to the historical context from which they issue.

To be able to read *Tel Quel* means to understand the times in which it was embedded and upon which it left its distinctive mark. In order to view literature and politics concurrently, one must account for the particular intellectual and sociopolitical forces that shaped *Tel Quel*'s enterprise of cultural renewal. Abstracted from historical circumstances, theory remains obscure. Viewed from only one perspective, *Tel Quel* appears incoherent. As problem-laden as the notion of a coherent and long-term *Tel Quel* cultural project may appear, it is one that I have entertained. Such an eccentric view forms the basis for this work. It is my contention that there has been not only a coherent cultural program operant in *Tel Quel* for more than twenty years, but that such a program was already in place in the review's inaugural issue.

To dismiss *Tel Quel*'s beginnings is to fail to recognize the origins of a bold cultural project fashioned by particular historical circumstances. Critics, for the most part, have bypassed *Tel Quel*'s founding years, alluding only to their "aesthetic ambiguity" or "eclectic confusion" (*confusionnisme*). In so doing, they have failed to explain why *Tel Quel* immediately attracted writers and intellectuals from very different ideological backgrounds. Jean Paulhan, Alain Robbe-Grillet, Ponge, Cayrol, Foucault, Barthes, Aragon, and Mauriac are but a few of the early admirers of *Tel Quel*. To neglect *Tel Quel*'s beginnings is ultimately to be incapable of explaining how a small literary magazine founded by a group of young writers—most of whom never achieved literary prominence—became a symbol of intellectual power in France and abroad during the 1960s and early 1970s. Nevertheless, *Tel Quel*'s founding years have received almost no critical attention. They have been eclipsed by studies of the review's later influential phase from the mid 1960s to the early 1970s. At that time, *Tel Quel* elicited the attention of intellectual circles in Europe, North and South America, Asia, and Australasia. In bypassing *Tel Quel*'s formative years, critics failed to account for what had prompted the theoretical tempest of *Tel Quel* in the mid and late 1960s and subsequently led the group to its revolutionary posturings of the late 1960s and early 1970s. This synchronic view of the *Tel Quel* enterprise not only resulted in the usual accusations of political opportunism, but also led to faulty hypotheses, such as the one that *Tel Quel* had suddenly struck up a relationship with the French Communist Party (PCF) in 1967–68, when in fact relations between the two had begun a decade earlier, even before the actual founding of the review. Furthermore, this narrow perspective of *Tel Quel* tended to situate the journal within a trend, thereby disregarding the role that *Tel Quel* might have played in initiating a new cultural direction.

In 1972, Jean-Jacques Brochier, editor of the popular *Magazine Littéraire*, ventured: "Without *Tel Quel*, literature and the Left would not be what they are today in France."[14] Such a statement may strike us as somewhat excessive. What possible constancy could there be in *Tel Quel*'s changing relationship to the Left: from its founding years, when it set out to disengage literature from politics in the wake of a "tempsmodernistic" cultural hegemony to its rapprochement with Marxism in the mid and late 1960s—via theory (Althusser, Gramsci, Mao Tse-tung) and the PCF—and finally to the exorcism of Marxism by way of the Chinese Cultural Revolution, May 1968, the new philosophers, and dissidents? Nevertheless, there is one constant: *Tel Quel* has *always* defined its enterprise of cultural renewal in relation to the French Left. Barthes maintained that it is not what changes that must be analyzed—as critics eager to dismiss *Tel Quel* have done over the years—but what remains the same. If that is so, then Brochier's observation may be provocative less for the presumably exaggerated importance attributed to *Tel Quel*, than for the relationship established between literature and the Left because of *Tel Quel*. Now, anyone even vaguely familiar with the story of avant-garde movements and engagement knows what a sorry relationship this has been. The political Left has been profoundly suspicious of the formalist nature of avant-garde art and conservative in its artistic tastes. In 1979, as the *Tel Quel* experience came to an end, Sollers affirmed that "culturally, the Left—which was all evolution, progress, generosity, and humanism—had with respect to questions of art and literature, the most regressive, reactionary, and conservative opinions."[15]

Then why would a cultural enterprise like *Tel Quel*, which saw itself as the offspring of literary modernity, ever become caught up in politics? One very important reason lies in the historical nature of its form: the "review-form" (*forme-revue*, Debray, *Teachers, Writers; Celebrities*) as a means of cultural renewal. This form is, in fact, one reason for the delay of a systematic and comprehensive examination of *Tel Quel* and its historical context. Such an instrument of cultural renewal has not been an object of critical study in the

14. Jean-Jacques Brochier, "tel quel, du nouveau roman à la révolution culturelle," *Magazine Littéraire* 65 (June 1972): 10.

15. Sollers, "Gauche, droite . . ." in *La Droite aujourd'hui*, ed. Jean-Pierre Apparu (Paris: Albin Michel, 1979), 329.

United States. There have been only a few critical works on New York literary magazines and on the *Partisan Review*. Recent studies on *Les Temps Modernes* have been published in Europe, where cultural journals have always played a formative role in the production, diffusion, and transformation of intellectual thought. American academics have focused on Telquelians such as Barthes and Kristeva and on currents such as poststructuralism and deconstruction, rather than on *Tel Quel* the journal. Debray contends that the history of literature has too often been the "history of literary genres and doctrines, as though they contained within them their own laws of succession."[16] But isn't that letting go of the prey for the shadow and prolonging the idealist reversal in the artistic field? (133).

As a periodical publication, the review is by its very nature bound up with current events. Even the purely literary review is a social creature. It cannot discount temporal matters. Although it may opt to preserve a safe distance from sociopolitical events, in order to assure its periodicity, the review must account for the production and diffusion of culture. Cultural renewal is a function of acoustics: "The history of acoustics is not the history of music. It tells of the sound and the fury: of the best channel of speech in each historical period, the one that will facilitate the loudest sound and the greatest fury" (Debray, *Teachers, Writers, Celebrities* 128). Even if it is not interested in having broad appeal, as a periodical phenomenon the review cannot forget that "full speech is hollow if it has no support" (78). To be influential, one first has to be heard; that is, to have access to the forms and places with the best audience (128). Indifference to acoustical concerns on the part of small literary magazines has significantly contributed to the ephemeral nature of their enterprise. On the other hand, the great lesson of the *Nouvelle Revue Française* was the realization that symbolic power had to be translated in the institutional realm. Launched on 15 November 1908, this literary review almost concurrently established (in 1910) the most powerful of French publishing houses: Gallimard. The *NRF* placed literature and the writer at the pinnacle of French culture. The supremacy of literature was bound up with the hegemony of the publishing world, which supplanted, in fact, the power of the university institution in the realm of intellectual life in France (Debray, *Teachers, Writers, Celebrities* 65–66).

Ironically, the importance of the *NRF* was perhaps best summed up by the notorious remark of German ambassador Otto Abetz upon his arrival in occupied Paris in 1940: "France has only had three powers: the Catholics,

16. Debray, *Teachers, Writers, Celebrities*, 133.

the Communists, and the *NRF*. Let us begin with the *NRF*."[17] In effect, Abetz seized the journal, entrusting its direction to Drieu La Rochelle, a Fascist. With this single, concrete, yet highly symbolic gesture, he succeeded in bringing to naught everything the *NRF* represented and had struggled to preserve from its very founding: the separation of art and politics, the belief in an intrinsic notion of literature that could remain untouched by social and political changes. In *The Obstructed Path*, H. Stuart Hughes argues that the social and political examination of conscience that should have taken place after World War I was postponed to the 1930s.[18] The French basked in the dying embers of an Indian summer of glory that was already menaced by autumn winds. The delayed realization of the war's impact was reinforced by a corresponding overvaluation of the cultural situation (2). For Hughes, "an assertion of artistic or philosophical pre-eminence served as psychic compensation for the relinquishment of an active international role." As the French withdrew from foreign commitments to the cultivation of their own garden, the nation's sense of cultural primacy became more pronounced (3). But by the 1930s these illusions were shaken: the "purist definition of the writer's aim seemed dated; indeed the métier as such came under question as ethically insufficient for an apocalyptic era" (5).

French writers and intellectuals did not wait for the Occupation to learn the lessons of history. It was in the 1930s that "most Frenchmen were stupified on discovering their historicity."[19] As Jean-Paul Sartre writes: "From 1930 on, the world depression, the coming of Nazism, and the events in China opened our eyes. It seemed as if the ground were going to fall from under us, and suddenly, *for us too*, the great historical juggling began" (*What Is Literature?* 212). History erupted on the intellectual scene, leaving the notion of pure literature trampled underfoot. A vast terrain for cultural renewal, heretofore guarded by the *NRF*, opened up. A new generation came of age in Europe's darkest hours: a generation that felt "situated" and collectively responsible in the face of history: "All at once we felt ourselves abruptly *situated*. The detachment which our predecessors were so fond of

17. Abetz cited in C. Lesbats, " 'La Nouvelle Revue Française': Humanisme et Esthétique," in *Manuel d'historie littéraire de la France*, ed. Pierre Abraham and Roland Desne (Paris: Editions Sociales, 1982), 6:203.

18. H. Stuart Hughes, *The Obstructed Path: French Social Thought in the Years of Desperation, 1930–1960* (New York: Harper and Row, 1966, 1968), 2.

19. Jean-Paul Sartre, *What is Literature?* trans. Bernard Frechtman (New York: Philosophical Library, 1949), 211–12. Originally published in *Les Temps Modernes* and subsequently as *Qu'est-ce que la littérature?* (Paris: Gallimard, 1948).

practising had become impossible. There was a collective adventure which was taking form in the future and which would be *our* adventure" (Sartre, *What Is Literature?* 213). This brutal encounter with history would leave an indelible mark on French letters, henceforth dominated by the notions of social responsibility and political commitment.[20] Claude-Edmonde Magny observes that "[a]fter 1930, literature returns to face the times."[21] The political mobilization of the 1930s that led writers such as André Malraux to join forces with Republican loyalists in the Spanish civil war found its full expression in the European Resistance of World War II.

The contradictory solutions envisioned by writers in the postwar years were a response to questions previously raised in the 1930s and tested in the realm of collective action during World War II. The war diverted individuals materially from their habits: it forced them to acknowledge, in a terribly concrete fashion, the dangers that menace the presuppositions of individual existence; it persuaded them that there is no possibility of salvation in neutrality and isolation.[22] Many European writers and intellectuals were obliged to test the validity of their ideals in the brutal reality of armed combat. Those who had given privilege to the contemplative realm and had found refuge in their isolation were compelled to unite their abstract beliefs with concrete and collective action. Cultural renewal and political action were seen as necessarily bound up with one another in the immediate postwar years. A new form of cultural militancy came into its own, and with it a writing that emphasized the concrete and collective. Even philosophy, by nature abstract, had to be concrete. Thus the initial shock and consequent popularity of existentialist philosophy, insofar as it strove to establish a direct relationship with material, everyday reality. The demand for a concrete literature and philosophy reflected the dominant cultural mood of a society in which all that remained was the individual, bare and terror-stricken, stripped of all the values of Western humanism that had heretofore constituted identity. Auschwitz and Hiroshima symbolized the complete failure of a cultural tradition unable to stand by its proclaimed principles

20. The notion of "engagement" as we know it today was first used by Paul Nizan in April 1932 and not—as most critics claim—by Emmanuel Mounier's Catholic personalist review *Esprit*, which was founded in October of that year. See David Schalk, *The Spectrum of Political Engagement* (Princeton: Princeton University Press, 1979), 15.

21. Claude-Edmonde Magny, *Historie du roman français depuis 1918* (Paris: Editions du Seuil, 1950), 61.

22. Letter of Giaime Pintor to Luigi Pintor, 28 November 1943, in *Il sangue d'Europa*, ed. Valentino Gerratana (Turin: Einaudi, 1966), 186.

and values. It was therefore only natural that postwar philosophy and literature would make the individual the root of all meanings: an individual situated in a barren wasteland that had to be repopulated; an individual whose meaning and freedom were entirely in his or her actions, who existed only insofar as he or she acted. As Sartre put it: "man is nothing other than what he makes of himself—that is the first principle."[23] For Sartre, it was not a "matter of choosing one's age but of choosing one's self within it," so that one could act upon the times rather than be acted upon.[24] Concerned with "chang[ing] both man's social condition and his conception of himself,"[25] *Les Temps Modernes* aspired to establish a direct relationship between sociopolitical events and literature: it aimed to give back to literature the social function that it never should have relinquished. The need to reflect on events perpetually, on the meaning to give and the action to oppose them, resulted in a new conception of literature: a "literary pragmatism" or "dynamics of commitment" that we have come to know as "engagement."

Despite the fall of the *NRF* in 1940, and with it the cultural supremacy for which it stood, the review-form would continue to be an essential resource in the struggle for the conquest and preservation of symbolic power in the postwar years.[26] Writing on *Les Temps Modernes*, Anna Boschetti noted that among the phenomena that mattered in the postwar years, and behind the protagonists themselves, there was usually a group, and this group identified itself through a common publication (*Intellectual Enterprise* 138). For Michel-Antoine Burnier, the review, as a collection of writings, is unique, for "it can express the meaning of an age, indeed almost the entire body of knowledge of that age. Provided its editors are vigilant, nothing is foreign; it can give an account of everything."[27] To follow the trail blazed by intellectuals bound to the activity of reviews in the postwar years is to procure a comprehensive view of both the cultural and the political history

23. Sartre cited in James Wilkinson, *The Intellectual Resistance in Europe* (Cambridge: Harvard University Press, 1981), 81.

24. Sartre, *What is Literature?* 239.

25. Sartre, "Présentation," *Les Temps Modernes* 1 (October 1945): 7–8.

26. Anna Boschetti, *The Intellectual Enterprise: Sartre and "Les Temps Modernes,"* trans. Richard McCleary (Evanston: Northwestern University Press, 1988), 138. Originally published as *L'Impresa intellettuale: Sartre e "Les Temps Modernes"* (Bari: Edizioni Dedalo, 1984).

27. Michel-Antoine Burnier, *Choice of Action*, trans. Bernard Murchland (New York: Random House, 1968), 20. Originally published as *Les Existentialistes et la politique* (Paris: Gallimard, 1966).

of that period.[28] Cultural renewal, political action, and the review-form became synonymous forces in postwar Europe.

The notion of engaged literature would be intimately tied up with the review-form: the latter would represent a common meeting-ground for literature and journalism, domains as opposed as they are bound by the notion of writing. Sartre would "militate in favor of the literary status of journalism—better still, in favor of reporting being acknowledged as the 'pilot' genre of present literature."[29] In the presentation to *Les Temps Modernes*, he stated: "We feel, in effect, that reporting is one of the genres of literature and can become one of the most important of them."[30] As a reporter, the engaged writer must be capable of "seizing meanings, intuitively and instantaneously, and of regrouping them such that the reader can be afforded immediately decipherable synthetic totalities."[31] He is a descendant of the eighteenth-century revolutionary writer, or what Barthes has called an "écrivant": "the writer's function is to say at once and on every occasion what he thinks."[32]

Journalism, like journal writing, "roots the movement of writing in time, in the humility of the daily, dated and preserved by its date."[33] By removing the writer from the nontemporal solitude of literature, the journal places him in touch with the person he is when he does not write, the individual living his everyday existence (20, 22). It thereby liberates writers from the "prisonhouse of language," by giving them the illusion of being closer to the event itself than to the act of writing. Journalism also requires a notion of writing in absolute proximity to the event: it seeks to minimize as much as possible

28. Mario Valente, *Ideologia e potere: da "Il Politecnico" a "Contropiano"* (Turin: Edizioni radiotelevisione italiana, 1978), 7.

29. Denis Hollier, *The Politics of Prose*, trans. Jeffrey Mehlman (Minneapolis: University of Minnesota Press, 1986), 82. Originally published as *Politique de la prose* (Paris: Gallimard, 1982).

30. Sartre, "Présentation," 20. Julia Kristeva would, in fact, later praise Simone de Beauvoir, the "chronicler" for her extraordinary capacity "to construct an entire cultural phenomenon." See "My Memory's Hyperbole," in *The Female Autograph*, ed. Domna Stanton and Jeanine Parisier Plottel, trans. Athena Viscusi (New York: New York Literary Forum, 1984), 261. Originally published as "Mémoire" in *L'Infini* 1 (Winter 1983).

31. Sartre, "Présentation," 20.

32. Barthes, "Authors and Writers," in *Critical Essays*, trans. Richard Howard (Evanston: Northwestern University Press, 1972), 148. Originally appeared as "Ecrivains et écrivants," in *Essais critiques*, which was published in Collection Tel Quel (Paris: Seuil, 1964).

33. Maurice Blanchot, *L'Espace littéraire* (Paris: Gallimard, 1955, 1968), 21, my translation. Available in English as *The Space of Literature*, trans. Ann Smock (Lincoln: University of Nebraska Press, 1982).

the distance between language and reality, words and things. Denis Hollier argues that "the structure of journalistic writing joins up with the most persistent Sartrean fantasy—that of a writing without difference, stripped of any time gap and clinging to the present, a writing rigorously contemporary with whatever it would speak about."[34] Sartrean engagement is diametrically opposed to the notion of literature that came into being in the nineteenth century: a literature "enclosed within a radical intransitivity," in a form of language "difficult of access, folded back upon the enigma of its own origin and existing wholly in reference to the pure act of writing."[35] Sartre's objective was to rid writing of the unfortunate crease that it had acquired; commitment would put an end to self-referentiality.[36] If literature had a specific content, it would no longer have to indulge in self-meditation.[37]

Although *Les Temps Modernes* is clearly not the *NRF*, both reviews nevertheless succeeded in maintaining cultural hegemony in two different historical contexts. Perhaps it was less a question of putting the review-form in touch with history than recognizing once again its essentially historical nature. As the cultural organ common to literary schools, political parties, and scientific organisms, capable of representing both "the closure of the avant-garde and the openness of the militant,"[38] and embracing a broad spectrum of ideologies from "art for art's sake" to engagement, from Fascism to Communism, the review has served, particularly since the turn of the century, as the ideal battleground for intellectual confrontation. In an article devoted to reviews and the intelligentsia in France, Paul Thibaud, former editor of *Esprit*, contends that reviews, before being instruments of information or discussion, represent a means for intellectuals to organize themselves and become aware of their roles.[39] Thibaud believes that each time the intelligentsia is forced to reexamine its positions, striking new reviews are born (519).

Even though reviews often depend on institutions such as political parties, national centers of scientific research, the university, and the church, the

---

34. Hollier, *The Politics of Prose*, 82.
35. Michel Foucault, *The Order of Things* (New York: Vintage, 1973), 300. Originally published as *Les Mots et les choses* (Paris: Gallimard, 1966).
36. Hollier, *The Politics of Prose*, 63.
37. Sartre, *What is Literature?* 122.
38. Debray, *Teachers, Writers, Celebrities*, 75.
39. Paul Thibaud, "Texte de travail: à propos des revues, à propos de l'intelligentsia, à propos de cette revue," *Esprit* 3 (March 1977): 519.

most original reviews are marginal or even against social institutions (519). According to Thibaud, this is because reviews do not merely exist to defend or illustrate existing doctrines; more often they constitute a sort of proving-ground for a fundamentally new apprehension of reality, a new way of seizing the moment by different intellectuals rallied around the common questions of a period (520). The review allows intellectuals to go beyond conventional institutional cloisters as well as do away with disciplinary police. What ensues is a melting-down process "in which many of the contrasts in terms of which we have been accustomed to think may lose their relevance."[40] Allowing the various disciplines to come into contact with and contaminate one another through the review-form implies coming to terms with traditional definitions of literature and science, culture and politics.

The review-form thus becomes a privileged site for contesting traditional dichotomies of Western idealist thought: not only culture and politics, but also thought and action, the spiritual and the temporal. The demise of the *NRF*, and with it that of liberal humanism, taught European intellectuals that no serious spirituality could afford to overlook the temporal.[41] In his opening article to *Les Temps Modernes*, Maurice Merleau-Ponty stated that World War II and the Occupation had taught him and his generation "that values remain nominal without an economic and political infrastructure which allows them to come into being—especially insofar as values are nothing in concrete history than another manner of designating relations among men, as they are established by the modality of work, love, hope, in brief their coexistence."[42]

The review is by its very nature irrefutably bound up with current events. Unlike the book, which is definitive in form, the review has the capacity to evolve and change, react and denounce. Not even the apolitical literary review can afford to ignore the material conditions of its existence. The review is a creature of the moment; its very survival depends on its ability to weather a generally inauspicious cultural climate. It cannot ignore the temporal sphere, nor the question of the conquest and preservation of intellectual power: "It is not freedom of speech which is lacking but rather the freedom to be heard."[43] Consequently, it cannot separate itself from

40. Walter Benjamin, "The Author as Producer," *Understanding Brecht*, trans. Anna Bostock (London: New Left, 1973), 89.

41. Debray, *Teachers, Writers, Celebrities*, 71.

42. Maurice Merleau-Ponty, "La guerre a eu lieu," *Les Temps Modernes* 1 (1 October 1945): 65.

43. Gianni Scalia, "L'esempio del Politecnico," *Letterature moderne* 10, no. 5 (1960): 639.

politics. Such a realization inevitably leads to the contestation of certain idealist conceptions of literature and culture. The review cannot dissociate its theory from its practice. It is as though by its very nature the review were engaged. This was the lesson that the demise of the *NRF* during the Occupation taught an entire generation of European postwar writers. This was also the guiding notion behind the establishment of an "organ of research"—*Les Temps Modernes*—devoted to "the study of the concrete problems of [its] time."

In choosing to write a book on *Tel Quel*, one of my major objectives has been to situate a cultural organ and intellectual movement within the broader framework of twentieth-century French letters and intellectual thought. In the specific context of contemporary French letters, two reviews immediately stand out: *La Nouvelle Revue Française* and *Les Temps Modernes*. If the *NRF* and *Les Temps Modernes* are the references to which many of my remarks on *Tel Quel* ultimately lead, it is because these two cultural reviews became the symbols of intellectual power in the inter- and postwar periods. In order to secure the literary hegemony that it did, *Tel Quel* had to define its program of cultural renewal in light of these two powers. With its unconditional defense of literature for over two decades, *Tel Quel* represents, in many respects, an attempt to resuscitate *La Nouvelle Revue Française* in the wake of *Les Temps Modernes*.

The critique of engagement by the *Tel Quel* generation was central to a mission whose purported aim was the rehabilitation of the literary modernity of the late nineteenth and early twentieth centuries. As they had boldly stated from the onset—in none other than Aragon's *Les Lettres Françaises*—they wanted to take literature seriously the way Hölderlin, Flaubert, Mallarmé, Proust, Joyce, and Valéry had done. They were going to be *écrivains*, not *écrivants*. In seeking to relaunch a literary movement that had been under attack by Fascism, Nazism, and Stalinism, and that had been occulted in the postwar years by socialist realism and Sartrean engagement, the founding Telquelians were put in a position where they had to account for the repression of certain literary and artistic manifestations—to which they had inherently been drawn—by political ideologies. No wonder Brochier would claim, in 1972, "I even suspect *Tel Quel* of having the ambitions of a *NRF* 1980 that had understood that literature is the privileged sector of ideology."[44] In comparing *Tel Quel* in this manner to the *NRF*, Brochier, a

44. Brochier, "Tel Quel, du nouveau roman à la révolution culturelle," 9. Brochier appears to be using the date 1980 in reference to the *NRF*'s founding date, 1908.

former Sartrean, was implicitly recognizing that one could no longer refer to the *NRF* without also taking *Les Temps Modernes* into account. By 1972, *Tel Quel* was certainly acquainted with the intricate twists and turns of literature and ideology, but even in 1960, *Tel Quel* already knew that literature was reactionary only to the degree that political criteria were applied to it. In calling for the critical examination of literature and its powers, independently of any particular ideological or political context, *Tel Quel*'s opening declaration opposed the dominant literary mood of its time, and, in particular, the subordination of literature to politics that characterized the 1940s and 1950s: "Ideologues have ruled long enough over expression. . . . It's about time a parting of the ways took place; let us be permitted to focus upon expression itself, its inevitability, and its particular laws."[45] The emphasis on the moral and ideological dimensions of literature had ultimately led to a failure to account for questions of language and form.

For the committed writer, language appears almost to go without saying. If, for Sartrean engagement, man is *Homo significans*, "it is not because he speaks, but because he exists. Meaning is the characteristic medium of his life, not the effect of his speech."[46] Contrasting postwar literary concerns with those of the early 1960s, Foucault contended that the "humanist" literature of the 1940s and 1950s was essentially a literature of signification (What is the meaning of man? Of the world?). Then came "something very different, almost resistant to meaning, which is the sign, or language itself."[47] Hollier has perceptively remarked that in not wanting to miss anything of his times, Sartre, nevertheless, remained indifferent to its major ideological theme, "the tiresome problem of language" (*Politics of Prose* 59).

If *Tel Quel* was ever going to come close to realizing its grandiose ambition of resuscitating the golden age of literature, it had to contest a mode of thought which it felt had not only devalorized literature (by having made it the handmaiden of political ideologies), but had also led to the demise of the writer who, if he was not also an intellectual (that is, on the Left), was inevitably on the Right. The founding Telquelians defiantly positioned themselves on the literary front, that is, on the Right. Unlike

45. "Déclaration," trans. Bettina Knapp, *Tel Quel* 1 (Spring 1960): 3.
46. Hollier, *The Politics of Prose*, 59.
47. Foucault, "Débat sur le roman" ("Une littérature nouvelle?" Décade de Cerisy, September 1963), in *Tel Quel* 17 (Spring 1964): 38.

Sartre and Aragon's generation, the Telquelians were not interested in transforming the world. If literature had any subversive potential for them, it was to be found not in its relation to political reality, but in the "thickness of words," in precisely what engagement had relegated to an aestheticizing ideology. What had in effect drawn Communist militants like Jacques Henric, Jean-Louis Houdebine, and Guy Scarpetta to *Tel Quel* in the early 1960s was its rejection of both Sartrean engagement and Aragonian socialist realism. These militants had the impression that nothing good in the way of literature had come out of these politicized currents. If postwar engagement was unsuccessful in reconciling literature and the revolution, was it perhaps because it failed to see that cultural revolutions disinter otherwise profoundly inaccessible truths and do so through the vehicle of style?[48]

In its contest with Sartrean engagement and its effort to supplant the intellectual hegemony wielded by *Les Temps Modernes*, *Tel Quel* surprisingly benefited from the aftermath of 1956. It received the enthusiastic support of a broad range of writers with different ideological leanings, who neverthelesss seemed to share a passion for literature and even, in several instances, a nostalgia for those times when writers had not had to dirty their hands in politics. Was the turn to literature another way of not dealing with the Stalinist truth after 1956? In the way that many historians and sociologists such as François Furet, Tony Judt, Jacques Julliard, and Edgar Morin have claimed that the turn to Third Worldism (*tiersmondisme*) was? If this had not been the case, *Tel Quel* would not have been able to draw attention away from the polarizing role played by the Algerian War in the French Left's attempt to deal or not deal with de-Stalinization. Since almost no critical attention has been devoted to *Tel Quel*'s founding years and the relation of the journal to the intellectual climate in France after 1956, I begin my study on *Tel Quel* by situating *Tel Quel*'s beginnings within the sociopolitical and intellectual context of de-Stalinization and decolonization. I show how the sociopolitical and cultural forces of the late 1950s helped to shape *Tel Quel*'s literary program and contributed to its success. Although these years were propitious for the disengagement of literature, I seek to dispel the popular misconception that *Tel Quel*'s beginnings were reactionary. More than a literary parenthesis, *Tel Quel*'s initial apolitism is indicative

---

48. In "La psychanalyse et son enseignement," Lacan writes, "Any return to Freud that gives substance to a teaching worthy of this [Freud's] name will be produced only by way of a path from which the most hidden truth manifests itself in the revolutions of culture. This path is the only formation we can claim to transmit to those who follow us. It is called: a style." In *Ecrits* (Paris: Editions du Seuil, 1966), 458.

of the changing literary and intellectual climate of the late 1950s. Dated March 1960, the first issue of *Tel Quel* inaugurates a new spring, a new literary temper. I demonstrate how it is the response of a new literary generation—the one born just before or during World War II—that refuses the history bequethed on it by its elders.

Chapter 1 focuses on *Tel Quel*'s inaugural issue and opening declaration. I contend that the road map for the course of its twenty-two-year trajectory can be unfolded in the very first issue. I show how *Tel Quel* challenged the dominant literary paradigm of its time, engaged literature versus "art for art's sake," by defending literature per se—a notion that had acquired right-wing connotations since the late 1930s—as a progressive force. In effect, what was dismissed by Sartrean engagement and relegated to an aestheticizing ideology became the subversive potential of literature for *Tel Quel*.

In Chapter 2, I consider *Tel Quel*'s early years (from 1960 to 1965) from the perspective of language. What collapses, in the 1960s, is the notion of language as an instrument or decor. The collapse of such a notion coincides with a theoretical *aggiornamento* in the human sciences and with a cultural renewal bound up with the avant-garde experiences of the first half of the century. I analyze how *Tel Quel*'s interest in the workings of language enables it to dismantle the paradigm of engagement, which made "reality" the concern of the novel and "words" the preoccupation of poetry (Barthes). Chapter 2 thus explores *Tel Quel*'s relationship to the novel and poetic language. It examines how, from the beginning, *Tel Quel* rejected the "ideology of the text as reflection," inherent in the novel and central to debates on literary realism, and an aestheticizing ideology attributed to poetry by a belletristic tradition bound up with Western metaphysics. I illustrate how *Tel Quel*'s initial interest in the formal questions posed by the *nouveau roman* is superseded by the exploration of poetic language as the questioning of meaning and identity through the experience of writing. I devote extensive consideration to the polemics of the Cerisy Colloquium of September 1963 ("A New Literature?"), which marks *Tel Quel*'s official break with the *nouveau roman* as well as its transition to a new phase characterized by the articulation of the practice of writing to philosophy. From 1963 to 1965, *Tel Quel* explored the linguistic and philosophical implications of writing (*écriture*) and began to elaborate a critical theory that transcended generic and disciplinary boundaries.

Chapter 3 examines *Tel Quel*'s evolving relationship to theory from 1965 to 1968. The intellectual terrorism of the mid 1960s brought *Tel Quel* into the international limelight. The years 1965–66 were marked by the explosion of French intellectual thought. If, in the wake of engagement, *Tel Quel* had turned to theory to wrestle literature from the political imperative, it subsequently used literature to challenge the structuralist hegemony of the 1960s. Chapter 3 analyzes the importance of the Barthes-Picard polemic for *Tel Quel*, their dissemination of the Russian formalists, and the impact of the Cluny encounter of April 1968 ("Linguistics and Literature") on the theoretical and political evolution of *Tel Quel*. At the end of the 1960s, theory became the missing link between the essentially bourgeois class origins of the *Tel Quel* team, their elitist practice of writing, and the class struggle. *Tel Quel* came to the class struggle via theory.

Chapter 4 looks at *Tel Quel*'s relationship to politics from 1967 to 1971. In 1967, *Tel Quel* took on the avant-garde wager of revolutionizing literature and transforming society, seeing itself as the logical successor of surrealism, whose philosophical and political errors it set out to rectify. A fellow traveler of the French Communist Party from 1967 to 1971, *Tel Quel* then became Maoist, devoting numerous articles to China until 1974. In this chapter, I consider *Tel Quel*'s relationship to Marxism, the French Communist Party, May 1968, and the Chinese Cultural Revolution.

In Chapter 5, I analyze *Tel Quel*'s turn from a political to a cultural perspective in the 1970s. From the mid to late 1970s, *Tel Quel* befriended the dissidents and *nouveaux philosophes*, relinquished Marxism, and declared the avant-garde dead. In 1986, the former Communist militant Henric, who joined up with *Tel Quel* in 1971, affirmed that, contrary to the avant-garde writers who had preceded them, they had caught themselves in time: "Whatever may have been our mild or not so mild ideological deliriums, we never sacrificed our literary and artistic convictions to the political slaughterhouse. Literature is what saved us."[49] Henric is not only implying that literature saved the *Tel Quel* generation from engagement as he says—"We never gave in there. We were engaged but we never made engaged literature"—but also from politics itself. *Tel Quel*'s literary and aesthetic program enables us to understand its cultural politics. It is not a question of literary choices remaining untouched by politics (art for art's sake), but rather of literary choices dictating political ones. To a notion of literature conceived from a political perspective, which equates in the instances of postwar engagement and socialist realism with the subordina-

---

49. Jacques Henric, "Quand une avant-garde (littéraire) rencontre une autre avant-garde (politique) . . . ," unpublished paper (December 1986).

tion of literature to a political ideology, *Tel Quel* opposes an ethics stemming from the literary experience itself. Such an ethics is founded on the premise that questions of political oppression and ideological totalitarianism are initially implanted "in the relation that each subject holds with his language and his culture, and with that which goes beyond them."[50]

By focusing on *Tel Quel* as an organ of cultural renewal, I aim to show that literature—even when it claims to be disengaged—can never sever its historical ties. The historical perspective of this book will help elucidate the intricate twists and turns of French intellectual life in the 1960s and 1970s, and the role played by *Tel Quel* in the evolution of intellectual thought and writing during this period. *Tel Quel*'s cultural politics have been fashioned as much by the historical vicissitudes of the period following the post- and cold war years, as they have by the theoretical advances in literary studies, semiotics, philosophy, and psychoanalysis of this era. Although *Tel Quel* is clearly the product of a particular time and place, its cultural enterprise can be viewed from a broader historical perspective. Founded in the wake of and in contraposition to Sartrean engagement, *Tel Quel* came to its end shortly before the dissolution of Marxism-Communism marked by the demolition of the Berlin Wall, the reunification of Europe, and the collapse of the Soviet Union. In many respects, *Tel Quel* signals the end of an era. As such, its cultural venture provides some significant parting thoughts on a period of European literary and intellectual history in which—despite the obfuscations of theory—Marxism continued to cast its shadow on cultural enterprises, writers still had to account for their politics, and the belief that cultural and political revolutions needed to go hand in hand lingered on.

50. Guy Scarpetta, *Eloge du cosmopolitisme* (Paris: Grasset, 1981), 290.

CHAPTER ONE

REQUIEM FOR THE POSTWAR YEARS

literature, forever despised and yet triumphant
—Tel Quel, *"Declaration"*

Dated Spring 1960, the inaugural issue of *Tel Quel* hardly draws attention to its debut "at the worst possible moment of the worst of colonialist wars."[1] The only allusion to the Algerian War is a fictional piece by Sollers entitled "Requiem" that describes, in an objective and austere fashion characteristic of the *nouveau roman*, the funeral of a friend recently killed in battle. Sollers's "Requiem" seems to be directed more at the literary mood of the late 1950s than at the sociopolitical reality of 1960. The first issue of *Tel Quel* is marked not only by a lack of political statements pertaining to the war, but also by its opening "Declaration," which demands that literature, "forever despised and yet triumphant," be once again taken seriously and freed from the ideological determinations of the cold-war years: "Ideologues have ruled long enough over expression . . . it's about time a parting of the ways took place; let us be permitted to focus upon expression itself, its

---

1. Jean-Pierre Faye cited in Jean Ristat, *Qui sont les contemporains* (Paris: Gallimard, 1975), 187.

inevitability, and its particular laws."[2] Commenting on *Tel Quel*'s initial "Declaration," which he compared to a "letter of candidacy to the Académie Française,"[3] Jean-Pierre Faye stated: "At a time when 'expression' freed from 'political and moral directives' chose to take care of itself alone, the French army was busying itself by occupying Algeria, killing a million people and torturing thousands of others."[4]

Tel Quel would never be forgiven for its apolitical beginnings: "In France, the development of a political position remains the decisive test, disclosing as it does the definitive meaning of a mode of thought."[5] *Tel Quel*'s initial apoliticism was interpreted as a form of complicity with right-wing (pro–French Algeria) forces. If advocating the disengagement of literature in a nation divided by war was at best tolerated as paradoxical, and at worst denounced as reactionary, it was because of the extenuating political circumstances *and* the manner in which literature was perceived as inextricably bound up with politics: "The presupposition that all literary and philosophical attitudes inevitably have political implications is, of course, yet another reflection of how deeply Sartre's ideas on commitment in literature had affected the literary climate in postwar France."[6] With respect to literature and ideology, *Tel Quel*'s beginnings coincided with the end of the postwar era. Until then the major debate had been between the old right-wing literature and engaged—or Sartrean—literature.[7]

By making its debut on the historical stage in the guise of an exclusively literary review, *Tel Quel* inadvertently positioned itself on the right, for literature in and of itself was seen as reactionary.[8] Sartrean engagement had imposed not only the notion that " 'pure' literature is a dream,"[9] but also that such a view serves society's most conservative forces. Literature had to

2. "Déclaration," trans. Bettina Knapp, *Tel Quel* 1 (Spring 1960): 3.

3. Faye, personal interview, Paris, 23 May 1979.

4. Faye cited in Bettina Knapp, *French Novelists Speak Out* (Troy, N.Y.: Whitston, 1976), 84.

5. Vincent Descombes, *Modern French Philosophy*, trans. L. Scott-Fox and J. M. Harding (New York: Cambridge University Press, 1980), 7. Originally published as *Le Même et l'Autre: quarante-cinq ans de philosophie française* (Paris: Editions de Minuit, 1979).

6. Philip Thody, *Roland Barthes* (Chicago: University of Chicago Press, 1977), 90.

7. Sollers cited in Louis-Bertrand Robitaille, " 'Tel Quel,' ou comment peut-on être Chinois?" *La Presse* (5 April 1975): D2.

8. "To have founded a review of 'pure' literature seemed conservative; as though literature were, in essence, reactionary." Sollers, *Vision à New York* (Paris: Grasset, 1981), 83.

9. Sartre, "The Purposes of Writing," in *Between Existentialism and Marxism*, trans. John Mathews (New York: Random House, 1974), 13. Originally published in Madeleine Chapsal, *Les Ecrivains en personne* (Paris: Julliard, 1960).

be something other than itself. In fact, by stating, "If literature is not *everything*, it is worth nothing. This is what I mean by 'commitment'" (13–14), Sartre was implicitly suggesting that literature had to be everything *but itself*: committed literature had to be as unliterary as possible. The alternative was to be either "revolutionary" without "literature," or—since "literature" is "bourgeois"—conservative.[10]

Disengaging literature from the ideological perspectives of the postwar years was an audacious but paradoxical task. For Barthes, a fellow traveler of *Tel Quel* for twenty years, "to create a review, even a literary review, is not a literary act, it is an entirely social act: it is to decide that you will, in some sense, institutionalize reality."[11] If the review-form had become synonymous with cultural renewal bound up with social change and political action, what role could it now play in a cultural context of disengagement? Given its historical role, it was at risk in remaining unengaged, for even literary journals professing a purely literary orientation, such as *La Nouvelle Revue Française*, had inevitably been drawn into the political arena. Thus, by contending that engaged journals were perfectly justified in reducing the space accorded to literature (157), Barthes appeared to reiterate the notion that literature and commitment are fundamentally incompatible.

For *Tel Quel*, however, the dislodging of literature from the reigning postwar ideologies did not imply an inevitable reversion to an idealized notion of art. The review was opposed to any sanctification of literature, especially to writing as a purely aesthetic practice.[12] Like Sartre, who urged that writers cease being taken for charlatans who make people believe there is something magical about writing,[13] *Tel Quel* wished to dispense with "the neoromantic eloquence that deifies the writer, making him into a creator."[14] Both Sartre and the *Tel Quel* group strove to divest writing of its creative and metaphysical connotations in order to render literature explicable as a social process and a stake (*enjeu*) of political struggle: to them literature was a progressive force. For *Tel Quel*, however, literature did not require justification by extraliterary criteria: the subversive thrust of literature was in the

10. Sollers, "Le réflexe de réduction" in *Théorie d'Ensemble*, which was published in Collection Tel Quel (Paris: Seuil, 1968), 398. Originally published in *La Quinzaine Littéraire* (January 1968).

11. Barthes, "Literature Today," *Critical Essays*, 156. Originally published as "La littérature, aujourd'hui," *Tel Quel* 7 (Autumn 1961).

12. Sollers, "Le réflexe de réduction," 398.

13. Sartre, "The Purposes of Writing," 14.

14. Jacques Henric, "Ecriture et révolution," (interview with Sollers), in *Théorie d'Ensemble*, 67. Originally published in *Les Lettres Françaises* (24 April 1967).

inherent practice of the text. Over the years, the history of *Tel Quel* would coincide increasingly "with the systematic defense that literature is subversive *per se*. No longer as "art for art's sake," but rather as the site from which the truth of reality can be told, whether that reality is political, economic, or sexual. A truth that concerns the species in its smallest details."[15]

Tel Quel's mission was a most ambitious one. The dismissal of extraliterary justifications was part of a program of cultural renewal aimed at restoring the status that literature had lost after the discredit of the *Nouvelle Revue Française* during the Occupation. As a journal that had founded its own publishing house and symbolized the height of publishing hegemony, the *NRF* had succeeded in placing literature among the highest of French values and in giving the writer a status to which he would never again lay claim. In appropriating a cultural organ with historical antecedents, *Tel Quel* had to take its place in the wake of *NRF* and *Les Temps Modernes*, which represented the hegemonic cultural forces of the inter- and postwar years.

The founding objective of *Tel Quel*, manifest in the desire for the most literal, neutral, and material title possible, was to extricate literature from both its metaphysical and ideological overtones.[16] Barthes clearly understood the *Tel Quel* project from the onset. In an interview granted to the review in 1961, he remarked that *Tel Quel* had to confront, on the one hand, literary reviews of the previous generation and, on the other, encyclopedic journals exhibiting an increasing indifference to literature. It was thus forced to react against a certain type of literature as well as a certain contempt for literature,[17] which accounts for the apologetic tone of *Tel Quel's* opening declaration. In calling for the disengagement of literature through the historically engaged review-form, the *Tel Quel* group is obviously well aware of the questionable nature of is endeavor. There is, nevertheless, a provocative resonance in *Tel Quel's* defensive tone. Conceding that to speak of a "passion for literature" or a "literary quality" is not merely anachronistic but, even worse, suspect in 1960, the "Declaration" urges literature to stop defending itself with a guilty conscience and part company with the ideologues who have sufficiently policed literary expression (3).

The contempt for literature at the time of *Tel Quel's* founding was very

15. Sollers, "On n' a encore rien vu," 26.

16. Sollers, personal interview, Paris, 5 July 1979. *Tel Quel* also brings to mind the work of Paul Valéry, an important precursor for the group.

17. Barthes, "Literature Today," 156.

much a result of the Manichaean oppositions of the cold-war years, in which literature and philosophy were subordinate to political concerns, caught up as they were in the power struggle between existentialism and Marxism. Dictated by the question of Stalinism, the cold-war years divided French intellectuals into two irremediably opposed camps. Philosophical and literary questions were dispelled by the ever-resounding "With whom are you?" (Pierre Daix). In his famous preface to *Signes* [Signs], Merleau-Ponty maintained that there had been "a political mania among philosophers which had produced neither effective politics nor good philosophy."[18] The same criticism holds true for literature. For the most part dismissing questions of style and form, the various ideologies of commitment did not succeed in producing a truly alternative literary practice. On the whole, they failed to recognize that language itself must be questioned if a social order is to revolutionize and not merely repeat: "Revolutionary politics, when it isn't repetition, should be the time when politics (the common measure, thus language) severs."[19]

If Sartrean engagement succeeded in grounding literature once again in the social context, from which it never should have been removed, it nevertheless failed to free language from an idealist framework where it is considered a mere instrument or ornament. For the engaged writer, language is essentially instrumental: words are "useful conventions, tools which gradually wear out and which one throws away when they are no longer serviceable."[20] They are transparent signs quickly passed over in favor of the represented object or transmitted idea. Style must pass unnoticed: "Since words are transparent and since the gaze looks through them, it would be absurd to slip in among them some panes of rough glass" (25). In reducing language to an instrument and discarding style as excess, the committed writer fails to take language seriously.

Tel Quel argued that literature would continue to have a secondary status so long as it remained subordinate to politics or aesthetics—that is, insofar as language was reduced to being "the convenient instrument or sumptuous decor of a social, emotional or poetic 'reality' which preexists it and which it is responsible, in a subsidiary way, for expressing, provided it abides by a

18. My translation. Merleau-Ponty, *Signs*, trans. Richard McCleary (Evanston: Northwestern University Press, 1964), 6. Originally published as *Signes* (Paris: Gallimard, 1960).
19. Kristeva, "Sujet dans le langage et pratique politique," *Tel Quel* 58 (Summer 1974): 22. Revised and reprinted as "Politique de la littérature" in *Polylogue*, which appeared in Collection Tel Quel (Paris: Seuil, 1977).
20. Sartre, *What is Literature?* 13.

few rules of style."[21] Barthes maintains that Sartre answered the question "What is literature?" from the outside, and in so doing held an ambiguous literary position.[22] In order to circumvent the ornamental dimension of literature, Sartre kept his distance from the literary object. There was no place for the "ponderous, awesome materiality" (Foucault) of language—which Sartre equated with "style" or "poetry"—in a literature that had to be about something other than itself. In urging that literature only be concerned with itself and its particular laws, *Tel Quel's* opening declaration was, in effect, a direct response to Sartrean engagement. Unlike Sartre, the *Tel Quel* group would remain as close as possible to the literary object by raising "the fundamental problems of language, without which [literature] would not exist."[23]

Tel Quel's opening declaration, which can be read as a manifesto for its first phase from 1960 to 1963, calls for the critical examination of literature and its powers, independently of any particular ideology or political context. It places poetry, intended in the broadest sense of the term to encompass all literary genres, at the highest level: "One must concede today that it is no longer possible to conceive of writing without a clear estimate of its powers, a composure measuring up to the chaos where it manifests itself, a determination that will place poetry on the highest spiritual plane. Everything else will not be literature" (3). *Tel Quel* was obviously challenging the literary conceptions of its time, particularly, the notion of the subordination of literature to politics that so characterized the 1940s and 1950s. If the "Declaration" is provocative, it is not merely because a group of apolitical aesthetes were advocating the autonomy and supremacy of literature in the midst of a society ravaged by social and political turmoil occasioned by war. This is, after all, a position that we have come to accept as inherent in Western humanism under the many guises of "art for art's sake." What is perhaps equally if not more unsettling is that a new generation of writers was challenging the dominant literary paradigm of the time, engaged literature versus "art for art's sake," by trying to pass off literature per se—a notion

21. Barthes, "From Science to Literature," in *The Rustle of Language*, trans. Richard Howard (New York: Hill and Wang, 1986), 4. Originally published in the *Times Literary Supplement* (1967) and subsequently in *Le Bruissement de la langue* (Paris: Seuil, 1984).

22. Barthes, "Literature and Metalanguage," in *Critical Essays*, 98.

23. Barthes, "To Write: An Intransitive Verb?" in *The Languages of Criticism and the Sciences of Man*, ed. Richard Macksey and Eugenio Donato (Baltimore: Johns Hopkins University Press, 1970), 145. Reprinted in *Le Bruissement de la langue* and *The Rustle of Language*.

that had acquired right-wing connotations since the late 1930s—as a progressive force.

The rehabilitation of literature in 1960 implied the liquidation of postwar ideologies and, particularly, of engagement. With respect to literature and ideology, *Tel Quel* marks a closing chapter in French intellectual history. It constitutes a requiem for the postwar years. If the crisis of the *NRF* coincides with the bankruptcy of liberal humanism symbolized by the fall of the Third Republic, and the founding of *Les Temps Modernes* represents the hopes and illusions of the Fourth Republic, then *Tel Quel* is very much an offspring of the Fifth Republic. Referring to the *Tel Quel* project, which dates back to October 1958, François Wahl stated: "We are entering the Second Empire, and there is going to be a new *Parnasse*. This new *Parnasse* must express itself; it is part of the laws of history. This new *Parnasse* will be *Tel Quel*."[24] Hallier even went so far as to say that his group had founded a right-wing journal at Seuil,[25] a publishing house noted for its resistance to the Algerian War and for housing the engaged Catholic journal, *Esprit*.[26] By taking on *Tel Quel*, Seuil had agreed to sponsor a review devoted exclusively to literary concerns. In addition to legitimating a new generation of writers, Seuil was acknowledging—through the peculiar cohabitation of *Esprit* and *Tel Quel* at 27 Rue Jacob—the changing cultural mood of the late 1950s and early 1960s during which the orthodoxies of the post- and cold-war years were rapidly being refuted.

The founding years of the Fifth Republic (1958–60) were propitious both to an intellectual current such as structuralism and to the resurgence of a literary movement—spearheaded by *Tel Quel*—that advocated the disengagement of literature. These years were characterized by a political restoration that attempted to disarm the political militancy of French intellectuals.

24. François Wahl cited in Jean-Pierre Faye, *Commencement d'une figure en mouvement* (Paris: Editions Stock, 1980), 68.

25. Hallier cited in Faye, *Commencement d'une figure en mouvement*, 69.

26. Not since the Occupation had publishing houses been engaged in such a political struggle. The Editions de Minuit, Maspero, and Seuil became symbols of intellectual resistance during the Algerian War. Seuil became involved in the Algerian War in 1957, publishing a number of texts against the war and the colonial legacy. *Esprit* published more than two hundred articles on the war from December 1954 to October 1962. The journal also published the first testimonial text against torture in April 1957. Beginning in 1954, Seuil also began publishing novels by Algerian writers of French expression, such as Mohammed Dib, Kateb Yacine, and Mouloud Feraoun. Three bombs were planted at Seuil by the French Right. See Anne Simonin, "Les Editions de Minuit et les Editions du Seuil," in *La Guerre d'Algérie et les intellectuels français*, by Jean-Pierre Rioux and Jean-François Sirinelli (Paris: Editions Complexe, 1991): 219–45.

The intellectuals' sense of powerlessness in the framework of the new political regime was further compounded by a profound disillusionment with Marxism and Communism as alternative forces. Affirming that Marxism remained "the unsurpassable horizon of our time," yet admitting that as an official state doctrine, "Marxism was at a standstill,"[27] Sartre was, in effect, acknowledging a changing French intellectual climate characterized by the de-Stalinization of French thought. The founding year of Tel Quel— 1960—marks an intellectual thaw (dégel) as well as a paradigm shift in French intellectual thought, as evidenced by the publication of such key works as Sartre's Critique de la raison dialectique [Critique of dialectical reason] and Merleau-Ponty's Signes, followed shortly by Foucault's Folie et déraison. Histoire de la folie à l'âge classique [Madness and civilization] (1961), Frantz Fanon's Les Damnés de la terre [The wretched of the earth] (1961), and Claude Lévi-Strauss's La Pensée sauvage [The savage mind] (1962).

With their emphasis on language instead of mankind, intemporal structures instead of historical evolution, the disciplines of semiotics, psychoanalysis, and ethnology were repeatedly accused of dealing underhanded blows to philosophical and historical thought—the hegemonic forms of discourse in the immediate postwar years. The shift in focus from history to science, from evolution to the search for invariants and systematicity, led many left-wing intellectuals, including Henri Lefebvre and Sartre, to equate the theoretical developments commonly referred to as "structuralism" with the dominant ideology of a technocratic society of experts and with the process of legitimation that is characteristic of the consolidation of capitalism.[28] Sartre even ventured to say, in his critique of Foucault's Les Mots et les choses [The order of things], that "Foucault gives the people what they needed: an eclectic synthesis in which Robbe-Grillet, structuralism linguistics, Lacan and Tel Quel are systematically utilized to demonstrate the impossibility of historical reflection. Behind history, of course, it is Marxism which is attacked. The task is to come up with a new ideology: the latest barrier that the bourgeoisie once again can erect against Marx."[29] While

27. Sartre, "Questions de méthode," in Critique de la raison dialectique (Paris: Gallimard, 1960), 1:29, 25. Translated as Search for a Method, trans. Hazel Barnes (New York: Knopf, 1963).

28. See Henri Lefebvre, L'Idéologie structuraliste (Paris: Seuil, 1971, 1975), 25ff.

29. Sartre, "Replies to Structuralism: An Interview with Jean-Paul Sartre," trans. Robert D'Amico, Telos 9 (Fall 1971): 110. Originally published as "Jean-Paul Sartre répond," in L'Arc 30 (1966).

history had been a revolutionary concept in the nineteenth century and a watchword for an entire generation of writers and intellectuals who came of age in the 1930s and into prominence in the postwar years, language now assumed this role.[30] The new interest in semiotics and psychoanalysis led to a reevaluation of language, which was no longer viewed as a mere instrument or decoration, but rather as a sign and a truth.[31] Everything affected by language was thus called into question: philosophy, literature, and the social sciences (66).

In *Les Mots et les choses*, Foucault controversially asserts that "man is neither the oldest nor the most constant problem that has been posed for human knowledge."[32] In fact, for Kristeva, "the conception of language as the 'key' to man and to social history and as the means of access to the laws of societal functioning constitutes perhaps one of the most striking characteristics of our era, and as such is definitely a new phenomenon."[33] According to Kristeva, whereas the Renaissance substituted the cult of Man for the medieval cult of God, "our era is bringing about a revolution of no less importance by effacing all cults, since it is replacing the latest cult, that of Man, with language, a *system* amenable to scientific analysis" (4). Linguistics (or semiotics) thus serves as the lever for the demystification of mankind insofar as "it introduces science into the complex and imprecise zone of human activities where ideologies and religions are (usually) established" (4).

Although often dismissed as a form of disengagement, the preoccupation with language during the late 1950s and early 1960s was, in effect, a political gesture. Describing his initiation into semiotic theory, Barthes affirmed: "The origin of semiology was political for me. Weary of the immobile, oratorical character of ideological denunciations, I glimpsed with bedazzlement, in reading Saussure (it was in 1956), that there could be an elegant method (as one says of a solution to a mathematical problem) for analyzing social symbols, class distinctions, and ideological cunning."[34]

30. Foucault, "Débat sur la poésie" ("Une littérature nouvelle?" Décade de Cerisy, September 1963) *Tel Quel* 17 (Spring 1964): 77.

31. Barthes, *Criticism and Truth*, trans. Katrine Pilcher Keuneman (Minneapolis: University of Minnesota Press, 1987), 66. Originally published in Collection Tel Quel as *Critique et vérité* (Paris: Seuil, 1966).

32. Foucault, *The Order of Things*, 386.

33. Kristeva, *Language: The Unknown*, trans. Anne Menke (New York: Columbia University Press, 1989), 3. Originally published as *Le langage, cet inconnu* (Paris: Seuil, 1981).

34. Barthes, "L'aventure sémiologique," *Le Monde* (7 June 1974): 28.

Kristeva maintains that the formalist reaction of the late 1950s and early 1960s, exemplified both by structuralist theory and the practice of the *nouveau roman*, served to purge "that subjective or rhetorical edema that our parents had set up to protect themselves against the devastating suffering of wars, or that they had used to construct their martyrdom."[35] It was, she argues, a reaction against the romantic, grandiloquent, and pathetic rhetoric (263) of the postwar years, and against engagement, an attitude that *Tel Quel* considered sentimental, unscientific, and typically bourgeois.[36] Highly critical of the notion of Sartrean engagement, Alain Robbe-Grillet contended in 1957 that commitment for the new novelist now implied "full awareness of the present problems of his own language, the conviction of their extreme importance, the desire to solve them from within."[37]

Several years later in an interview granted to *Tel Quel*, Robbe-Grillet affirmed that Sartrean engagement and Aragonian socialist realism were incompatible with the exercise of literature.[38] Robbe-Grillet's conception of literature would be shared not only by apolitical aesthetes such as the founding members of *Tel Quel*, but also by a new generation of Communist militants who had been bequeathed a distinct feeling—as a result of the cold-war years—that it was impossible to be "modern" in literature *and* "militant" in politics. As the literary father of his party, Aragon had left a new generation of Communist writers with the firm conviction that revolutionary literature had absolutely nothing in common with political militancy. Just as Aragon had abandoned the surrealists for the Communist Party and Stalinism, Sartre too, in the postwar years, sacrificed literature in the name of politics. Although Sartre had attempted to bypass the doubt about the redemptive role he had accorded to the writer by shifting it to the intellectual,[39] the crisis of the writer inevitably caught up with him. His ambiguous response to the question "What is literature?"—by which he kept a safe distance from his object—consequently led to his pessimistic remarks in *Que peut la littérature?* [What are the powers of literature?], also

35. Kristeva, "My Memory's Hyperbole," 263.

36. *Tel Quel*, "Réponses à la 'Nouvelle Critique,'" *Théorie d'Ensemble*, 386. Originally published as "*Tel Quel* nous répond," in *La Nouvelle Critique* 8–9 (1967).

37. Alain Robbe-Grillet, *For a New Novel*, trans. Richard Howard (New York: Grove, 1965), 41. Originally published as *Pour un nouveau roman* (Paris: Minuit, 1963).

38. Robbe-Grillet, "La littérature, aujourd'hui—VI," *Tel Quel* 14 (Summer 1963): 39–40.

39. Jean-François Lyotard, "Foreword: A Success of Sartre's," in *The Politics of Prose*, by Hollier, xi. Originally published in *Critique* 432 (February 1983).

summarized in *Les Mots* [The words]: "For a long time, I took my pen for a sword; I now know we're powerless."[40]

In fact, a new generation of Communist militants such as Jacques Henric, Jean-Louis Houdebine, Guy Scarpetta, and Jean Thibaudeau was attracted to *Tel Quel* in the early 1960s precisely because from the very onset the review rejected Sartrean engagement and Aragonian socialist realism: "*Tel Quel* was born of the refusal of these currents."[41] Did *Tel Quel* share the sentiment that engagement was perhaps less a literary program than a moral excuse? That engagement was the retrospective word of a philosophical and literary generation that felt guilty for not having resisted, for having allowed the Occupation?[42] Jacques Julliard argues that after the Liberation, joining up with left-wing parties, and particularly the Communist Party, represented a certain form of exorcising a bad conscience for many writers and intellectuals who had continued to write during the Occupation (192).

In endeavoring to disengage literature, *Tel Quel* sought to demarcate itself from an era plagued by a variety of crises that resulted in the demise of literature in the name of politics. In the era preceding the new *Parnasse*, French intellectuals were swept up in historical events that compelled them to make politics their leitmotiv, with Marxism-Leninism as the life jacket helping them to remain afloat in the aftermath of a cataclysmic war. Despite the large number of Communist intellectuals and fellow travelers who continued to uphold the French Communist Party, believing that they would be in limbo without it, doubts that Stalinist Russia was the answer began to sprout during the 1950s. These doubts were translated into certitudes when Nikita Khrushchev indicted Stalin at the twentieth Soviet Party Congress, and when Hungary was invaded by Soviet troops in 1956. The indictment of Stalinism and the surge of an imperialist Soviet Union left many French intellectuals disillusioned by the Soviet model that they had continued, for the most part, to uphold.

While still immersed in this crisis, French intellectuals were thrown back by yet another drama into the murky waters of political engagement. In Algeria, a revolution initially seen as an insignificant and distant event developed into a raging war that began to threaten the French intellectual in

40. Sartre, *The Words*, trans. Bernard Frechtman (New York: George Braziller, 1964), 253–54. Originally published as *Les Mots* (Paris: Gallimard, 1964).

41. Henric, "Quand une avant-garde (littéraire) rencontre une autre avant-garde (politique) . . ."

42. Jacques Julliard, "La réussite gaullienne," in *Le Débat: Les Idées en France (1945–1988)* (Paris: Gallimard, 1989), 191–92.

his own backyard. The Algerian War was a second blow to the already fissuring French Left. Indeed, the political triumph of the Left that led to the French Communist Party vote on Algeria was to have a major impact on French Communists and sympathizers. While the Marxist-Leninist crisis was the "epicenter of the earthquake that shook the conscience"[43] of French intellectuals and began to sway their convictions in a multifaceted reality— composed at once of the work of Marx, Engels, and Lenin; the orthodoxy of the Soviet Union; the politics of Communist parties bound up with or opposed to this orthodoxy; and the struggle against imperialism throughout the world[44]—the Algerian War caused the tremors that deepened the cracks initiated by this crisis. Indeed, by granting the Guy Mollet-Lacoste government full powers for its North African policy, the vote of the French Communist Party not only resulted in the escalation of the colonial war, but also caused a schism in the traditional Left. The war marked the birth of a New Left (*gauchisme*) that had heretofore been confined to Trotskyite circles and to groups rallied around such reviews as Cornelius Castoriadis's *Social-isme et Barbarie*. The Algerian War of liberation thus represented a significant setback for the traditional Left: both the Communist and Socialist Parties showed themselves to be not only prudent but reactionary, capable of being simultaneously Stalinist and imperialist, and of "missing" the revolution because of their ethnocentricity.[45]

43. Michel Winock, *Chronique des années soixante* (Paris: Seuil, 1987), 58.

44. See François Châtelet, "Récit," *L'Arc* 70 (1977): 6.

45. One of the strongest indictments of ethnocentrism and cultural imperialism in the French Communist Party came from the renowed Martinican poet and Communist militant, Aimé Césaire. In his famous 24 October 1956 letter of resignation addressed to Maurice Thorez, the secretary-general of the French Communist Party, Césaire challenged the exclusive right of the West to make and interpret history. Like other French Marxist intellectuals, Césaire criticized the party's reluctant attitude toward de-Stalinization. This reluctance was even more problematic considering that the Communist parties of Italy, Poland, Hungary, and China had already initiated the process of de-Stalinization: "Never have I had so strong a feeling of a major people lagging so painfully in arrears of history," wrote Césaire (66). Unlike other French intellectuals, however, Césaire did not limit his criticism to the question of Stalinism, which he viewed as "the bankrupcy of an ideal and the pathetic illustration of a whole generation's failure" (6).

In its assimilationist and chauvinist policies, the French Communist Party shared the fundamental belief of the European bourgeoisie "in the omnifarious superiority of the West": "[the] belief that evolution as it has come about in Europe is the only sort possible; the only desirable sort . . . to summarize it all, [the] rarely avowed but nonetheless real belief in civilization with a capital C; in progress with a capital P" (10). Césaire claimed that the party's scornful rejection of "cultural relativism" was but a function of its Stalinism, for Stalin himself had "reintroduced the notion of 'advanced' and 'retarded' peoples into socialist thinking" (10). If the aim of progressive politics was to one day restore freedom of colonized peoples, then

The years from 1954 to 1962 symbolized an era, essentially defined by the convergence of de-Stalinization and decolonization, that would change the face of France and the world. It was an era of chaotic and vagrant French intellectual thought in search of a new horizon. A product of this chaos, particularly of the disenchantment with the Soviet model, the New Left turned to liberation struggles in the Third World. A number of French historians, including Jean-François Sirinelli, contend that the Algerian War cushioned the blows of the Khrushchev report and the Hungarian autumn by diverting attention from the totalitarian question that had mobilized French intellectuals until the mid 1950s.[46] As de-Stalinization challenged Communism and socialism from within, revealing that the "bastards" (*salauds*) were not just the "bourgeois" and that the Soviet Union was not necessarily in the vanguard of history, a new universalist mirage—a substitute messianism—presented itself to revolutionary intellectuals who were unable to relinquish Marxism completely: the independence struggles of the Third World.[47] A number of historians, including François Furet, explained the deviation of the wandering left-wing intelligentsia toward the Third World as one way of coming to terms with "the Stalinist truth." Shifting from Russia to the Third World was certainly one of the New Left's ways of bolstering Marxism while condemning both Stalinism and colonialism. As the symbol of this intelligentsia in search of political truth, Sartre turned from Moscow to the Third World: for a moment, the Algerian National Liberation Front appeared as the detonator of a new French revolution.[48] Furet viewed the transfer of revolutionary hopes (especially after the devastation of World War II) to Russia and then to the Third World as an avowal

---

progressive parties should not go against their supposed objectives (11). Césaire concluded that the very anticolonialism of French Communists bore the stigma of the colonialism they were combating (13). See *Letter to Maurice Thorez* (Paris: Présence Africaine, 1957). Originally published in French.

46. See Jean-François Sirinelli, "Les intellectuels français en guerre d'Algérie," in *La Guerre d'Algérie et les intellectuels français*, Jean-Pierre Rioux and Jean-François Sirinelli (Paris: Editions Complexe, 1991): 25. Tony Judt also adheres to this line of thought in *Past Imperfect: French Intellectuals, 1944–56* (Berkeley and Los Angeles: University of California Press, 1992). His book appeared after I had already completed this chapter. I do refer to it, however, in Chapter 5.

47. François Furet, "Les intellectuels français et le structuralisme," *Preuves* 192 (February 1967): 4. Furet qualifies this shift as one of ideological extremism characteristic of left-wing intellectual milieux who ended up isolating themselves from both the PCF and the working classes.

48. Edgar Morin, "Le symbole d'une errance," *Libération*, special issue on Sartre (1980): 37.

of the implicit impotence of national possibilities; it also implied the survival of Jacobinism: one day, France would once again guide revolutionary history.[49] Nonetheless, despite Charles de Gaulle's spectacular return to the political scene, France had already lost its political supremacy: "Expulsed from history, France accepts all the better to expulse history from French thought" (Furet, "Les intellectuels français" 6). As a result, it can now "cast a glance at a world that is no longer shielded by its own example and by a civilizing obsession: an almost spatial, henceforth skeptical glance on the 'lessons' and 'meaning' of history . . . this mistress for so long tyrannical and then unfaithful" (Furet, "Les intellectuels français").

Dethroned from his superior seat, the French intellectual of the 1960s was forced to come to terms with the notions of history and mankind that had underpinned French thought in the postwar years. But just how eager was a Marxist like Sartre to undertake such a venture? To what degree did the shift to the Third World adopted by the New Left represent an attempt to safeguard precarious Western notions of history and mankind in the midst of decolonization? Even though Sartre was forced to admit, in his preface to Fanon's *Les Damnés de la terre*, that the European had become a man only by fabricating slaves and monsters,[50] he hesitated to undertake a systematic reexamination of Western humanism, which became apparent in his defense of historical reflection and Marxism in the face of the structuralist advances of the early 1960s. Active in politics, eager to salvage philosophy, history, and Marxism from the reactionary forces of his time, Sartre had little time for literature in the late 1950s. And yet as the illusory expectations of the Fourth Republic evaporated, Sartre wrote *Les Séquestrés d'Altona* [The condemned of Altona] (1959), a play protesting the institutionalization of torture during the Algerian War. By focusing upon the dilemma of a Nazi trying to exonerate his guilt, Sartre was also alluding to the fact that the French, the

49. Furet, "Les intellectuels français," 6.

50. Sartre, preface to *The Wretched of the Earth* by Frantz Fanon, trans. Constance Farrington (New York: Grove, 1963), 22. Originally published as the preface to *Les Damnés de la terre* (Paris: Maspero, 1961). Reprinted in *Situations, V* (Paris: Gallimard, 1964). In the *Discourse on Colonialism*, Césaire contends that before being the victims of Fascism, Nazism, and Stalinism, Europeans were their accomplices: they tolerated barbarism, shut their eyes to it, and even legitimized it when it was applied only to non-European peoples. According to Césaire, "[what the European] cannot forgive Hitler for is not *crime* in itself, the *crime against man*, [but rather] the crime against the white man, the humiliation of the white man, and the fact that he applied to Europe colonialist procedures which until then had been reserved exclusively for the Arabs of Algeria, the coolies of India, and the Blacks of Africa." *Discourse on Colonialism*, trans. John Pinkham (London: Monthly Review, 1972), 14. Originally published as *Discours sur le colonialisme* (Paris: Présence Africaine, 1955).

former victims of Nazi Occupation, had themselves become, in little more than a decade, executioners (torturers).[51] Despite the belief in mankind as the maker of history that underlies the *Critique de la raison dialectique*, one has the sense in *Les Séquestrés d'Altona* (as in Albert Camus's Algerian stories of *L'Exil et le royaume* [The exile and the kingdom], written just before or at the time of the outbreak of the Algerian War) that the individual feels surpassed by history. History has now become synonymous with catastrophe and tragedy. The protagonists of *Les Séquestrés d'Altona* are no longer those of Sartre's earlier engaged theater: individual freedom is now impaired by a tremendous sense of guilt.

At the other extreme of the literary spectrum in the late 1950s lies the new novel and Robbe-Grillet, with his so-called objective realism, ostensibly devoid of human subjectivity and sociopolitical reality. Robbe-Grillet's rescinding of politics from literature was evident throughout his early novels and screenplays, which were deliberately devoid of any political content. Of these texts, *L'Année dernière à Marienbad* [Last year at Marienbad] was written in the midst of the Algerian War, yet Robbe-Grillet refused to refer to the Algerian War in that work. Was he insensitive to the political upheaval generated by the Algerian War? Or was he merely expressing his discontent with engaged literature? Robbe-Grillet's refusal to acknowledge Algeria in *Marienbad* was certainly not a claim for apoliticism. His association with the politicized Alain Resnais and with Minuit (one of the publishing houses most opposed to the war) was already indicative of his penchant for politics. Furthermore, in September 1960, along with such committed intellectuals as Sartre, Beauvoir, Châtelet, Lefebvre, and Duras, he signed the "Manifesto of the 121,"[52] which was a declaration of the right of insubordination and represented an act of civil disobedience. The manifesto had significant resonance; it was even said to hail the birth of an intellectual party. Endorsed by *Les Temps Modernes*, it was condemned by the Communist and Socialist Parties.

Robbe-Grillet nevertheless insisted on keeping Algeria out of *Marienbad*. Preoccupied on the one hand with formal innovation—considered secondary by Marxist literary paradigms—while on the other hand opposed to war and its political connotations, Robbe-Grillet found himself in a quandary over the mingling of literature and politics. By intentionally omitting Algeria from

---

51. Sartre, "Une victoire," in *Situations, V* (Paris: Gallimard, 1964), 73.

52. Although 121 French intellectuals signed the first manifesto on 4 September 1960, there were an additional 58 signatures by 29 September.

Marienbad, he was not so much displaying apoliticism as advocating the responsibility of forms that would become the leitmotiv of Barthes and *Tel Quel* during the 1960s. Besides, had Robbe-Grillet referred to Algeria in his screenplay, he would have acknowledged that the only way to be revolutionary in literature is to talk about class struggle or anticolonialist war. Adamantly opposed to the engaged notion that literature can only be about a certain content, Robbe-Grillet continually fought off this content with a narrative technique that prevented a story from being told and tried to suspend meaning: a technique characterized by endless repetitions, gaps, and interior duplications (*mises en abyme*). He believed that the subordination of form to content inevitably resulted in a socialist realism that was a revolutionary parody of nineteenth-century (Balzacian) bourgeois realism. Nevertheless, his preoccupation with form and his rejection of the coexistence of literature and politics earned him, from Marxist critics such as Lucien Goldmann, the reputation of being a technocratic, capitalist writer.

Other sociological readings of Robbe-Grillet shed a different light on his work. Jacques Leenhardt was one of the first critics to do a political reading of Robbe-Grillet based on an analysis of language and form. Leenhardt was thus led to say that *Marienbad* "is a world of conventions and stucco, a world of idle chatter and impotence," whereas *Jealousy* "gives us the old colonial empire, with its racism and myths, its incapacity to assure its domination in the face of rising forces that anguish it."[53] Leenhardt claims that far from being mere formalist exercises, Robbe-Grillet's works capture the morbid mood of a dying empire and republic and reflect the crisis of history and mankind, the decomposition of bourgeois society and its philosophical and literary tenets: humanism and realism (165–66).

In a retrospective, autobiographical text, *Le Miroir qui revient* [Ghosts in the mirror] (1984), Robbe-Grillet notes how surprised he is that so many literary critics, including Barthes who launched the revolutionary notions of "objective literature" and "literal literature," lost sight of the political unconscious of his early novels. How could so many readers fail to see the monsters against which he was struggling? Were they, too, grappling with their personal demons, braving them in seeking a degree zero of writing? Robbe-Grillet claims that his so-called whiteness was merely the color of his armor, and he was thus consecrated an "objective novelist." He contends

53. Jacques Leenhardt, "Nouveau Roman et Société," in *Nouveau Roman: Hier, aujourd'hui*, ed. Jean Ricardou and Françoise Van Rossum-Guyon (Paris: Union Generale d'Editions, 1972), 1:164. See also his *Lecture politique du roman* (Paris: Minuit, 1973).

that Barthes sought to reduce the cunning dislocations, implicit phantoms, and autoerasures of his novels to a universe of things that would merely affirm its own objective, literal solidity. This aspect, Robbe-Grillet now maintains, was only one of two irreconcilable poles of a contradiction in his writing. Barthes decided not to look at the monsters hidden in the shadows of the hyperrealist tableau. And when in *Marienbad* the ghosts and phantasms invaded in too visible a fashion, Barthes pulled back. Perhaps, suggests Robbe-Grillet, Barthes—like other writers (including himself)—was at grips with similar conflicts.[54] All were haunted by the ghosts of the recent past. Caught between the death throes of engagement and the much-awaited birth of a new literary spring in the early 1960s, writers and critics of the 1950s found an enterprise of spring cleaning in Robbe-Grillet's descriptive formalism. Sequestered by the political domination of the postwar years, the writer now turned "back towards his or her proper home in language," in order to display "its resources rather than naively attack the representation of an external object."[55]

Robbe-Grillet's influence on *Tel Quel* stemmed from his decision to free literature from the grips of politics: it was this common concern for disengagement that attracted *Tel Quel* to Robbe-Grillet and the new novel. Following in the footsteps of Robbe-Grillet, *Tel Quel*'s founding team was also confronted with the dilemma of the Algerian War. But unlike Robbe-Grillet, who still seemed troubled by the phantoms of World War II, *Tel Quel*'s founding group resolved the dilemma of the Algerian War by absolving themselves of the sense of guilt that prevailed among French intellectuals of the postwar era. We may interpret *Tel Quel*'s imperviousness to the Algerian War as a negation of the World War II legacy that, according to Sartre, had turned victims into executioners (or perhaps, as Aimé Césaire and Sartre had in effect shown, the victims had been executioners from the start). Clearly, the *Tel Quel* founding team had felt from the onset that they had not committed any sins—those of Fascism and Stalinism—and therefore did not need to assume the guilt of their elders. By disengaging from politics, by means of language, *Tel Quel* rejected history itself, a history created not by them but by their elders—the generation of Sartre and

54. Robbe-Grillet, *Le Miroir qui revient* (Paris: Minuit, 1984), 38, 69. Subsequently translated as *Ghosts in the Mirror*, trans. Jo Levy (London: John Calder, 1988), 34, 54–55.
55. Kristeva, "The Pain of Sorrow in the Modern World: The Works of Marguerite Duras," *PMLA* 102, no. 2 (March 1987): 139. Also in *Soleil noir: Dépression et mélancholie* (Paris: Gallimard, 1987).

Aragon—and in which they had been thrust. Even if the *Tel Quel* generation had not waged war, it had been cast into its throes.

Although no statements pertaining to World War II appear in the early issues of *Tel Quel*, the war nevertheless had a profound impact on the founding group. Huguenin (b. 1936) acknowledged that although he and his contemporaries no longer spoke of war, it was a legacy that weighed heavily on them. Addressing his generation in an article provocatively entitled "Aimer la vie, vivre l'amour!" [To love life, to live love!] that appeared in May 1961 in the art journal *Réalités*, Huguenin confessed that at the age of four, he was less frightened by the Nazi occupants than by French masses fleeing; at nine, after having witnessed a collective panic, he discovered the collective lie of Liberation: "My generation was born of this chaos. This war we did not wage has left us with scars from which we have yet to heal. As the children of abdicators, we were first injured in our pride."[56] Huguenin believed that he and his contemporaries were less marked by fear, humiliation, or suffering than by the realization that their pain was useless and, at most, had merely "paid the debts of their elders, their miserable between-the-wars happiness" (56). He noted that his generation "grew up without help and guidance. It had to sort things out by itself; its elders left it without ideals, principles, or mysticism" (61). The words of this twenty-year-old are clearly those of a so-called lost generation: the generation born just before or during World War II, that is, the *Tel Quel* generation.[57] Considering that this generation felt vanquished, which way would it turn? Was a reactionary stance the only logical solution? Is it just a generational law that it would go against its elders? That it would as a consequence reject engagement? Is it as simple as that? Or were the notions of engagement and socialist realism already on trial during the cold-war years and particularly in 1956, and for reasons that were not just literary in scope?

In revalidating literature as such, *Tel Quel* authors were essentially refusing a history they had not made, but that had nevertheless profoundly marked them. One of the leading spokespersons for the *Tel Quel* generation

56. Huguenin, "Aimer la vie, vivre l'amour!" *Réalités* no. 184 (May 1961): 56. In a letter of 21 February 1961 to François Mauriac—the literary father that launched him and Sollers—Huguenin stated that they were living in an "era in which any spiritual restlessness, any heartfelt craving pass[ed] for a reactionary stupidity." In *Le Feu à sa vie*, 55.

57. Between November and December 1976, *France-Culture* interviewed a number of writers such as Sollers, Hallier, Faye, and Lévy. The hypothesis put forth by the broadcast interviews was that the generation that turned twenty around 1960–62 was more than other generations (including the one that turned twenty in 1968) a "lost generation." See *Génération perdue*, interviews with Jacques Viansson-Ponté (Paris: Robert Laffont, 1977).

was the former Communist militant Jacques Henric (b. 1938), who joined *Tel Quel* in 1971. In 1986, Henric claimed that, contrary to the avant-garde writers who had preceded them, the Telquelians never sacrificed their literary and artistic convictions to the political slaughterhouse in the name of false gods like Stalin and Zhdanov. If the Telquelians succeeded, it is only because they caught themselves in time. They never resorted to engaged literature the way surrealists defected to socialist realism, Sartrean existentialism, or Camusian moralism.[58] Engagement developed in the 1930s to fight off the political barbarism of Fascism that intellectuals felt had resulted from the separation of powers (humanist or idealist culture). But this literary panacea, which had been conjured up to dispel the ghosts of a tinged past, was not the best elixir. Incarnated in the guilty conscience of intellectuals such as Sartre and Aragon, engagement ended up serving the "alter ego" of Fascism: Stalinism. By defending Communism at all costs during the late 1940s and early 1950s, engaged writers contributed to the perpetuation of historical barbarism through the support of Stalinism, thereby becoming the intellectual guardians of the gulag. By having sacrificed literature in the name of politics and freedom of thought in the name of the party, those writers were perceived as having sold their souls to the devil. Hence, Henric's (and *Tel Quel*'s) verdict on engagement did not merely concern the failure of literary and artistic convictions, but—worse—the writers' role in legitimating further historical barbarism.

The *Tel Quel* generation wanted to be freed of this *mea culpa*. This did not imply, however, that it remained impervious to the diabolical history that had begotten it. A fellow traveler of *Tel Quel* and *L'Infini* since the mid-1970s, Bernard-Henri Lévy defined himself as "the bastard son of a diabolical couple, Fascism and Stalinism."[59] And Henric states: "Think about it: it's no small matter to check into one of the most diabolical depressions that the history of humanity has ever known. The evil powers were crushed, of course, but the traumatism continues, henceforth symbolized in the name of Auschwitz." Indeed the war against Fascism and Nazism deeply affected Henric's generation: "Here is the factual and existential fabric of which we're made. Those who tomorrow will trace the history of

---

58. Henric, "Quand une avant-garde . . ."
59. Bernard-Henri Lévy, *La Barbarie à visage humain* (Paris: Grasset, 1977, 1979), my translation, 7. Subsequently translated as *Barbarism With a Human Face*, trans. George Holoch (New York: Harper and Row, 1979).

our generation while forgetting from what mire it arose risk a lot of sidetracked blab."[60]

While striving to exorcise the specters of World War II, the *Tel Quel* generation had to contend with the situation in Algeria, "the only war that France gave them as adults": a "dirty war" characterized by "racism, massacres, institutionalized tortures, the Left in power, censured newspapers, banned books" Henric concludes that "whoever looks into our intellectual drifts and forgets the political landscape in which they occurred, can already put his pen away. It is from the neglect of this concrete history of our contemporaries that roaring ideological discourses, abstract theories completely detached from reality were *almost* right about our thought, our art, our most elementary, moral honor."[61] If they were only *almost* right, it was because "unlike the avant-garde that preceded us, we caught ourselves in time. Whatever may have been our mild or not so mild, ideological deliriums, we never sacrificed our literary and artistic convictions to the political slaughterhouse. Literature is what saved us" (Henric, "Quand une avant-garde . . .").

From its first to its last issue, *Tel Quel* affirmed its unflinching belief in the powers of literature. Was this a convenient way of avoiding historical reality (art for art's sake as apoliticism), or rather a means of fashioning a safeguard against ideological deliriums (politicized literature leading to a subordination to totalitarian politics)? In an interview with *Les Lettres Françaises* in February 1960, Huguenin affirmed that *Tel Quel* stood for the new sensibility of a generation that distanced itself from the one of the Resistance. While the preceding era was marked by a guilt complex concerning the role of the writer and the function of literature in society, "[t]oday, with us, with our generation in any case, we're delivered from an exaggerated sense of responsibilities, themselves exaggerated."[62] The new literary generation represented by *Tel Quel* refused to be held accountable for the errors of their elders, and their desire to dissociate literature from politics stemmed precisely from the belief that they had no reason to feel guilty about their artistic vocation.

Unlike their elders who had wanted to transform society, the *Tel Quel* generation had other aspirations. These aspirations were delineated in *Tel*

---

60. Henric, "Quand une avant-garde . . ."
61. Ibid.
62. Huguenin cited in Hubert Juin, "Pourquoi une nouvelle revue?" *Les Lettres Françaises* (18 February 1960): 4.

Quel's opening issue, which began with an epigraph from Nietzsche—"to want the world and reality as it is [*tel quel*]"—and a declaration calling for "expression" freed from "political and moral directives." Numerous critics considered *Tel Quel*'s heralded ambitions as narcissistic, irresponsible, and presumptuous, and the fact that the first epigraph was from Nietzsche led more than one critic to accuse the group of fascist leanings. In December 1960, the Italian critic Aldo Rossi devoted twelve pages in the well-known literary journal *Paragone* to the first two issues of *Tel Quel* and to the clamor caused by the founding group. Although Rossi's piece is extremely detailed, he nevertheless maintains a cautious ideological distance from this new avant-garde. He states that *telquelisme* ("talqualismo") is just a step away from "qualunquismo" and situates *Tel Quel* between *La Ronda* and the Hermetic movement ("Ermetismo").[63] In a review of *Tel Quel* for *L'Europa Letteraria* of June 1960, Giancarlo Vigorelli nevertheless distinguishes between *Tel Quel*'s neohermeticism, which accepts the world "as is," and his own hermetic generation of 1938, which rejected the Fascist reality of its time.[64]

Faye, who joined the *Tel Quel* editorial board in 1963, cast them as reactionary. Following his departure from the group in 1967, Faye claimed that the only writers who managed to escape from the antifascist movement of the times were the "Hussards" and *Tel Quel*.[65] His assertion was unfounded for two reasons. *Tel Quel*'s founding members not only did not sign the "Counter-Manifesto of the 185," that is, the "Manifesto of French Intellectuals" of 7 October 1960 in *Le Figaro*, which represented a right-wing response to the "Manifesto of the 121," along with the "Hussards" Antoine Blondin, Roger Nimier, and Jacques Perret (all three of whom did sign the Counter-Manifesto); they also did not adopt the neoclassical literary positions of that group. *Tel Quel*'s inaugural issue can hardly be considered reactionary in its literary selections. It contains two prose poems by Ponge,

63. Aldo Rossi, "La ragione letteraria delle ultime leve francesi, 'Tel Quel,'" *Paragone* 132 (December 1960): 127. The term "qualunquismo" comes from the newspaper *L'Uomo Qualunque*, which was founded in 1944. It insisted that the ordinary man on the street could run the government better than the professional politician. By extension, it designates indifference to larger political questions. *La Ronda* was a literary review published from 1919 to 1923. It advocated a return to the classics (Leopardi, Manzoni, the prose writers of the sixteenth century) and the autonomy of literature from the sociopolitical problems of its times.

64. Giancarlo Vigorelli, "Il 'Telquellismo' francese," *L'Europa Letteraria* 1, no. 3 (June 1960): 126.

65. Faye, in Knapp, *French Novelists Speak Out*, 84. Faye was, nevertheless, not among those who signed the "anti-fascist" "Manifesto of the 121."

an essay on "Flaubert and Modern Sensibility," fictional pieces by Claude Simon and Cayrol, the results of a literary survey administered to such writers as Jean Cocteau and Gracq, and positive reviews of books by Maurice Blanchot, Natalie Sarraute, and Robbe-Grillet.[66] If *Tel Quel* was reactionary, it was because of its call for the separation of literature and politics. Despite the crisis of Marxism and engagement in the late 1950s, appraising a writer still meant first of all assessing his politics. And *Tel Quel* was strictly literary.

While the negative responses to *Tel Quel* cannot be disregarded, they circumscribe an even more important issue. It is not merely a question of whether *Tel Quel* was "reactionary." More important, we must ask whether *Tel Quel's reaction* was just the reaction of a few up-and-coming writers and therefore inconsequential—a mere literary parenthesis in the midst of a sordid sociopolitical reality—or rather the expression of the shifting mood of a new generation that had nothing in common with the one that had been forced to confront history during the 1930s and 1940s. After all, this literary parenthesis succeeded in attracting Faye, who claimed he joined the review for purely literary reasons, and, more specifically, because of a common love for Mallarmé and an interest in the Russian formalists.[67]

Of *Tel Quel*, Barthes said: "The (straight and narrow) path for a review like yours would then be to see the world as it creates itself through a literary consciousness, to consider reality periodically as the raw material of a secret work, to locate yourselves at that very fragile and rather obscure moment when the relation of a real event is about to be apprehended by literary meaning."[68] There was undoubtedly something seductive about the purely literary quality of *Tel Quel* that captivated the left-winger Faye; the ex-deportee Cayrol, who published the first works of Sollers, Boisrouvray, and Coudol in the *Ecrire* collection at Seuil; the engaged Catholic Mauriac, who launched Sollers and

66. Blanchot, Cayrol, Sarraute, and Simon had also signed the original "Manifesto of the 121." Other well-known intellectuals who signed the first Manifesto include Adamov, Beauvoir, Boulez, Breton, Damisch, Duras, Glissant, Claude Lanzmann, Henri Lefebvre, Leiris, Jérôme Lindon, Mascolo, François Maspero, Maurice Nadeau, Resnais, Jean-François Revel, Christiane Rochefort, Signoret, and Vercors. The second list included Butor, Châtelet, Ollier, Sagan, Truffaut, Tzara. François Wahl, an editor at Seuil, also signed this second list. This gesture of solidarity nevertheless concealed a number of ideological differences among the signatories. Wahl, for example, claims that he was neither a Marxist nor an existentialist. But he was always a left-winger (*un homme de gauche*) and fiercely anticolonialist. Cited in Rémy Rieffel, "L'empreinte de la guerre d'Algérie," in *La Guerre d'Algérie et les intellectuels français* by Rioux and Sirinelli, 209.

67. Faye, personal interview, Paris, 23 May 1979.

68. Barthes, "Literature Today," 157.

Huguenin; and the Communist Aragon, who officially introduced Sollers to the Left and whose journal, *Les Lettres Françaises*, would go down in history as the first newspaper or magazine to interview the *Tel Quel* founding team. But the list of admirers does not stop there. *Tel Quel*'s initial supporters also include the ex-Communist Ponge as well as Barthes and Robbe-Grillet. Such a list is surely a testament to the unblemished quality of the literature *Tel Quel* was advocating. This array of engaged and not so engaged French intellectuals paid tribute to *Tel Quel* from the onset, because—far from being reactionary—it was offering something very different from the austere literature of engagement, which was perceived not only as obsolete, but as an ally of totalitarian politics.

Certainly no one can accuse Seuil of being a reactionary publisher. Like Minuit, it played a leading role in opposing the Algerian War. With respect to its literary orientation, Seuil was to a large degree following in the footsteps of Minuit. In the early 1950s Minuit had promoted a new literature by publishing such novels as Samuel Beckett's *Molloy* (1951), Robert Pinget's *Mahu ou le matériau* [Mahu or the material] (1952), Robbe-Grillet's *Les Gommes* [The erasers] (1953), and Sarraute's *Martereau* (1953). Duras's *Moderato cantabile* and Henri Alleg's *La Question* [The question] were both published in 1958. Anne Simonin argues that this was not by chance; rather, it manifested a subversive publishing strategy, both in the literary and the political realms that assured the temporal coincidence of an aesthetic and political avant-gardism within the same publishing house.[69] By promoting the "new wave" of writers represented by *Tel Quel*, several of whom initially positioned themselves in the direction of the *nouveau roman*, Seuil was in many respects adopting the publishing strategy of Minuit.

Tel Quel's aspiration for a literature free from political constraints, a literature that apprehends the wor(l)d as it is—"tel quel"—brought back, for a number of writers, including Mauriac and Aragon, the memory of a literary youth that had been lost in the meanders of political engagement. In launching Sollers, Mauriac and Aragon wrote of "a drop from the new wave" and "an eternal spring." Mauriac conceded that although Sollers was not engaged, he was, nevertheless, a good writer, and Aragon went even further by exclaiming, "Who cares about politics anyways!" Pronounced in 1957 and 1958, such statements clearly indicate a shifting literary temper initiated by Robbe-Grillet and Ponge—*Tel Quel*'s forefathers—but brought forth by *Tel Quel*.

69. Simonin, "Les Editions," 236.

In welcoming Sollers and other Telquelians, were Mauriac and Aragon merely manifesting nostalgia for their youth? Or was *Tel Quel* the long-awaited answer to an unavowed disenchantment with the times and with a literature that had been instrumentalized by Stalinism? "I would be the first to write this name," Mauriac wrote enthusiastically in a review of *Le Défi* that appeared in the 12 December 1957 issue of *L'Express*.[70] In so doing, he launched Sollers's literary career. Mauriac's fellow *Bordelais* had just published *Le Défi* in *Ecrire* 3. It was rather surprising to see a major literary figure like Mauriac, a progressive Catholic and a firm critic of the Algerian War, devote an entire article to Sollers. This rather unexpected literary parenthesis was curiously inserted between two entries devoted to the struggle against the injustices of the Algerian War. The 2 December "Bloc-Notes" was devoted to the Sorbonne in absentia dissertation defense of the Communist mathematician Maurice Audin, who had mysteriously disappeared (and who had, in fact, been tortured and killed by the French army for siding with Algerian nationalists). How could someone like Mauriac, who in his 14 November 1957 "Bloc-Notes" entry wrote, "History will say that torture was reestablished in France by those who kept silent,"[71] endorse a self-centered writer like Sollers who had, in effect, "kept silent"? Of Sollers's politics, Mauriac wrote, "For him, to be left-wing is to be against his family and his milieu. . . . But I fear that no injustice will distract him from himself. It's because God doesn't interest him."[72]

A year later, Sollers published his first novel, *Une curieuse solitude*, which was well received by Académie Française member Emile Henriot as well as by the Communist writer Aragon. While he never objected to being reviewed by an *académicien*, Sollers never quite forgave Mauriac and Aragon for discovering him: "When one is led to the baptismal font at once by the Vatican and the Kremlin—the Kremlin in the process of becoming pink—as was the case for me at the age of twenty, it's a sign that one must react."[73]

70. François Mauriac, "Une goutte de la vague," *L'Express*, 12 December 1957, 36. Reprinted in *Bloc-Notes* (Paris: Flammarion, 1958).

71. Mauriac, *Bloc-Notes*, 384.

72. Mauriac, "Une goutte de la vague," 36. Years later, Sollers would praise Mauriac for his politics: "Mauriac's *politics*, beyond the left-wing romanticism that was mine, on principle, seem, in the final analysis, evident to me. Catholicism included, now evident too. Like Judaism for others, each his fiber . . ." Untitled preface, *Le Magazine Littéraire* 215 (February 1985): 15.

73. Sollers, "Ebranler le système," *Magazine Littéraire* 65 (June 1972): 10. Despite his polemical relationship with Aragon and Mauriac, Sollers nevertheless finally gave the latter his due in 1985. In the prefatory article to a special number on Mauriac of the *Magazine Littéraire*

Sollers subsequently repudiated *Le Défi* and *Une curieuse solitude* because they were too traditional. He claimed that these early texts were not so much written by him as "by a specific social group (the bourgeoisie), whose spokesman [he] happened to be at a given moment because of [his] class origins."[74]

The immediate acclaim of an apolitical writer by two politicized members of the literary establishment, who represented respectively the Catholic and Communist Left, and Sollers's subsequent need to repudiate his early texts in order to negate his fathers present a phenomenon that needs to be explored. Critics writing on Sollers and *Tel Quel* have totally neglected these early years and have failed to account for the reviews by Mauriac and Aragon. Aragon's review is especially important: it allows us to understand better the relationship of *Tel Quel* to the Communist Party, which did not begin, as most critics have stated, around 1966–67, but rather in 1958 when Aragon launched Sollers—and launched him as a distinctly bourgeois writer—for the Communist Left.

Was Sollers just a literary spell in the midst of the Algerian crisis as Mauriac seemed to indicate? Or was something more dramatic taking place in French culture, as a close reading of Aragon's review would indicate? Why would a militant Communist who had only recently defended socialist realism be launching a "bourgeois" writer? Aragon's initial interest in Sollers is symptomatic of an undercurrent in French culture in the late 1950s that could also explain *Tel Quel*'s subsequent relationship to the Communist Left. Apoliticism was perhaps an unavowed desire of the time even for writers and intellectuals outside of the *Tel Quel* group. In 1972, Brochier claimed that "without *Tel Quel*, literature and the Left would not be what

---

(February 1985), Sollers acknowledges that they were, after all, bound by the "solidarity of provincials" and their Catholicism. Sollers even states that *Portrait du joueur* (1984) is "silently dedicated" to him. Sollers's reconciliation with the dying Mauriac coincides with the death of his own father: "He died almost at the same time as my father. I've said enough" (15).

74. Sollers, "Réponses," *Tel Quel* 43 (Autumn 1970): 71. In 1972, he stated: "One must distinguish the first published texts from those that I consider to be the first written texts. I am unusual in that I published texts before writing them. . . . I don't disown them, I deny them, and it seems to me that it is my fundamental right to invalidate objects that I was led to produce, in a state of unconscious reproduction" ("Ebranler le système," 10). Sollers's second novel, *Le Parc*, was published a year after the founding of *Tel Quel* (1961). A "novelistic poem" in the wave of the new novel, it was awarded the Médicis Prize. Although it is a departure from his first two texts and already reflects the preoccupations of *Tel Quel*, for Sollers, the "first real book" is *Drame* (1965).

they are today in France."[75] One could add that without Aragon and the
PCF, Sollers and *Tel Quel* would not be where they are today either. Literary
critics and journalists have unanimously claimed that *Tel Quel*'s relation to
the Communist Left began in 1966–67. We are thus left wondering how a
belletristic journal subsequently became avant-garde and supported the
Communist Party during the May 1968 events. Most critics dismiss the
question by saying that Sollers and *Tel Quel* merely adopted various
ideological disguises to suit the needs of the moment. This view, however, is
too simplistic. The fact remains—one that has not yet been analyzed—that
relations between *Tel Quel* and the PCF actually began before the first issue
of *Tel Quel* came out.

"Why a new review?" On 18 February 1960, just a few weeks before the
inaugural issue of *Tel Quel*, the Communist intellectual Hubert Juin interviewed Sollers, Hallier, Huguenin, and Coudol for *Les Lettres Françaises*.
This Communist literary journal was the first periodical to interview the *Tel
Quel* team. The early interest in *Tel Quel* by the Communist Left is quite
remarkable, especially in view of the journal's purely literary and apolitical
beginnings. And yet we must remember that on 20 November 1958, Aragon,
the editor-in-chief of *Les Lettres Françaises*, had launched Sollers in a
laudatory review of *Une curieuse solitude*, qualifying Sollers as "a genuine
writer," "a noble soul, one that knows what it is to dream."[76] Aragon's early
interest in Sollers reveals a changing cultural mood, characterized by the
de-Stalinization of the French Communist Party and the crisis of socialist
realism in the 1950s.

A rather lengthy review containing many revealing digressions, Aragon's
"Un perpétuel printemps" [An eternal spring] tells us more about his own
identity crisis as a writer in the late 1950s than it does about Sollers's *Une
curieuse solitude*. Aragon even asks himself if his fondness for the novel is
spurred by Sollers or by the memory of his own youth. The review begins
with a quote from Michel Zéraffa's novel, *Les Doublures* (1958): "two
essential forces were fighting for control of the world: the class struggle and
love; there was one too many" (15). Not only does Aragon criticize Zéraffa
for being too obsessed by the class struggle, but he also openly admits to
liking love stories: "too bad for those who take them for some sort of
cowardliness during revolutions and wars" (16). Aragon would like to speak

---

75. Brochier, "Tel quel, du nouveau roman à la révolution culturelle," 9.
76. Louis Aragon, "Un perpétuel printemps," in *J'abats mon jeu* (Paris: Réunis, 1959).
Originally published in *Les Lettres Françaises* (20–26 November 1958).

of Sollers "as if he were his age" (30). He admits to having reached that age where one awaits each new spring with less certainty, that age where he no longer finds the depth that he experienced in his youth: the marvelous slowness of life (24–25). The incantatory words of *Une curieuse solitude* nevertheless succeed in transporting Aragon back to the memory of his own spring. Thanks to Sollers, Aragon once again finds his youth; he discovers the surrealist past of his *vingt ans*. Despite the quarrels and schisms that characterized the surrealist group, Aragon refers to them as *les miens*. Not only does he claim that despite his Communist militancy he never sacrificed the surrealist horizon of his youth; he also admits to committing the crime of liking bourgeois literature (28, 38).

Aragon's concluding remarks on *Aurélien* (1944), considered one of his finest novels, are most revealing: "Of *Aurélien* people had already said, with that offended look of those who know and live outside of sin, how could you write *that* between 1941 and 1943?" (37). In fact, what they implied was that the class struggle was not sufficiently exposed in this novel. For Aragon, a more specific accusation appears to underlie these political objections to his work: "these manifestations of the modern *cant* can be summarized by a more precise accusation, which can only reinforce the good things I say or will say about the book of this *young bourgeois*, Philippe Sollers. It's that *Aurélien* is bourgeois literature, and I'm committing the crime of liking bourgeois literature. And so what?" (37–38). Aragon's fondness for Sollers's bourgeois writing was clearly not just a rebuttal of his long-held engaged principles. He obviously saw in the founder of *Tel Quel* the resurgence of something he had cherished but that had been battered and long repressed: a literary passion reminiscent of his surrealist youth: "And little by little, I am overtaken by this fragrance . . . by this transparent story, like cool water after a long walk" (26).

With Sartrean engagement and Aragonian socialist realism as literary paradigms for left-wing culture in the 1940s and 1950s, surrealism had never really succeeded in recovering the avant-garde dream of the 1920s and 1930s: "By 1960 surrealism was a dream of the past struggling to maintain the illusion that it still had something to offer the present."[77] *Tel Quel*, however, would revive the avant-garde wager left behind by surrealism. *Tel Quel*'s beginnings are as bound up with the *nouveau roman* of the 1950s as they are with surrealism and the 1920s, and behind this confluence, with the

77. Susan Suleiman, "As Is," in *A New History of French Literature*, ed. Denis Hollier (Cambridge: Harvard University Press, 1989), 1013.

literary modernity of the late nineteenth and early twentieth centuries. *Tel Quel's* objective of joining up with literary modernity was put forth unambiguously by Sollers in his interview with Juin in *Les Lettres Françaises: Tel Quel* was not just a "youth journal" reflecting the aspirations of a new up-and-coming literary generation, but rather an attempt to take literature seriously once again the way Flaubert, Baudelaire, Mallarmé, Proust, Valéry, Gracq, Ponge, and Robbe-Grillet had done. *Tel Quel* sought to revive a literary modernity that had essentially been dormant since the 1930s.

The avant-garde cultural experiences of the first half of the century once again became the real centers of passion and interest in the 1960s: "the nineteenth century is only officially over in literature sixty years later. What's essential for poetry is still Mallarmé, Lautréamont, surrealism; for the novel, Kafka, Joyce, Faulkner."[78] Why this gap? For Sollers, the period from the end of World War I to the 1960s forms a historical bloc and represents forty years of dissolution.[79] The latter half of this period joins up with and prolongs the surrealist era defined by André Breton in *Situation du surréalisme entre les deux guerres* [The situation of surrealism between the two wars]; that is, "surrealism can only be historically understood as a function of war—from 1919 to 1938—in relation both to the war it came from and the one it returned to."[80] If, for surrealism, everything begins with the senseless and cruel disaster of World War I, it does not end in the aftermath of World War II. If the immediate postwar years revolve around the question of Fascism and its extirpation from political institutions and cultural forms, French writers and intellectuals, during the late 1940s to the early 1960s, discover the aforementioned alter ego of Fascism: Stalinism. Sollers maintains that intellectual historians have not sufficiently accounted for the fact that "the twentieth century has known the two greatest experiences of cultural barbarism ever recorded by humanity: Fascism and Stalinism."[81] These two political forces have relentlessly opposed cultural modernity, labelling it formalist, bourgeois, decadent, pederast, and Jewish. The aversion to modernity is clearly more than a matter of artistic taste when it becomes associated with nationalism and xenophobia, racism, homophobia,

78. Sollers, "Littérature: le retour des précieux," *Le Nouvel Observateur* 525 (2–8 December 1974): 73.

79. Sollers, *Vision à New York*, 73.

80. André Breton, *Situation du surréalisme entre les deux guerres* (Paris: Editions de la Revue Fontaine, 1945), unpaginated. Originally a lecture delivered at Yale University on 10 December 1942.

81. Sollers, "Littérature: le retour des précieux," 73.

and anti-Semitism. Scarpetta argues that "the subjective motivating force behind anti-Semitism and xenophobia is in fact the same one that invests the resistance to modern art."[82]

Sollers claims that "it is only around 1964–66 that one can say that memory is revived."[83] (73). The "revival of memory" is bound up with language, for what path does memory take if not the one of language?[84] Hasn't every culture always suspected that language doesn't just say what it says? Isn't it symptomatic that the literary and artistic currents most suppressed by Fascism and Stalinism share a profound concern for the workings of language? Shouldn't the cultural renewal of a decade marked by the political phenomena of decolonization and de-Stalinization pay particular heed to the "detour taken through language by repressed thought?"[85] What collapses in the 1960s is, in effect, "the naive and instrumentalist conception of language,"[86] whose political ramifications need to be explored. The collapse coincides with a rebirth of the avant-garde: "It is only with delay, and after so many censors and obliterations, that our era takes note of Russian futurism and Formalism, surrealism, the great endeavors of narrative, linguistics, and even of psychoanalysis" (73). This revival is a function of a theoretical *aggiornamento*—a renewal in the human sciences at whose center is language. In a text symptomatically entitled *Lire le Capital* [Reading capital], Louis Althusser placed the question of language at the center of cultural renewal in the 1960s, contending that those years were "marked by the most dramatic and difficult trial of all, the discovery of and training in the meaning of the 'simplest' acts of our existence: seeing, listening, speaking, reading . . ."[87]

The revival of memory resulted in nothing less than the explosion of

82. Scarpetta, *Eloge du cosmopolitisme*, 291–92.

83. Sollers, "Littérature: le retour des précieux," 73.

84. Where path is intended in its etymological purity—from the Sanskrit *panthah*: "The panthah . . . is not simply the road as a space to cover from one point to another. . . . It is rather a 'crossing' attempted over an unknown and often hostile region . . . in short, a way into a region forbidden to normal passage, a means of going through a perilous or rough expanse." Emile Benveniste cited in Sollers's "Lautréamont's Science," *Writing and the Experience of Limits*, trans. Philip Barnard and David Hayman (New York: Columbia University Press, 1983), 143. Originally published in *Logiques* in Collection Tel Quel (Paris: Seuil, 1968) and subsequently in *L'Ecriture et l'expérience des limites* (Paris: Seuil, 1971).

85. Sollers cited in Monique Charvet and Ermanno Krumm, *Tel Quel: Un'avanguardia per il materialismo* (Bari: Dedalo, 1970), 31.

86. Sollers, "Littérature: le retour des précieux," 73.

87. Louis Althusser, *Reading Capital*, trans. Ben Brewster (New York: Pantheon, 1970), 15. Originally published as *Lire le Capital* (Paris: Maspero, 1965).

French intellectual thought in 1965–66, as signaled by the publication of Lacan's *Ecrits*, Foucault's *Les Mots et les Choses*, Althusser's *Pour Marx* [For Marx] and *Lire le Capital*, Barthes's *Critique et vérité* [Criticism and truth] and *Essais critiques* [Critical essays], Benveniste's *Problèmes de linguistique générale* [Problems in general linguistics], and Derrida's *De la grammatologie* [Of grammatology] (in *Critique*). Underlying this intellectual explosion was an acute attention to the workings of language, which gave *Tel Quel* its theoretical basis for reactualizing the avant-garde dream. A new conception of writing (*écriture*) began to permeate literature, linguistics, philosophy, and psychoanalysis, and the works of Jakobson, Benveniste, Derrida, Foucault, Lacan, and Althusser provided *Tel Quel* with a theoretical orientation that mirrored its own literary preoccupations. With this theoretical armor, *Tel Quel* was ready to pick up the avant-garde wager abandoned by surrealism. Whereas the surrealists had Marx and Freud, *Tel Quel* had Althusser and Lacan. Furthermore, the avant-garde venture spearheaded by *Tel Quel* was not to be the only beneficiary of the theoretical explosion of the mid-1960s: *Tel Quel* would meet up with the Communist Party as it began to undergo cultural de-Stalinization, and Communist intellectuals would also shift their attention to linguistics and psychoanalysis. Thus, language became the missing link that joined together notions, practices, and groups that had previously been judged incompatible. French intellectual thought and its institutions would never be the same again after these close encounters of the 1960s, whose common ground was language.

CHAPTER TWO

EXCESSES OF
LANGUAGE

The excesses of languages, to which the practice of literature
gives rise when it accedes to the rank of great art,
bring about with them as many excesses of thought.
— Jean-Louis Houdebine

From its onset, *Tel Quel* endeavored to bring together a fictional current originating in the great figures of modernity—Flaubert, Proust, Joyce, Kafka, Céline—and culminating in the works of Gracq and Robbe-Grillet; and a poetic one whose representatives were Baudelaire, Mallarmé, Lautréamont, Hölderlin, and Ponge. Such an undertaking was evident in *Tel Quel*'s inaugural issue, with an essay on "Flaubert et la sensibilité moderne" by Renaud Matignon. Matignon analyzes how Flaubert revolutionized the novel and established a new line of writing passed down to Robbe-Grillet. The first issue also contained fictional texts by new novelists and Minuit writers such as Simon, Thibaudeau, and Cayrol. In addition, there were two prose poems, "La Figue (sèche)" [The (dry) fig] and "Proème" by the marginal surrealist Ponge, who, thanks to *Tel Quel*, finally received the recognition due him.[1] These inaugural

1. Although Ponge also launched Sollers, Sollers is credited with having rediscovered Ponge, so to speak. In the mid-1950s, Sollers attended Ponge's lectures at l'Alliance Française. In 1960, he gave a lecture at the Sorbonne in which he stated that Ponge was a poet who needed to be better known. He also devoted two works to Ponge, *Francis Ponge* in the "Poètes d'aujourd'hui" collection at Seghers (1963) and *Entretiens de Francis Ponge avec Philippe*

texts were supplemented by a survey on writing and by the fiction of Sollers, Boisrouvray, and Jacques Coudol.

If Flaubert was the "patron" of *Tel Quel*, its fathers were the new novelist Robbe-Grillet and the surrealists Ponge and Gracq. In the only essay he ever devoted to *Tel Quel*, "Distance, Aspect, Origin," which later became the strategic opening piece of *Théorie d'Ensemble* [A comprehensive theory] (1968), Foucault highlighted the importance of Robbe-Grillet for the group by claiming that *Tel Quel* had found "in this father, a trap where [it] remained captive, captivated" (11). Foucault was also the first to publicly recognize—at the Cerisy Colloquium of 1963—*Tel Quel*'s debt to surrealism and, in particular, to Georges Bataille and Ponge. Robbe-Grillet and other new novelists showed *Tel Quel* how the novel could bring together a creative activity and its intellectual project. The surrealists, on the other hand, imbued *Tel Quel*'s founders with a distaste for a prosaic realism that is devoid of the poetic dimension, and with a consideration for the transgeneric dimension of writing. The avant-garde articulation between art and politics subsequently followed.

As his disciple and former student at the Claude-Bernard lycée in Paris, Huguenin expressed his admiration for Julien Gracq: a mentor who had succeeded in crossing the entire prewar, war, and postwar period while remaining a writer *and a poet*.[2] In emphasizing Gracq's importance as a poet, Huguenin was, in effect, alluding to the distinction made by Sartre fifteen years earlier in *Qu'est-ce que la littérature?* [What is literature?] where he had rejected poetry in favor of prose. Huguenin, nevertheless, recognized that for *Tel Quel* it was not just a question of returning to poetry—a genre that had been neglected in the postwar years—but, more important, of transcending the traditional generic distinctions of prose and poetry and looking for the poetic dimension in the novel and essay. This new way of looking at the poetic—outside of generic qualifications—would be one of the distinctive and lasting trademarks of the *Tel Quel* enterprise. In time, it was to assume linguistic, philosophical, and political dimensions, thanks to the pioneering work of Roman Jakobson, Denis Roche, Bataille, Kristeva, Pleynet, and other *Tel Quel* affiliates.

Sollers (12 interviews transmitted on Radio *France-Culture* from 18 April to 12 May 1967), which were published in 1970. Another Telquelian, Jean Thibaudeau, published *Francis Ponge* (1967). Texts by and on Ponge were published in the following issues of *Tel Quel*: 1, 4, 6, 8, 10, 13, 18, 25, 33.

2. Huguenin interviewed by Juin in "Pourquoi une nouvelle revue?" 4.

More than providing the convergence point of the novelistic and the poetic, Coudol hoped that *Tel Quel* would fuse the two into a third movement. Anticipating the impact of the human sciences on literature, philosophy, and history in the 1960s, Sollers foresaw that the literary genres were about to fuse: "Each one of us more or less dreams of a text which would be the culmination of this fusion of all the genres." He added further, "We would like our review to be the site where the different attempts to fuse literary genres could come together."[3]

The first work to be published in the Collection Tel Quel at Seuil, which was directed by Sollers, was Flaubert's *La Première éducation sentimentale* [The sentimental education]. Heretofore only available in a limited scholarly edition, Flaubert's work was now made accessible to the general public. In welcoming the young Flaubert into their sanctuary, these Telquelians, in their mid-twenties, were honoring their debt to literary modernity. In an essay on "Le Travail de Flaubert" [The work of Flaubert] published in *Tel Quel* 14 (Summer 1963), Gérard Genette declared that all Flaubert was already in the work of this twenty-three-year-old (51). In his preface to the Flaubert book, François-Régis Bastide proclaimed: "We knew it, but now we know it even better: the 'Patron' is Flaubert." In acknowledging Flaubert as their mentor, the young Telquelians were rediscovering the poetic art of the young Flaubert—what the critic Albert Thibaudet had qualified as Flaubert's ambition to move beyond genres and deal with the problem of expression in general.

Tel Quel subscribed to the notion that great literary texts could not be reduced to the restrictive categories of genres. As a "convention that underwrites all of our readings,"[4] genre is a discursive device that situates or programs the act of reading. It thereby defines the limits of readability. It is no coincidence that the great works of literature both defy generic classification and are considered unreadable. The compartmentalization of genres has inevitably resulted in the compartmentalization of the mind. Genres, like disciplines, are "discursive police" (Foucault, *L'Ordre du discours* 37) whose autonomy or identity is primarily determined by arbitrary regulations and limits. They function separately only to the degree that they exclude or repress fundamental aspects of other domains of knowledge. At the Cluny II Colloquium ("Literature and Ideologies") of 1970, Sollers stated: "If the

3. Coudol and Sollers interviewed by Juin, 4.
4. Marcelin Pleynet, "La poésie doit avoir pour but . . ." in *Théorie d'ensemble*, 95. Originally published in *Critique* (June 1968).

repressed of philosophy is politics, the repressed of literature would be philosophy."[5] Allowing the various genres and disciplines to come into contact with and contaminate one another implies coming to terms with traditional definitions of literature and culture. As a result, traditional concepts must be redefined or new terms coined. If disciplines have histori- cally been determined by particular worldviews that relate to social practices and conditions, then literature too has no intrinsic definition. Rather it is defined as what a particular society (or dominant group within such a society) in a particular historical moment conceives as literature.[6] Literature is thus a function of ideology; it is the manner in which a social class or group seeks to represent itself. *Tel Quel* dismissed "the historically deter- mined concept of literature,"[7] hoping to leave arbitrary dichotomies behind. By accentuating confluences and reevaluations, *Tel Quel* aimed to transform cultural practice, thereby producing new worldviews.

The transgeneric and transdisciplinary ambition of *Tel Quel* was only fitting for a group that had chosen the collective and hybrid review-form as its medium for cultural renewal. Initially the site for the recasting of literary forms, by the mid 1960s, *Tel Quel* would also bring together literature, art, philosophy, science, and politics. As a journal, *Tel Quel* never wanted to emphasize literary genres; instead, it endeavored to locate a site beyond the traditional distinctions of narrative, poetry, and criticism. This new site came to be called *écriture* and was subsequently integrated with other *Tel Quel* topologies such as the "text" and "signifying practice." These "keywords," which were fundamental to the *Tel Quel* enterprise, revealed a new relation- ship between literary practice and semiotic theory that was to have a profound impact on both. For *Tel Quel*, *écriture* always implied a theory *and* practice of writing—the coexistence of the two in the very same act or experience. In 1970, Sollers stated, "What we call *écriture textuelle* is the work site between a scriptural practice and its theory."[8] As a result, a new literary space emerged that defied not only generic divisions but also those divisions between writing and thought, creation and meditation, theory and practice.

Tel Quel's first phase (from 1960 to 1963) was necessarily an exploratory

---

5. Sollers, "La lutte idéologique dans l'écriture de l'avant-garde," *Littérature et idéologies* (Colloque de Cluny II, 2–4 April 1970) in *La Nouvelle Critique* special no. 39a (1970): 77.

6. Leon Roudiez, "With and Beyond Literary Structuralism," *Books Abroad* 49 (Spring 1975): 208.

7. Sollers, "Programme," *Tel Quel* 31 (Autum 1967): 5.

8. Sollers, "Ecriture et révolution," in *Théorie d'Ensemble*, 70.

one. The move from "literature" to *écriture* necessitated a new reference axis, a new way of looking at the literary text. The exploratory nature of this first phase is reflected in the technique, previously adopted by the surrealists, of interviewing and surveying writers and critics on their craft. *Tel Quel* believed that a new approach to the literary text could only come from the practice of writing itself, from writers not only reflecting on their own practice of writing, but incorporating this reflection into the very act of writing.

Often dismissed as eclectic, these early years actually served an important theoretical purpose. In addition to a vast array of fictional, poetic, and critical texts, as well as more significant pieces that transgress generic and disciplinary boundaries, the early issues of *Tel Quel* contain a number of surveys and interviews. *Tel Quel* sought to define a new literary spirit, inaugurated by the new novel of the mid-1950s, that was to influence the status of criticism in the mid-1960s. For example, the first issue of *Tel Quel* contains a survey administered to thirty-one writers entitled "Pensez-vous avoir un don d'écrivain?" [Do you think that you have a gift for writing?] Writers interviewed included Jean Cocteau, Philippe Jaccottet, Jean-Louis Bory, François Nourissier, Philippe Soupault, André Pierre de Mandiargues, Jean-Louis Curtis, François-Régis Bastide, Céline, Gracq, Paulhan, Sarraute, Robbe-Grillet, and Zéraffa.[9] Gracq replied that this question was meant to render the writer ill-at-ease (40). His response implicitly revealed what was to become *Tel Quel*'s mission: illuminating the conditions of literary creation through an analysis of the writing process and the factors that render it imponderable.[10] Indeed, *Tel Quel* was less interested in knowing whether writers thought that they had a special "gift" (a notion with all sorts of clairvoyant connotations), than in understanding why, over the centuries, the act of writing had been surrounded by a mystical aura. By the same token, it was not so much the psychological nature of the writer that intrigued *Tel Quel*, but rather the makeup of the literary experience itself.

Under the rubric "La littérature, aujourd'hui" [Literature, today] (a title that immediately brings to mind Robbe-Grillet's series of manifesto essays that appeared in *L'Express* in the mid-1950s), *Tel Quel* interviewed Barthes (no. 7), Sarraute (no. 9), Louis-René des Forêts (no. 10), Michel Butor (no.

---

9. Although the cover jacket indicates that thirty-two writers responded, in effect, only thirty-one responses are included in the issue.

10. Julien Gracq, "Enquête: Pensez-vous avoir un don d'écrivain?" *Tel Quel* 1 (Spring 1960): 39.

11), Cayrol (no. 13), and Robbe-Grillet (no. 14). Its purpose was to ascertain how writers arrived at theoretical positions from their own practice of writing. Robbe-Grillet, in fact, began his interview by claiming that he was a writer and not a theoretician. By interviewing writers and a critic like Barthes, the review sought to define a theoretical position stemming from the experience of writing itself. For *Tel Quel*, one could not be a writer without first acknowledging the very act that makes one a writer: the practice of writing.

Tel Quel took an interest in criticism early on. Inaugurating a series essentially devoted to writers with an interview of Barthes is indicative of a changing literary climate in which traditional distinctions between the writer and the critic were becoming obsolete. Barthes, in fact, argued that the writer could no longer be "defined in terms of his role or his value but only by a certain *awareness of discourse (parole)*.[11] While *Tel Quel*'s first survey was devoted to writers and their "gift for writing," its second and last survey (no. 14) was administered to forty critics who were asked: "Why are you a critic and what are your criteria? What did you learn from criticism and what did you expect from it?" Those interviewed included Gérard Genette, Claude-Edmonde Magny, Claude Ollier, R.-M. Albères, Hubert Juin, Eugène Ionesco, Pierre de Boisdeffre, Claude Simon, and many lesser-known critics. Interested in the dialectic between the creative and critical functions of language at work in the texts of writers and critics, *Tel Quel* categorized the forty responses as follows. There were first of all those critics (Genette was privileged among them) for whom criticism is an exercise of language: the writer considers himself a critic; the critic claims to be a writer. The second category established a division between writers and critics, among whom writers were the privileged group, even if they lacked a critical perspective, whereas critics were "pedagogical servants" who could be either paternalistic or overmodest. This group had the most respondents. The third group reflected the consequences of the second: a complete loss of identity on the part of critics. The last group views criticism merely in economic terms as a means of earning a living or of promoting oneself as a writer. *Tel Quel* noted that the generally mediocre responses to the two surveys seemed to provide sociological evidence favoring the dominant literary ideology of the time, which writers and critics for the most part refused to challenge. Their

---

11. Barthes, *Criticism and Truth*, 64. Barthes would be interviewed again by *Tel Quel* in numbers 16 ("Littérature et signification") and 47 ("Réponses").

answers revealed an implicit faith in literature as an institution that has been defined once and for all.

Published two years prior to the Barthes-Picard critical controversy, the "Survey on Criticism" (1963) led *Tel Quel* to foresee the day when criticism would no longer have literature as its object, for literature would have criticism as its object.[12] In challenging the traditional opposition between the writer and the critic, *Tel Quel* attempted to define a new notion of writing necessarily contingent on the interpenetration of the creative and critical functions of language. It is important to remember that *Tel Quel* was founded at a time when writers were still not expected to account critically for what they did, and critics were not supposed to "write." The "worn-out myth of the *'superb creator and the humble servant, both necessary, each in his place'* " was still in effect, as revealed by the Barthes-Picard polemic of 1965–66.[13] *Tel Quel* opposed the separation of the creative and critical functions of writing; in so doing, it demanded that writers "take a critical, virtually a scientific attitude toward themselves, that they break permanently with the individualism of the would-be creator of forms."[14] For *Tel Quel* there were "no innocent forms, no rough, original, pure, immediate, popular, first or last forms" (Sollers, *Writing and the Experience of Limits* 191). By dismissing "the neoromantic eloquence that deifies a writer, making of him a creator,"[15] *Tel Quel* sought to remove the literary experience from its pedestal. For the notions of the writer as a genius, a godlike figure conjuring his masterpiece out of the void, or of writing as creation ex nihilo obfuscate the notion of production: one has the impression that either nothing happens or something unexplainable happens.[16] So long as creative or metaphysical conceptions of literature and culture prevail, it will never be possible to consider these as social domains and stakes of political struggles. By relegating historical processes to a spiritual realm, we succeed in rendering them "timeless and classless," universal, eternal, and, consequently, irreproachable.

No wonder that the question of literature had become anachronistic and

---

12. Gérard Genette, "Enquête sur la critique," *Tel Quel* 14 (Summer 1963): 71.

13. Barthes, *Criticism and Truth*, 64.

14. Sollers, "The Novel and the Experience of Limits," in *Writing and the Experience of Limits*, 191. Originally published as "Le roman et l'expériences des limites" in *Tel Quel* 25 (Spring 1966). Subsequently published in *Logiques*.

15. Jacques Henric, "Ecriture et révolution (interview with Philippe Sollers)," in *Théorie d'ensemble*, 67.

16. Pierre Macherey, *Pour une théorie de la production littéraire*, 2d ed. (Paris: Maspero, 1978), 84–85.

irrelevant and, consequently, had been spurned, during the 1940s and 1950s by those interested in political passions and issues.[17] The problem with literature lay in its confinement "within the reductionist limits of the concept of 'belles lettres,' that offspring of middle-class liberalism" (Felman, *Writing and Madness* 15). Shoshana Felman maintains that those "who claim that the demystification of this liberalism does away with the very notion of literature as well" fail to recognize "that what we call the literary goes quite beyond the issues of bourgeois ideology, that literature not only surpasses, but in fact totally subverts the reductionist definition in which some have sought, and still seek, to imprison it" (*Writing and Madness* 15).

What dangers lurk behind the literary object, such that social institutions feel obliged to disarm it; that is, to surround it with a mysterious halo, thereby attributing to it an ornamental and consequently secondary place in our culture? According to Kristeva, it is in the name of magic, poetry, and literature that a certain practice in the signifier has throughout history been surrounded by a "mysterious halo," which, in valorizing such a practice or attributing to it an ornamental place, at once censors and ideologically recuperates it.[18] Relegated to the "sacred," "beautiful," or "irrational," the literary object or text ended up being subordinated to religion, aesthetics, and psychiatry ("Le texte et sa science" 7).

This is precisely what *Tel Quel* aimed to combat. Literature would continue to be scorned by the politically minded or held captive by a decorative halo so long as it remained subordinate to political ideologies or to an aestheticizing ideology that failed to consider the act of writing as a self-conscious activity and poetic language as an "opening up of beings" (Kristeva, "The Ethics of Linguistics" 25). For *Tel Quel*, only a radical exploration of language could help offset the secondary status held by literature in France. This obviously meant coming to terms with the content/form dichotomy that made possible such distinctions as fiction, poetry, and criticism. Such a dichotomy had also led to the conclusion that if literature was not engaged, it was frivolous. Sollers maintained that form and content had to be conjugated in a responsible manner. If content and

17. Shoshana Felman, *Writing and Madness* (Ithaca: Cornell University Press, 1985), 15. Originally published as *La Folie et la chose littéraire* (Paris: Seuil, 1978). *Tel Quel* also published the following by Felman: an interview with Sollers, "La chose littéraire, sa folie, son pouvoir" (nos. 80, 81), "Don Juan ou la promesse d'amour" (no. 87).

18. Kristeva, "Le texte et sa science," in *Séméiotiké: Recherches pour une sémanalyse*, which was published in Collection Tel Quel (Paris: Seuil, 1969), 7.

form were perceived as one and the same, committed writers could claim to deliver their thoughts without any concern for form. Likewise, frivolous writers could argue that their form was sufficient to absorb their ideas; consequently they were dispensed from questioning them. If the former were guilty of disrespect for the infinite richness of forms and resources of language, the latter were equally at fault for having recourse to the travesty of form in order to avoid calling their thought into question.[19]

In an interview with Communist intellectual Jacques Henric, Sollers maintained that literature, in France, was symptomatic of "a profoundly reactionary, decadent and, to sum it all, exhausted ideology."[20] This remark was made only in 1967, at the onset of *Tel Quel's* overtly politicized phase. Although *Tel Quel's* early years can be characterized by a lack of political positions, from its onset, *Tel Quel* nevertheless rejected two "ideologies" that underpinned the traditional notion of literature: (1) the "ideology of the text as reflection," inherent in the novel and central to debates on literary realism, and (2) an aestheticizing ideology attributed to poetry by a belletristic tradition bound up with Western metaphysics. In taking exception to these two apparently diametrically opposed ideologies, *Tel Quel* was in line with Barthes, for whom generic distinctions such as fiction and poetry were possible only insofar as they rested on a faulty premise that made "reality" the concern of the novel, and "words" the concern of poetry,[21] a paradigm essential to engaged literature. Therefore, in order to dispel the Manichaean opposition that made literature either engaged (subordinate to politics) or frivolous (the domain of an "aestheticizing obscurantism"), *Tel Quel* had to dismantle this paradigm. How? By taking language and, consequently, literature seriously. By recognizing that "language is the *being* of literature, its very world: all literature is contained in the act of writing, and no longer in that of 'thinking,' of 'painting,' of 'recounting,' of 'feeling.' "[22] The accent on language "specifically jeopardizes the assurance of a world which arrogantly sets 'realities' against 'words,' as if language were merely the futile decor of humanity's more substantial interests."[23] Barthes maintains that "it is solely by its passage through language that literature pursues the disturbance of the essential concepts of our culture, 'reality' chief

19. Sollers, "L'expérience 'Tel Quel,' " *Les Lettres Françaises* (23 January 1964): 5.
20. Sollers, "Ecriture et révolution," in *Théorie d'Ensemble*, 67–68.
21. Barthes, "Literature Today," *Critical Essays*, 160.
22. Barthes, "From Science to Literature," 4–5.
23. Barthes, "The Indictment Periodically Lodged . . . ," in *The Rustle of Language*, 343.

among them."[24] Thus, any critique of literature must begin with its pretensions and claims to realism and expressivity.[25]

Tel Quel's first phase devoted considerable attention to the question of literary realism. Not only was this question raised in all the interviews of "La littérature aujourd'hui," but it was also central to the polemic on Robbe-Grillet that culminated in the "Débat sur le roman" [Debate on the novel] at the Cerisy Colloquium of 1963. It was also at the heart of Sollers's early essays on the novel, "Logique de la fiction" [The logic of fiction] (Tel Quel, no. 15) and "Le roman et l'expérience des limites" [The novel and the experience of limits] (Tel Quel, no. 25). The debate on realism is important for understanding how Tel Quel went beyond the nouveau roman and surrealism by articulating the relationship of literary experience to philosophy. As an alternative to postwar engagement, Tel Quel initially turned to the nouveau roman, which it considered as the only force to represent a new formal and ideological approach to literature in 1960.[26] Sollers went so far as to say, in 1962, that it was the experience of the new novel that had taught him how to be a serious writer.[27] His second novel, Le Parc [The park] (1961), which was awarded the Médicis Prize, departs from the classical style of Une curieuse solitude and clearly shows his debt to the new novel. Two Minuit writers were appointed to Tel Quel's editorial board at an early point: Jean Thibaudeau, who received the Fénéon Prize for his first novel, Une Cérémonie royale (1960), replaced Huguenin in 1960 (no. 3); Jean Ricardou, author of L'Observateur de Cannes [The observer of Cannes] (1961), which was excerpted in Tel Quel (no. 5), joined in 1962 (no. 9).

Tel Quel's beginnings coincide with the peak moment of the nouveau roman. Fundamental texts such as Robbe-Grillet's Dans le labyrinthe [In the labyrinth], Sarraute's Le Planétarium [Planetarium] and Ollier's La Mise en Scène were published in 1959; Simon's La Route des Flandres [The Flanders road] and Butor's Degrés [Degrees] in 1960. The first seventeen issues of Tel Quel contain fictional pieces by Robbe-Grillet, Simon, Ollier, Cayrol, and Ricardou, as well as interviews with and critical texts by Sarraute, Butor, Robbe-Grillet, Ricardou, and des Forêts. Although texts by new novelists would cease to appear in Tel Quel after 1964, Ricardou, considered the

---

24. Barthes, "From Science to Literature," 5.
25. Sollers, "Literature and Totality," Writing and the Experience of Limits, 71. Originally published as "Littérature et totalité," in Tel Quel 26 (Summer 1966).
26. Sollers, "Tel Quel aujourd'hui," France Nouvelle (31 May 1967): 21.
27. Sollers, "Où va le roman?" Le Figaro Littéraire (22 September 1962): 3.

theoretician of the *nouveau roman* group, would continue to be a driving force behind the review until his resignation in November 1971. Ricardou, whose first *Tel Quel* publication dates back to 1960 (no. 2), published both fictional and theoretical pieces in the journal. A number of these theoretical pieces were subsequently incorporated into *Problèmes du nouveau roman* (1967) and *Pour une théorie du nouveau roman* (1971), both published in Collection Tel Quel. Ricardou was especially important to the *Tel Quel* enterprise of the early 1960s for his exploration of the novel in terms of "auto-representation" and "anti-representation," and for his work on metaphor and analogy (including *mise en abyme*). He spoke out against the realist illusion and the premises of engaged literature at a debate in 1964 entitled "Que peut la littérature?" that had been organized by the Union of Communist Students (UEC) and their journal *Clarté*. The debate brought together the champion of engagement, Sartre, along with Beauvoir, Communist writers Yves Buin (the editor of *Clarté*) and Jorge Semprun, Yves Berger, and another Telquelian, Faye.[28] As the sole practitioner *and* theoretician of the new novel—all the other new novelists disclaimed that they were theoreticians—Ricardou, who considered the work of *Tel Quel* a radicalization of the *nouveau roman*, provided *Tel Quel* with a formalist orientation (Sollers even situated Ricardou's work in the wake of the Russian formalists) that would be central to *Tel Quel's* phase of the mid- and late 1960s.

Tel Quel's reputation as "a radical advance on and a critique of the nouveau roman"[29] is also due to historical circumstances. According to Ricardou, the new novel came of age in a period characterized by a theoretical void: the work of Blanchot and Barthes was still occulted by engagement. The new novel established itself in a very adverse ideological climate, and did so only with difficulty.[30] *Tel Quel*, on the other hand, benefited from the weakening hold of existentialism and engagement on French culture (64). The demise of engagement can be attributed, in part, to the work of the new novel in contesting literary realism, specifically the notion that literature passively reflects social practice. The critique of realism inevitably led to an awareness of language per se, at a time when semiotics was asserting itself as a new discipline. With its attention to

---

28. See *Que peut la littérature?*, ed. Yves Buin (Paris: Union Générale d'Editions, 1965).

29. Stephen Heath, *The Nouveau Roman: A Study in the Practice of Writing* (Philadelphia: Temple University Press, 1972), 216.

30. Jean Ricardou, "Nouveau Roman: Un entretien de Jean Thibaudeau avec Jean Ricardou," *La Nouvelle Critique* 60 (January 1973): 64.

narrative technique and forms, the new novel, as self-referential writing, represented a coming together of the creative and critical functions of writing: every new novel was, to a degree, a theory of the novel.

Although *Tel Quel* acknowledged the undeniable role played by the new novel in reawakening literary consciousness in the mid-1950s, it came to suspect its formalism of being a diversion from more urgent philosophical and political questions that had been raised previously by Sade, Mallarmé, Lautréamont, Joyce, Artaud, and Bataille. If *Tel Quel*'s break with the new novel was based on literary and philosophical reasons, and not political reasons as Sollers would later claim, an important question still remains: If the break in 1963 was not the result of political differences, is there any remote connection between that break and the separation of literature and politics for which Sollers criticized the new novel years later? That is to say, did the reasons for the break at Cerisy ultimately point a way out of the impasse of both the *nouveau roman* and Sartrean engagement, when it came to the question of bridging an innovative literary practice and political militancy?

In September 1963, *Tel Quel* organized a colloquium at Cerisy entitled "Une nouvelle littérature?" [A new literature?] with the purpose of reassessing the literary situation in France, beginning with the *nouveau roman*. Participants included Foucault, the musician Gilbert Amy, the novelist and musician Maurice Roche (who collaborated with *Tel Quel* before founding *Change* in 1967 with Faye), the philosopher Maurice de Gandillac, the new novelist Ollier, the poet Jean Tortel, the Italian avant-garde *Novissimi* writers Edouardo Sanguineti and Alfredo Giuliani, and a number of Telquelians, including Sollers, Pleynet, Faye, Thibaudeau, and Baudry. Thibaudeau also notes that there were several young German writers present, whose names unfortunately he does not recall.[31] In *Mes Années "Tel Quel"* [My *Tel Quel* years], Thibaudeau deplores the selective published accounts on Cerisy, which he attributes to the rival ambitions of Sollers, Pleynet, and Faye (93–94). The special issue devoted to Cerisy (no. 17) contains only the presentations of Faye, Pleynet, and Amy (the opening presentation by Sollers, "Logique de la fiction" appeared in *Tel Quel* 15), and the debates on the novel and poetry. It does not account for all participants and discussions at the colloquium.[32] According to Thibaudeau, no mention is made of the

---

31. Jean Thibaudeau, *Mes Années "Tel Quel"* (Paris: Editions Ecriture, 1994), 94.
32. Thibaudeau accounts for the presence of Giuliani and Roche, whose names do not appear in no. 17. He also mentions the presence of German writers. However, he fails to

two presentations by Giuliani and Sanguineti (*Mes Années "Tel Quel"* 93–94). As we shall later see in our discussion of the debates on the novel and poetry, Sanguineti was at odds with Foucault and the Telquelians because of his Marxist positions. Thibaudeau writes that "Sanguineti, in effect, during the sessions, was alone against all. The only 'Marxist'" (97). Nor was any mention made of the presentations and discussions on painting and film (94). *Tel Quel's* special issue on Cerisy scarcely calls attention to the various arts and the somewhat international dimension of the colloquium. But "A New Literature?" constitutes a strategic moment in the history of *Tel Quel*: the beginning of a period that culminated in *Théorie d'Ensemble* in 1968. Cerisy 1963 represents a turning point in the history of *Tel Quel*: it concurrently marks its official break with the *nouveau roman* and, in particular, Robbe-Grillet, as well as its transition to a new phase (1963–67) characterized by the articulation of the practice of writing (*écriture*) with philosophy.

This articulation of writing with philosophical thought would be legitimized, so to speak, by Foucault's role as moderator, along with Faye, at Cerisy. Foucault's presence at this *Tel Quel* gathering may appear surprising since he published only one essay in the review, "Le langage à l'infini" [Language to infinity] (no. 15), and devoted only one text to the *Tel Quel* team in *Théorie d'Ensemble*: "Distance, Aspect, Origin." These were, nonetheless, the years (1962–67) in which Foucault published a significant number of texts devoted to authors such as Roussel, Hölderlin, Bataille, Klossowski, Robbe-Grillet, Mallarmé, Verne, and Blanchot, not to mention the transgressive function accorded to literature in *Histoire de la folie*. At the time of his encounter with the *Tel Quel* group, Foucault was not yet the intellectual guru that he was to become with the publication of *Les Mots et les choses* in 1966. Today, ten years after his death, critical interest in Foucault still focuses, for the most part, on his relationship to structuralism and his contribution to the human sciences.[33] Few would venture to call Foucault a writer, even if that made him famous in the first place (Revel, "Histoire d'une disparition" 82). In fact, Sollers would be one of the first to consider Foucault a writer. Perhaps, remarks Judith Revel, the problem is not that Foucault wrote well, but that he allowed the practice of writing— his "grand baroque style" (Blanchot, *Michel Foucault as I Remember Him*

---

account for de Gandillac and Tortel whose names appear in the special issue. *Mes Années "Tel Quel,"* 93–94.

33. Judith Revel, "Histoire d'une disparition," *Le Débat* 79 (March–April 1994): 82.

64)—to be an integral part of the process of knowledge (83). The Western philosophical tradition has, over the centuries, sought to contain the "wakefulness of writing," that writing which for idealist, logocentric thought has always been scorned as "a decorative exteriority, a dangerous possibility of non-truth."[34] Consequently, to place philosophical discourse—essentially pivoted on the question of truth—at the periphery of writing, in the materiality of language, is already to have begun to subvert Western thought.

According to Pierre Macherey, Foucault did not just reflect *on* literature; he worked *with* literature.[35] Foucault repeatedly acknowledged that it was thanks to his reading of Roussel in 1957 that he was able to break definitively with the phenomenological hold of the postwar period[36] and its conception of language and the subject. And if Nietzsche became the new *maître à penser* of the philosophical generation of the 1960s, Foucault confessed, nevertheless, that he had read Nietzsche because of Bataille, and he had read Bataille because of Blanchot.[37]

Foucaldians, for the most part, have lost sight of the important theoretical and transgressive function that the practice of writing occupies in the work of Foucault.[38] *Raymond Roussel*, the sole book that Foucault devoted entirely to a writer, went almost unnoticed. It was, however, most favorably reviewed by Sollers in *Tel Quel* 14 (Summer 1963): "The scope of his investigation, the subtlety and depth of his reflection, coupled with a writing (*écriture*) of great beauty already give Michel Foucault, and lead us to foresee for him as a writer, an extremely important place (it is obvious). His *Roussel*, in any case, is with Maurice Blanchot's *Lautréamont* the most brilliant critical (but poetical) book in recent years. One is almost tempted to call it, in reference to *The Birth of the Clinic*, *The Birth of Criticism*."[39] In his appraisal of Foucault's *Roussel*, Sollers makes several noteworthy remarks. First of all, Foucault is a writer. And he is a writer because he is a

34. Sollers, "L'écriture fonction de transformation sociale," in *Théorie d'Ensemble*, 401. Originally published in *La Nouvelle Critique* 12.

35. Pierre Macherey, *A quoi pense la littérature?* (Paris: Presses Universitaires de France, 1990), 177.

36. Foucault cited in Revel, "Histoire d'une disparition," 85.

37. Foucault, "How Much Does it Cost for Reason to Tell the Truth?" in *Foucault Live*, ed. Sylvère Lotringer (New York: Semiotext(e) Foreign Agents Series, 1989), 239. Originally published in *Spuren* (May–June 1983).

38. Revel, "Histoire d'une disparition," 82.

39. Sollers, "Logicus Solus," *Tel Quel* 14 (Summer 1963): 50. Subsequently reprinted in *Logiques*.

critic. For Sollers, Foucault establishes critical discourse as an independent genre. In his attempt to determine why the critical essay was developing more and more independently of the literary works to which it referred, Yves Bertherat, writing on Foucault's *Roussel* and Butor's *Essais sur les modernes* for *Esprit*—the other journal at Seuil—claims that there is something behind the mystery of the work (*l'oeuvre*) that entreats us more than the work itself. Bertherat views this resistance within the work in terms of the surreal, marvelous, or transcendent—notions that continue to place the problematic nature of literature outside of language.[40] These terms would, in fact, be contested by Foucault and the *Tel Quel* group at Cerisy. Nevertheless, Bertherat shares, to some degree, *Tel Quel's* earliest preoccupations when he states, two years later, again in reference to the work of Foucault, that literature solicits us only insofar as it remains inexplicable.[41] Explaining literature, he notes, has nevertheless become a major obsession of the 1960s, and has resulted in the advent of a science of literature, conflicts among critical schools, and the displacement of literature into philosophical space. In discussing the latter, Betherat recognizes the importance of Foucault's "mad thought" (*pensée folle*), that "thought from the outside" which contests the terrorism of Western reason and which *Tel Quel* would claim is perhaps nothing other than literature. For Foucault, literary practice opens up, beneath the edifice of knowledge, a breathtaking, refractory space that needs to be thought, that is, also brought into play.[42] Foucault attempts to define a new writing space for himself, while also making it visible in the works of others, so that a redefinition of traditional nomenclature of discourses can take place: a new typology whereby the act of writing would found another distribution of disciplinary languages and where the production of speech would no longer be merely the last refuge of a subjectivity and henceforth excluded from the body of science (83–84).

Sollers sees this shift taking place in Foucault's *Roussel*, through what he terms the birth of criticism in relation to the birth of the clinic.[43] In fact, Sollers is one of the rare reviewers to establish a relationship between two apparently distinct works published contemporeaneously—apparently at Foucault's request—in May 1963. In so doing, he situates criticism as a new

---

40. Yves Bertherat, "Essais," *Esprit* 33, 334 (January 1965): 285.
41. Bertherat, "La pensée folle," *Esprit* 35, 360 (May 1967): 862.
42. Revel, "Histoire d'une disparition," 83.
43. Jacques Derrida further examines the relationship between critical and clinical discourse in "La parole soufflée"—the first piece he published in *Tel Quel*—in a special issue devoted to Artaud (no. 20) in the winter of 1965.

form of discourse at the confluence of space, language, and death—the subject of *Naissance de la clinique* [The birth of the clinic], where he examines death not only through the medical gaze but also through the art and literature of modernity. In that study, Foucault points out that since the nineteenth century, both medical and lyrical experience have been a function of death:

> In what at first sight might seem a very strange way, the movement that sustained lyricism in the nineteenth century was one and the same as that by which man obtained positive knowledge of himself; but it is surprising that the figures of knowledge and those of language should obey the same profound law, and that the irruption of finitude should dominate, in the same way, this relation of man to death, which, in the first case, authorizes a scientific discourse in a rational form, and in the second, opens up the source of a language that unfolds endlessly in the void left by the absence of the gods.[44]

Roussel obviously captivated Foucault because he revealed the "profound relationship that all language maintains with, disengages itself from, takes up, and repeats indefinitely with death."[45] In fact, in "Le langage à l'infini," the only piece he published in *Tel Quel*, Foucault examines the death that is at the heart of all writing (particularly with reference to Hölderlin, an author of central importance to *Tel Quel* in the 1960s, as we shall see further on in this chapter). *Tel Quel* published Hölderlin's "Retour" [Return] as well as an extract from Heidegger's work on Hölderlin in issue 6 (Summer 1961); the poet Michel Deguy's "Sur le commentaire Heideggerien de Hölderlin" [On the Heideggerian commentary of Hölderlin] appeared in issue 8 (Winter 1962); Hölderlin's "Fragments" appeared in *Tel Quel* 68; and Houdebine's *Excès de langages* [Excesses of languages] devotes numerous pages to Hölderlin. Could Foucault's tribute to Roussel be situated, as Macherey claims, in the wake of Heidegger's work on Hölderlin?[46]

A philosopher working on Hölderlin, Mallarmé, Kafka, Artaud, Bataille,

---

44. Foucault, *The Birth of the Clinic: An Archaeology of Medical Perception*, trans. A. M. Sheridan Smith (New York: Pantheon, 1973), 198. Originally published as *Naissance de la clinique: Une archéologie du regard medical* (Paris: Presses Universitaires de France, 1963).

45. Foucault, *Death and the Labyrinth: The World of Raymond Roussel*, trans. Charles Ruas (Garden City, N.Y.: Doubleday, 1986), 54. Originally published as *Raymond Roussel* (Paris: Gallimard, 1963).

46. Macherey, *A quoi pense la littérature?* 193.

Roussel, or Sollers was something unheard-of in relation to what classical philosophy had led us to expect.[47] And yet, with the accent on language in the 1960s, the articulation of philosophical thought with the practice of writing (and vice versa for *Tel Quel*) became common practice for a number of philosophers, such as Foucault, Derrida, and Gilles Deleuze, who ventured to challenge the so-called supremacy of Western rationality. The passage through literature (fiction and poetry) was significant; it permitted philosophers to bypass the authority of the philosophical tradition[48]—a tradition that has systematically sought to exorcize the machinations of language by relegating them to literature. By investigating what Western rationality had systematically excluded over the centuries, Foucault, Derrida, and Deleuze were inevitably looking at "thought from the outside" (Foucault), from the "excesses of language." According to Jean-Louis Houdebine, "the excesses of languages to which the practice of literature gives rise when it accedes to the rank of great art, bring about with them as many excesses of thought."[49]

Foucault's pioneering work on the division between reason and madness in Western culture would be fundamental in redefining the place of literature in French intellectual thought of the 1960s and 1970s; as such it would leave its mark on the *Tel Quel* enterprise. The importance of Foucault's *Histoire de la folie* for *Tel Quel* cannot be overstated: Sollers considers it the major event of the 1960s.[50] Although Blanchot, Barthes, Pierre Klossowski, and other literary intellectuals took an immediate interest in Foucault's history of madness, the same cannot be said for psychiatrists and historians. According to Foucault, *Histoire de la folie* was poorly received in left-wing intellectual circles: no mention was made of it in *Les Temps Modernes*.[51] Perhaps this is not by chance. If the history of Western culture can be characterized

---

47. Jean-Louis Houdebine, "Positions" (interview of Jean-Louis Houdebine and Guy Scarpetta with Derrida on 17 June 1971) in Derrida, *Positions*, trans. Alan Bass (Chicago: University of Chicago Press, 1981), 67. This interview was originally published in *Promesse* 30–31 (Autumn–Winter 1971), a satellite journal of *Tel Quel* and subsequently reprinted in *Positions* (Paris: Minuit, 1972).

48. Dominique Grisoni, "Années soixante: la critique des philosophes," *Magazine Littéraire* 192 (February 1983): 44.

49. Houdebine, *Excès de langages* (Paris: Denoël, 1984), 11.

50. Sollers, "De *Tel Quel* à *L'Infini*," *Autrement* 69 (April 1985): 8. *Tel Quel*, however, did not review Foucault's book at the time of its publication. Only later did *Tel Quel* and *L'Infini* publish two important texts on Foucault that devote considerable attention to *Madness and Civilization*: "L'Autre Histoire: à partir de Michel Foucault," *Tel Quel* 86 (Winter 1980) and "Michel Foucault Singulier," *L'Infini* 11 (Summer 1985). Both texts are by Bernard Sichère.

51. Foucault, "On Power," in *Politics, Philosophy, Culture: Interviews and Other Writings*

essentially by "Reason's progressive conquest and consequent repression of that which it calls madness," Foucault's *Histoire de la folie* reminds us that it is not coincidental that "throughout our cultural history, the madness that has been socially, politically, and philosophically repressed has nonetheless made itself heard, has survived as a speaking *subject* only in and through literary texts."[52]

The "limit-texts" of writers such as Hölderlin, Nerval, Lautréamont, and Artaud, or thinkers on the "outer frontier" (Foucault) of philosophy, like Nietzsche, play out what was heretofore relegated to madmen, dreamers, or mystics. Their writing contests the very reason that underpins Western thought. What they recover is not an irrationalism, but rather those forms of the most profound reason—the forms of its contestation.[53] This contestation is necessarily situated in language; as Sollers states, "the defense mechanisms of society—as revealed by a certain criticism—are especially directed against language, the guaranty of agreed-upon rationality."[54] At Cerisy, Foucault contended that the division between reason and madness had been played out in a particularly intense and violent manner in the texts of modernity. Since the nineteenth century, and the advent of literature as we know it today, language itself, argues Foucault, has been the arena where the play of limit, contestation, and transgression has unfolded with the greatest intensity.[55]

In the "Debate on the Novel," which he moderated at Cerisy, Foucault continually drew comparisons between the writing of *Tel Quel*—particularly, of Sollers and Pleynet—and his own philosophy. Foucault was the first to show how the writing of *Tel Quel*, although influenced at its onset by both the new novel and surrealism, succeeded in giving literature a new philosophical dimension that was lacking in both. He was also the first to acknowledge the importance of Robbe-Grillet for *Tel Quel*. In "Distance, Aspect, Origin," Foucault wrote of the group's indebtedness to Robbe-Grillet. In the second issue of *Tel Quel*, Sollers published "Sept propositions sur Robbe-Grillet" (an essay on *Dans le Labyrinthe*), which, Foucault argued, read almost like a second "Declaration."

(1977–1984), ed. Lawrence Kritzman, trans. Alan Sheridan (New York: Routledge, 1988), 97. Originally published in *L'Express*, 6–12 July 1984.

52. Shoshana Felman, *Writing and Madness*, 38, 15.

53. Foucault, "Débat sur la poésie," 76.

54. Sollers, "Logique de la fiction," *Tel Quel* 15 (Autumn 1963). Presented at Cerisy, this text was reprinted, in slightly modified form, in *Logiques*, 27.

55. Foucault, "Débat sur la poésie," 75.

The "Debate on the Novel" at Cerisy was, in many respects, the culmination of a series of critical essays *Tel Quel* had devoted to Robbe-Grillet from 1960 to 1964.[56] The review's interest in Robbe-Grillet had been sparked by the lively critical debate surrounding his so-called evolution from a hyperrealist, thing-oriented (*chosiste*) writer of "l'école du regard" to an extremely subjective one, for whom the imaginary realm became primary. This evolution seemed particularly apparent in his screenplay for Alain Resnais's *L'Année dernière à Marienbad*, excerpted in *Tel Quel* (no. 5). Critics such as Bruce Morrissette thus spoke of two Robbe-Grillets, whereas Barthes attempted "Le Point sur Robbe-Grillet" [The last word on Robbe-Grillet]. Had Robbe-Grillet evolved or had critics misread his early novels? Had he abandoned the objective realism of *Les Gommes* (1953) for the purely imaginary realm of *Marienbad* (1961)? Did his work reflect a "positivist intelligence or a fundamentally poetic imagination?"[57]

A chronological reading of Robbe-Grillet's essays and interviews, a number of which were subsequently published in *Pour un nouveau roman* [For a new novel], points to an evolution. In 1953, Robbe-Grillet stated that "*Les Gommes* is a descriptive and scientific novel" and "the events take place in my book outside of psychology, which is the habitual instrument of novelists."[58] However, in 1961, he noted that the descriptions of *Le Voyeur* [The voyeur] and *La Jalousie* [Jealousy] "are always made by someone," and that this witness is "someone sexually obsessed or a husband whose distrust borders on delirium."[59] In his introduction to *Marienbad* he stated that "[t]he whole film, as a matter of fact, is the story of a persuasion: it deals with a reality that the hero creates out of his own vision, out of his own words."[60] Such statements led to the conclusion that his descriptions are

56. *Tel Quel* interviewed Robbe-Grillet in no. 14 (Summer 1963). Texts on Robbe-Grillet include: Sollers's "Sept propositions sur Robbe-Grillet," *Tel Quel* 2 (Summer 1960); Gérard Genette's "Sur Robbe-Grillet," *Tel Quel* 8 (Winter 1962), reprinted in revised form as "Vertige fixe" in *Figures I* (Paris: Seuil, 1966); Faye's "Nouvelle Analogie?" *Tel Quel* 17 (Spring 1964); Sollers's review of *Pour un nouveau roman* in *Tel Quel* 18 (Summer 1964); Ricardou's "Réalités variables," *Tel Quel* 12 (Winter 1963) and "La querelle de la métaphore," *Tel Quel* 18.

57. Genette, "Vertige Fixe," 89–90.

58. Robbe-Grillet, "Alain Robbe-Grillet: géomètre du temps," *Arts* (20–26 March 1953): 5; and *Combat*, 6 April 1953.

59. Robbe-Grillet, interview in *Le Monde*, 13 May 1961, 9.

60. Robbe-Grillet, *Last Year at Marienbad*, trans. Richard Howard (New York: Grove, 1962), 10. Originally published as *L'Année dernière à Marienbad* (Paris: Minuit, 1961).

"absolutely subjective" and that "this subjectivity is the essential characteristic of what's been called the *nouveau roman*."[61]

An informative analysis of Robbe-Grillet's evolution was undertaken by
Genette in "Sur Robbe-Grillet" (*Tel Quel* 8). Regardless of whether critics
had misread Robbe-Grillet or whether he actually evolved, the revision of
the Robbe-Grillet myth was significant. The implications of such a revision
had to be analyzed, and that is precisely what Genette and other Telquelians
set out to do. To what degree must Robbe-Grillet's two phases be made to
coincide? Must one, Genette asks, look for a "realist" intention, a desire,
that is, to describe reality as it is or as it appears; or rather for a "fantastic"
proposal, one that is exterior to this reality and the result of an arbitrary
fiction?[62] Robbe-Grillet's entire work appears to be guided by a profound
concern for realism. Did he then merely pass from objective realism (a reality
independent of the consciousness that the characters in the novels have of it)
in *Les Gommes* and *Le Voyeur* to subjective realism (a reality grasped and
described through the perceptions, memories, and fantasies of the characters) in *La Jalousie* and *Marienbad*? Did the latter solution represent a way
of salvaging a realist position (72–73)? Genette concludes that all of
Robbe-Grillet's contradictory protests proceed from a refusal of classical
psychology and the fantastic. His equivocal relation between object and
subject is the perpetual alibi whose oscillation between the two permits him
to escape these two stumbling blocks by playing one against the other. Hence
his initial pretensions to integral objectivity and his subsequent conversion
to pure subjectivity serve the same function: they constitute the realist point
of honor of an author who is not a realist but cannot accept that he is not
(90). For Genette, this dilemma represents the exemplary malaise of a
literature besieged by a world it can neither refuse nor admit. In his review
of *Pour un nouveau roman* (*Tel Quel* 18), Sollers concedes that Robbe-
Grillet and the other new novelists were right to contest the psychological
novel, but in so doing went to the other extreme. They fell prey to the "realist
error"; that is, an excessive privilege was accorded to the so-called exterior
world in their works.[63] In his 1956 piece "Pour un réalisme de la présence"
[For a realism of presence], which would later be incorporated into *Pour un
nouveau roman*, Robbe-Grillet stressed how he sought to move beyond a
world of psychological or social meanings characteristic of the nineteenth-

61. Robbe-Grillet, *Le Monde*, 9.
62. Genette, "Vertige Fixe," 72.
63. Sollers, "A. Robbe-Grillet: Pour un nouveau roman," *Tel Quel* 18 (Summer 1964): 93.

century realist and naturalist novel. Instead, he hoped to construct a more solid and immediate world: "In this future universe of the novel, gestures and objects will be *there* before being *something*."[64] He noted that "since it is chiefly in its presence that the world's reality resides, our task is now to create a literature that takes that presence into account" (23).

In his essay on Robbe-Grillet's apparent evolution from an objective to a subjective writer, Barthes maintained that Robbe-Grillet's "[theoretical] error was merely to suppose that there is a *Dasein* of things, antecedent and exterior to language, which he believed literature was obliged to rediscover in a final impulse of realism."[65] For Barthes, "literary realism has always presented itself as a certain way of *copying* reality. As if reality were on one side and language on the other, as if reality were antecedent to language and the latter's task were somehow to pursue the former until it had caught up" (197). Robbe-Grillet's descriptive formalism (the objective or literal dimension of his early novels) was a means of purging his predecessors' realism of its moralistic, political, or passionate dimensions. What nevertheless remained was an attempt to *represent* the world, albeit through an apparently neutral, quasi-scientific language. Like the realists, Robbe-Grillet "copies or seems to copy a model; in formal terms, we might say that he proceeds as if his novel were only the event which satisfies an antecedent structure." Whether his realism is objective or subjective is not that pertinent, "for what defines realism is not the origin of its model but its exteriority in relation to the language which expresses it" (198). Sollers, in fact, argues that the absolute subjectivity of the second Robbe-Grillet is merely a "mental realism" that models itself on the outside world.[66]

In the "Debate on the Novel" at Cerisy, Foucault maintained that Robbe-Grillet's conception of reality placed him in an aesthetics of perception. Foucault argued that Robbe-Grillet expurgated metaphor because it embodied a certain relation of the writing subject to the world. Making metaphors was a means of appropriating the world, as though metaphor were between the subject and the world.[67] Robbe-Grillet refuses this bridge and seeks to restore the distance between the external world and mankind. He does so through a descriptive formalism: "the visual or descriptive adjective, the word that contents itself with measuring, locating, limiting, defining, indi-

64. Robbe-Grillet, *For a New Novel*, 21. Originally published as "Pour un réalisme de la présence," *L'Express*, 17 January 1956, 11. Reprinted in *Pour un nouveau roman*.
65. Barthes, "The Last Word on Robbe-Grillet?" in *Critical Essays*, 203.
66. Sollers, "A. Robbe-Grillet: Pour un nouveau roman," 94.
67. Foucault, "Débat sur le roman," *Tel Quel* 17 (Spring 1964), 40.

cates a difficult but most likely direction for a new art of the novel."[68] Robbe-Grillet purposefully resorted to description. He sought to place himself outside of things, rather than at the heart of them as in metaphor: "Posited, from the start, as *not being man*, they remain constantly out of reach and are, ultimately, neither comprehended in a natural alliance [metaphor] nor recovered by suffering [tragedy]" (*For a New Novel* 70). The gaze registers a distance and refuses any complicity between the subjective and the objective: "Optical description is, in effect, the kind which most readily establishes distances: the sense of sight, if it seeks to remain simply that, leaves things in their respective place" (73).

But even to privilege perception, to be content, in a positivist gesture, merely to measure, is, Faye argued at Cerisy, not to limit oneself to seeing but also to displace: "to measure, is already to cut into, deform, and transform the big object: the world."[69] It is not the objects in Robbe-Grillet's novels that are interesting, but rather their displacements. Moreover, notes Faye, it is not only the objects that are displaced by observation, but also the observer or *observatories*: "The novel is perhaps this disagreeable experimentation, where the observatories are of an unlimited number and all are in movement" (62). At each instant, the Observatory-Player is transformed. Subjectivity crops up insidiously in what began as a hygienic enterprise of disinfecting the world of man's presence (60).

Despite his eagerness to free himself from the traditional psychological novel, Robbe-Grillet could not completely dispel the psychologism in which his novels remained embedded. Indeed, his "realist illusion" continued to be rooted in psychologistic prejudices: "to lay claim to the objectivity of a vision that holds unilaterally, metaphysically, to an existence 'in itself' of the external world, paradoxically ends up reinforcing the least rigorous subjectivism," noted Sollers.[70] The quasi-equivalence between the subjective and objective in Robbe-Grillet's critical language merely betrays the intellectual impossibility of escaping from psychologism (Sollers, "A. Robbe-Grillet" 93). Sollers would thus be led to say, in 1968, that the positivist ideology of the new novel "oscillates between a survival from psychologism . . . and a decoratively structural 'descriptionism.'"[71] Faye would even contend, at Cerisy, that Robbe-Grillet was "perhaps more Cartesian than his enemies of

68. Robbe-Grillet, *For A New Novel*, 24.
69. Faye, "Nouvelle Analogie," in *Le Récit hunique* (Paris: Seuil, 1967), 62. Originally published in *Tel Quel* 17 (Spring 1964).
70. Sollers, "A. Robbe-Grillet: Pour un nouveau roman," 93.
71. Sollers, "Le réflexe de réduction," 392.

the Old Novel"; his "novelistic neo-positivism [had] its roots in the most noble of Cartesian theologies."[72]

Sollers concludes that Robbe-Grillet's so-called evolution from an objective to a subjective writer can be interpreted either as a psychologistic resurgence, of a most equivocal romanticism, or, quite simply, as a return to a hyberbolic verbal arbitrariness. Moreover, this arbitrariness clearly posits, from the start, the unreadability of the world and thereby deprives itself of a sufficient contestation of thought—in pretending to contest language and, at the same time, the world.[73] Never was the confusion greater. For Sollers, a new novel will only result from an integral practice of language and thought. This new practice, advocated at Cerisy, will be situated in the interstices between literature and philosophy, in a space where the "I think" of classical philosophy is contested by the "I speak" of modern literature; in the conjunction between "thinking *and* speaking," in that intermediary realm, which, for Sollers, is "always the intermediary state toward a site of reversal that is provoked, undergone, pursued," and which is bound up with a poetic strategy.[74]

Robbe-Grillet conceived of metaphor as exterior to language in the same way reality—the one he sought to represent without recourse to metaphor— was outside of language for him. Derrida has nevertheless shown how all language is metaphorical. To refuse metaphor is thus to refuse language; that is, to confuse a sign for a thing. In advocating the presence of things, Robbe-Grillet occults the reality of language and thereby adheres to traditional realism. Realism is bound up with idealism or logocentrism: "Realism or sensualism—'empiricism'—are modifications of logocentrism."[75] Derrida argues:

It is not only idealism in the narrow sense that falls back upon the transcendental signified. It can always come to reassure a metaphysical materialism. It then becomes an ultimate referent, according to the classical logic implied by the value of referent, or it becomes an "objective reality" absolutely "anterior" to any work of the mark,

---

72. Faye, "Nouvelle Analogie," 61.

73. Sollers, "A. Robbe-Grillet: Pour un nouveau roman," 94.

74. Sollers, *L'Intermédiaire*, published in Collection Tel Quel (Paris: Seuil, 1963), 8. See also Foucault, "Débat sur le roman," 13.

75. Derrida, *Positions* (Chicago: University of Chicago Press, 1981), trans. Alan Bass, 65. Originally published as *Positions* (Paris: Minuit, 1972).

the semantic content of a form of presence which guarantees the
movement of the text in general from the outside. (*Positions* 65)

Derrida's observation is paramount not only to the debate on realism and
language at Cerisy, but also to an understanding of *Tel Quel*'s later shift to
Marxism—via theory—and, in particular, Derrida's notion of *écriture* as a
critique of logocentrism and Althusser's critique of economism and reflection theories. It also shows how *Tel Quel*'s break with the new novel had
political undertones.

At Cerisy, Foucault and the *Tel Quel* group would be at odds with the
Italian Marxist and Gruppo 63 avant-garde writer Edouardo Sanguineti.
Thibaudeau subsequently translated Sanguineti's works for the journal and
Collection Tel Quel. Both Thibaudeau and Jacqueline Risset, who joined *Tel
Quel* in 1967, were proponents of Italian literature and culture. From the
beginning *Tel Quel* published a number of texts by Italian writers, critics,
and philosophers: Giuseppe Ungaretti, translated by Ponge (no. 8), and
Jaccottet (15), Carlo Emilio Gadda (no. 9), Umberto Eco (11, 12, 55),
Sanguineti (nos. 15, 23, 29, 48–49), Giambattista Vico (no. 23), Nanni
Balestrini (25, 48–49, 51), and Mario Lunetta (43).[76] In later years, *Tel
Quel* would also welcome Maria-Antonietta Macciocchi and join up with
the Verdiglione psychoanalytical circle.

Three of the Italian authors published by *Tel Quel* (Balestrini, Eco,
Sanguineti) were affiliated with Gruppo 63, an avant-garde literary current
officially formed at the Palermo Conference of 3–8 October 1963, which
brought together thirty-four writers and nine critics, in a manner that closely
followed *Tel Quel*'s September endeavor at Cerisy. Many of the Gruppo 63
had been affiliated with the avant-garde journal *Il Verri*, founded by Luciano
Anceschi in 1956, and with the anthology *I Novissimi* in 1961. In defining
an avant-garde for the 1960s, Gruppo 63 began by taking its critical distance
from the neorealist currents of the late 1940s and early 1950s and from a
hermetic (*Ermetismo*) revival in poetry. As a leading proponent of Gruppo
63, Sanguineti's presence at Cerisy (along with Giuliani's who, according to
Thibaudeau, also attended the gathering) could have been the occasion for a
productive encounter between two avant-garde literary currents formed in
the early 1960s that had similar concerns. Sanguineti shared *Tel Quel*'s

76. The following translations appeared in Collection Tel Quel at Seuil: Sanguineti's
Capriccio italiano and *Le Noble Jeu de l'oye*, both translated by Thibaudeau, and Ungaretti's *A
partir du désert*, translated by Jaccottet.

budding interest in linguistics and psychoanalysis, but he had a Marxist orientation that most Telquelians would not adopt until 1966–68. At that time, *Tel Quel* would endorse Sanguineti's Communist candidacy when the journal became pro-PCF.[77]

In the debates on the novel and poetry, Sanguineti accused both *Tel Quel* and Foucault of spiritualism. Foucault, who was adamantly anti-Communist, had provocatively replied: "I'm a materialist because I deny reality," to Sanguineti who had remarked that believing in reality made him a materialist.[78] The question of reality had been central to the colloquium. Sollers had read a paper entitled "Logique de la fiction," which had led to a discussion of reality. But then a fundamental distinction was established, reflected in the following question by Marcelin Pleynet: "How do you make reality come into language?"[79] How do those, like Sanguineti, find reality other than through language? Foucault notes that no matter how hard we try to deny it, we live in a world of signs and language: therein lies the problem ("Débat sur le roman" 45). Faye would in fact define literature as "being able to say by what signs our reality comes to us."[80]

The sign was the central problem of the 1960s. At Cerisy, Foucault distinguished between the humanist literature of the postwar years, which he referred to as a literature of meaning, and a new form of writing characterized by something that resists meaning, that is, the sign or language itself.[81] How ironic, claimed Faye, that the most penetrating critical pieces on Robbe-Grillet's early works were written by a theoretician of the sign: Barthes. And yet, added Faye, Robbe-Grillet attempted to evacuate the signified from his fictional universe. This neutralization of the sign, of the meaning of the world, is, for Robbe-Grillet, a sort of cleansing experience that draws a backdrop on which the imminence of the sign becomes particularly menacing and disturbing. Robbe-Grillet wanted to dehumanize the world of things in order to make it uncomfortable and prevent its too easy habitation by man.[82] But the discomfort of the world could not be accounted for by an aesthetics of perception. In his review of *For a New Novel*, Sollers argued that the notion of a "worldview" had become outdated for a decade characterized by the advent of the sign. The problem now

77. See "Appel au vote communiste de Sanguineti," *Tel Quel* 33 (Spring 1968): 95.
78. "Débat sur le roman," 46.
79. Pleynet, "Débat sur le roman," 45.
80. Faye in *Que peut la littérature?*, 63.
81. Foucault, "Débat sur le roman," 38.
82. Faye, "Débat sur le roman," 38.

was to come to terms with the modern presence of nonreason—brought to light by the writing of modernity and by the articulation of linguistics, anthropology, and psychoanalysis in the 1960s—which revealed that man is at heart more of a stranger to himself than he can ever be to others. As a truly contemporary investigation of meaning, the modern novel takes its place in an interrogation of language.[83]

If reality as such does not exist for Foucault and *Tel Quel*, it is because language enables us to speak. We must recognize the site from which we speak: language exists, argues Foucault, and that is what, in effect, we are speaking about—not reality.[84] We speak from within language: "It is the world of words that creates the world of things. . . . Man speaks, then, but it is because the symbol has made him a man."[85] From this perspective, metaphor is within language; it is a figure of language, and figures of language can only be understood from language and not from the world. What we have with *Tel Quel*, notes Foucault, is an aesthetics of language and not of perception.[86] The reality question is only valid for an aesthetics of perception. In introducing a third realm—the symbolic—between the real and the imaginary, structuralism taught us that "we never find a state where man is separated from language, which he then creates in order to 'express' what is taking place within him: it is language which teaches the definition of man, not the contrary."[87]

For *Tel Quel*, the limits of the new novel were bound up with the failure to properly account for the question of language. In fact, the back cover of the Cerisy issue (*Tel Quel* 17) reads:

> The time has undoubtedly come to take stock of the current situation of literature. Today, everyone acknowledges the importance of the

---

83. Sollers, "A. Robbe-Grillet: Pour un nouveau roman," 93.

84. Foucault, "Débat sur le roman," 45.

85. Lacan, "The Function and Field of Speech and Language in Psychoanalysis," in *Ecrits (A Selection)*, trans. Alan Sheridan (New York: Norton, 1977), 65. Originally published in *Ecrits* (Paris: Seuil, 1966).

86. Foucault, "Débat sur le roman," 51.

87. Barthes, "To Write: An Intransitive Verb?" 135. Barthes's words echo those of Emile Benveniste: "We can never get back to man separated from language and we shall never see him inventing it. We shall never get back to man reduced to himself and exercising his wits to conceive of the existence of an other. It is speaking man whom we find in the world, a man speaking to another man, and language provides the very definition of man." From "Subjectivity in Language," *Problems in General Linguistics* (Coral Gables: University of Miami Press, 1971), trans. Mary Elizabeth Meek, 224. Originally published as *Problèmes de linguistique générale* (Paris: Gallimard, 1966).

nouveau roman, the undeniable role of reawakening that it has played for the literary conscience. It is now time to recognize its limits, the fact that it has failed to comprehend the whole of the serious and original enterprises of the times, thus making it possible to situate it in a broader whole. A greater lucidity can in effect, in making *language* the principal subject of all writing, open new perspectives.

If *Tel Quel* was to take literature seriously, it could no longer neglect the linguistic and philosophical implications of the act of writing, "the thought that it aims and seeks to found, the interior experience it entails." Such a highly visible pronouncement on the back cover of the Cerisy issue reveals *Tel Quel*'s debt to the dissident surrealist Bataille. Although *Tel Quel* initially supported the *nouveau roman* as a viable alternative to Sartrean engagement, it also played an important role in reevaluating the dissident surrealists Artaud, Bataille, and Ponge. The impact of these three authors on *Tel Quel*, as well as their deviation from official surrealism, was publically recognized, for the first time, by Foucault at Cerisy.

In "Debate on the Novel," Foucault drew an explicit comparison between *Tel Quel* and its predecessor, surrealism. He noted that the writing of *Tel Quel* and the surrealists revolved around certain limit-experiences such as dreams, unreason, and madness. Unlike the surrealists, however, the *Tel Quel* authors did not bury these experiences in a psychological dimension. According to Foucault, *Tel Quel* succeeded in displacing these experiences from the realm of the psyche to that of philosophical thought, in the way that marginal philosophers, such as Blanchot and Bataille, had done. Furthermore, Foucault argues that the surrealists viewed language as a mere instrument of access, a surface of reflection for their experiences, a half-open door toward the real, whereas for *Tel Quel*, language represented an opaque and thick space within which these experiences take place.[88] Thus the importance of someone like Ponge for the *Tel Quel* team, for whom mankind can only be understood through language. As paradoxical as the double patronage of Ponge and Bataille may appear, it is actually an appropriate one for *Tel Quel*, in that both authors freed a series of experiences from the psychological realm and restituted them to the one of thought. These experiences derive from and find their space in language (13).

Foucault's remarks at Cerisy were largely in response to Sollers's presen-

---

88. Foucault, "Débat sur le roman," 13.

tation of "Logique de la fiction," published in the Autumn 1963 issue of *Tel Quel* and subsequently revised for *Logiques*. This text, along with "Le roman et l'expérience des limites," a lecture pronounced in December 1965 and subsequently published in the Spring 1966 issue of *Tel Quel*, is essential for understanding the early history of *Tel Quel*. In a manner and tone clearly reminiscent of the surrealists, Sollers attempted to undermine the traditional opposition between reality and fiction: "Nietzsche taught us that we would never be free so long as we had not 'unlearned' our antinomies."[89] Sollers began by rejecting the notion that reality and fiction, life and writing are necessarily opposed to one another. Like his surrealist predecessors, he devalued the notion of reality: What if our everyday lives were merely the unsuccessful realization of a broader, yet unactualized reality whose multiple possibilities need to be explored? In exploring the specificity of fiction, Sollers sought to contest the socially guarded and valorized notion of reality.

Two epigraphs set off Sollers's text. To Parmenides's "We cannot think what is not"—thought or fiction as a copy of the real—Sollers juxtaposes Nietzsche's "What can be thought is certainly fictitious." Sollers argues that our actualization as individuals is bound up with society's fictions. It is fiction that gives man his identity, by establishing his limits: "Man does not know at heart what he can think. Fiction is there to teach him."[90] This explains the tremendous importance attributed by society to fiction, and to its principal vehicle, the novel. As the strongest point of impact of social narration, the novel plays a fundamental role in determining the relationship of the individual to social practice.[91] If our society needs the myth of the "novel," it is not only for economic purposes. This myth does not merely allow for "a cheap recognition of literature while keeping it under tight control—in other words while carefully filtering its deviations." More important, it serves as "a means of instituting a permanent conditioning that goes much further than the book market alone. THE NOVEL IS THE WAY THIS SOCIETY SPEAKS [TO] ITSELF [SE PARLE], the way the individual MUST LIVE HIMSELF in order to be accepted there."[92]

For this reason the "novelistic" point of view must be "omnipresent, self-evident, inviolable." It is therefore no accident that society watches so vigilantly over fiction. The apogee of the novel and the social class that it

89. Sollers, "The Novel and the Experience of Limits," 194–95.
90. Sollers, "Logique de la fiction," 18.
91. Sollers, "Ebranler le système," 11.
92. Sollers, "The Novel and the Experience of Limits," 186–87.

represents—the bourgeoisie—has generated major literary battles over what does or does not constitute a novel, and over which novels are realist. The novel is irremediably caught up with the question of literary realism. In his famous article on realism, originally published in Russian in 1921 and appearing for the first time in French in *Tel Quel*'s *Théorie de la Littérature* (1965) and in *Tel Quel* 24 (Winter 1966), Roman Jakobson defines realism as an artistic current whose aim is to reproduce reality as faithfully as possible and to aspire to a maximum of verisimilitude.[93] Thus, works that seem verisimilar, faithful to reality are realistic. The ambiguity is evident. Jakobson breaks down the notion of realism into three categories. First, realism is an aspiration or tendency on the part of the author. Second, it is what others consider to be realistic. The individual viewpoint takes on an objective value. Third, in the nineteenth century, realism becomes a model by which the value of subsequent works is judged. The nineteenth-century novel thus becomes a model of realist writing for the twentieth century, a paradox that becomes particularly evident in the instance of socialist societies aiming for an alternative cultural practice.

Jakobson's categorization demonstrates that the notion of realism, tied up as it is with verisimilitude, is inevitably subject to common opinion, tradition, or authority, and does not necessarily coincide with historical reality or scientific truth.[94] Sollers, in fact, reduces realism to a mere "bias that consists in the belief that a writing must *express* something that would not be given in this writing, something that would be immediately and unanimously acceptable." Nevertheless, "this agreement is effective only by virtue of preliminary conventions, the notion of reality being one such convention and conformity, a kind of tacit contract between the individual and the social group."[95] Sollers raises two important issues. The first obviously concerns the notion of consensus implicit in literary realism. Our notion of reality, like the novel that circulates it, is a function of the dominant ideology: the real is "in given historical circumstances . . . that which the greatest number of those in power are obliged, for precise economic reasons, to hold as real" ("The Novel and the Experience of Limits" 194). It is only to the degree that reality is commonly understood that any form of consensus is possible. If the

93. Roman Jakobson, "Du réalisme artistique," in *Théorie de la Littérature*, ed. and trans. Tzvetan Todorov (Paris: Seuil, 1965), 98–108. Also published in *Tel Quel* 24 (Winter 1966). An English version, "On Realism in Art," appeared in Jakobson's *Language in Literature* (Cambridge: Harvard University Press, 1987), ed. Krystyna Pomorska and Stephen Rudy.

94. Barthes, *Criticism and Truth*, 34.

95. Sollers, "The Novel and the Experience of Limits," 194.

real is not questioned, it is because we ignore the language used to convey it: "Language is marvelous in that it makes us forget it."[96] It is precisely this marvel of language that makes consensus possible.

This brings us to the second issue: the emphasis placed on something apparently absent from the writing itself, a notion of reality characterized by its exteriority with respect to the discourse that produces it. Hence Barthes's contention that "what defines realism is not the origin of the model but its exteriority in relation to the language which expresses it."[97] We thus have "the assurance of a world, which arrogantly sets 'realities' against 'words,' as if language were merely the futile decor of humanity's more substantial interests."[98] Why is it that we persist in attributing reality to anything but language? Why is it that we have perpetuated for so long what Sollers considers to be the most tenacious prejudice: "[the one] which defines the novel, once and for all, as a reflection of the world or of the mind—a mirror walked along the street or around the brain; a reflection, consequently that would write itself, in a more or less structured manner, through a 'temperament,' an engineer or visionary, and under the influence of events that would be exterior to it."[99] As naive as this prejudice may seem, it is nonetheless an illusion not readily shaken off, for it is an "illusion of such power that in it we must recognize a very profound sort of law bearing on language itself: the necessity that compels us to remain unconscious of its radical operations, so that we retain only its superficial fiction" (201).

In taking fiction for reality, in perceiving narration as external to the forms that manifest it, we live "in a projected, deferred, delegated manner instead of confronting, as in a chess match, the ineluctable process that makes every one of our gestures a **written act,** the very fiction (and reality) of our existence" (202). What we are denying, in effect, is the central place of language in our lives. Perhaps this is what we do not want to acknowledge and what society does not want us to realize: that our identity is but a fictional form, just as our notion of the real is but a mere function of language. The real "is manifested nowhere else but in a language, and a society's language and myths are what it decides to take as reality" (194). According to Sollers, two options are open to us:

---

96. Merleau-Ponty cited in Jean-Joseph Goux, "Marx et l'inscription du travail," in *Théorie d'Ensemble*, 206.

97. Roland Barthes, "The Last Word On Robbe-Grillet?" 198.

98. Barthes, "The Indictment Periodically Lodged," 343.

99. Sollers, "The Novel and the Experience of Limits," 201.

—either we accept, as social individuals (and beyond simple material necessity), the guarantee of reality this society gives us in exchange for an implicit abandonment of all fundamental claims (of any attempt to alter this society's principles)—in which case language becomes a secondary phenomenon for us, becomes "art"; —or else we decide to live ourselves, regardless of the cost as **fiction,** at which time a decisive and undoubtedly scandalous reversal is produced, but a reversal whose singular nature constitutes the literary experience. Literature is nothing if it does not achieve this reversal.[100]

We must confront the fiction of our existence through the medium of language. Making language itself the principal subject of writing and critical inquiry, placing language at the primary level of attention, implies a critical revision of knowledge. Barthes maintains that "it is solely by its passage through language that literature pursues the disturbance of the essential concepts of our culture, 'reality' chief among them."[101]

In giving the appearance of mirroring reality, the novel denies the very literary and social conventions that make it possible. If the success of the novel clearly depends on its capacity to pass off its fiction as reality, our success as individuals, or subjects, depends on our capacity to read this reality as fiction. The fiction that we are inadvertently caught in and that we must either address or deliberately ignore is the one of writing and reading. For Sollers, we are continually in the process of reading and writing— whether we dream, act, or fantasize. If we remain unaware of the fact that we are reading and writing, it is because we believe that we know how to read and write. Sollers contends that we were deprived of reading and writing our lives the very day we were told that we knew how to read and write ("The Novel and the Experience of Limits" 202). We need to question the habitual forms taken by our reading and writing, those very forms that define or limit us: the fiction we live, which establishes what we deem readable, is merely the recognition of a limit from which intelligibility and meaning become possible: "Admit that you only read what suits you," urges Sollers in *Lois* [Laws].[102]

---

100. Sollers, "The Novel and the Experience of Limits," 192. I have altered a small error in the original translation.

101. Barthes, "From Science to Literature," 5.

102. Sollers, *Lois,* 111. Published in Collection Tel Quel in 1972.

No wonder the term *formalist* has been systematically attributed to those texts that call attention to the very forms by means of which reality becomes intelligible, readable, or "real"; in so doing the texts call into question a society's system of intelligibility (its "real"). If it is from within language itself that we must contest a culture, it is so that we may "lay bare the fiction and meaning of [an] era—along with the limits, codifications, and repressions this meaning undergoes. To be inside history's meaning, is to be inside its form."[103] The "fundamental aesthetic error—the political-economic error—consists in believing that language is a simple instrument of representation."[104] Language, Ponge taught us, is "first of all a *milieu*, the milieu where we're born, where we make ourselves, where we disappear. Language is our body and air, our world and thought, our perception and unconscious."[105] When "the reality of language is the only literary reality,"[106] distinctions between prose and poetry become obsolete. A new literary space emerges, one that defies the generic categories of narration, poetry, and criticism. Furthermore, theory and practice, creation and meditation, writing and thought need no longer be opposed to one another in a sterile and mechanical fashion.[107]

In an important theoretical piece entitled "La poésie doit avoir pour but . . ." [The objective of poetry is . . ."], published in *Théorie d'ensemble,* Pleynet raises a fundamental question: "What happens to the best theory of the novel once it finds itself cut off from the theoretical function of poetic discourse?"[108] Pleynet suggests that any attempts to come to terms with language are futile if they fail to consider the implications of the "poetic." No wonder, as we shall see in Chapter 3, *Tel Quel* would be profoundly marked by the work of Jakobson. If *Tel Quel* turned to poetry, it was precisely in order to dismantle the dichotomies (for example, prose/poetry, reality/language) that marked the dead ends of engagement and the *nouveau roman.* The literary debates of the 1940s and 1950s centered primarily on the novel, relegating poetry to an aestheticizing ideology. The pioneering work of Pleynet and Denis Roche would be instrumental in making poetry a central concern of *Tel Quel* from the very start.

103. Sollers, "The Novel and the Experience of Limits," 203.
104. Sollers, "Literature and Totality," 71.
105. Sollers, "La poésie, oui ou non," *Logiques*, 198.
106. Barthes, "Writers, Intellectuals, Teachers," in *The Rustle of Language*, 320. Originally published as "Ecrivains, Intellectuels, Professeurs," *Tel Quel* 47 (Autumn 1971).
107. Sollers, "Les grandes irrégularités du langage," *Logiques*, 199.
108. Pleynet, "La poésie doit avoir pour but . . . ," 95.

According to Pleynet, if theoretical considerations of the late 1950s and early 1960s succeeded in freeing the novel from a certain naturalist impasse and provided a new realist articulation, nothing of the sort occurred for poetry, which remained an accomplice of an aestheticizing reading that continued to mask textual activity.[109] In his survey of the poetry of the postwar years, Pleynet objected to the narcissistic fetal posture of the poet: given to sentimental outpouring or subjective release, the poet cuts himself off from social history and from the history of ideas. Pleynet thus contended that to remove oneself from events was to separate oneself from ideas.[110] But he also dismissed the engaged stance: In what is the poet engaged? What exactly is his relationship to the social and historical whole? Pleynet condemned engaged poetry less for its lack of formal innovation than for the mediocrity of its thought and the narrow historical perspective that it presupposes (225).

Hollier maintains that the poetry of the Resistance was followed by a resistance to poetry after the Liberation.[111] Pleynet would probably argue that Resistance poetry already constituted *a resistance to poetry*. At stake in poetry is not the question of genre, but rather a certain relation of the writing subject to language and history, which appears to be absent from the engaged writing of the 1940s and 1950s. The postwar years occulted the "revolution of poetic language" represented by Mallarmé, Lautréamont, Artaud, Joyce, and others. Although we can appreciate the suspicion directed at cultural manifestations of the first half of the century, it is nevertheless symptomatic that the transnational modernity of the nineteenth- and twentieth-century avant-gardes was evacuated from the postwar scene, as it had been a few years earlier under Fascism and Nazism. For Scarpetta, there is a parallel between the motivating forces behind nationalism and xenophobia, on the one hand, and resistance to modern art, on the other. He believes that questions of nationalism and xenophobia are fundamentally related to the manner in which the individual conceives of language and culture.[112]

The desire to surpass the sentimental-political vein of postwar poetry led to formal considerations. Nevertheless, formalism posed other problems. By emphasizing objectivity, the formalist work justified censorships, repressed

109. Pleynet, "La poésie doit avoir pour but . . . ," 94–95.
110. Pleynet, "Incipit Vita Nova," in *Art et littérature*, which was published in Collection Tel Quel (Paris: Seuil, 1977), 224, 226. Originally published in *Art Press International* 4 (May–June 1973).
111. Hollier, *The Politics of Prose*, 9.
112. See Scarpetta's *Eloge du cosmopolitisme*.

conflicts, and kept the subject and his language in a state of sterilizing retention.[113] Poetry, advances Pleynet, must be a practice of language in which "the exorbitance of the conflicting forces of the subject and his history" are reinvested ("Incipit Vita Nova" 231). The poet must therefore familiarize himself not only with the history of language and literature, but also with human sciences such as psychoanalysis and sociology, which can illuminate the place of the writing subject in his journey across writing and the ideological function of literature in the social whole (226).

Tel Quel's work on poetic language brought together the radical exploration of language by the nineteenth- and twentieth-century avant-gardes, as well as the theoretical advances in semiotics, psychoanalysis, and philosophy during the 1960s. Kristeva has demonstrated how the epistemological and sociopolitical transformations of the latter part of the nineteenth century can be discerned in the avant-garde "texts of rupture," where the subversion of language reciprocally implies the subversion of the writing subject and both imply a critique of the existing sociopolitical order. The avant-garde movements of this period "propounded a practice and sometimes even a knowledge of language and its subject, that kept pace with, when they did not precede, Freudian breakthroughs."[114] For *Tel Quel*, the question of subjectivity would be irremediably tied up with the notion of poetic language.

Whereas Sollers's "Logique de la fiction" had been the departure point for the "Debate on the Novel" at Cerisy, Pleynet's "La pensée contraire" [Contrary thought] introduced the "Debate on Poetry" that ensued. *Tel Quel*'s wager—to maintain the irrational aspect of poetic experience while liberating it from its sacred connotations—was at the heart of Pleynet's presentation. He notes that over the ages, poetry has had its share of disparagers. As evidence, he cites numerous philosophers and poets from Plato: "Poets are not guided in their creation by science, but by a sort of instinct and by divine inspiration"; to Diderot, "Poetry seeks something enormously barbarian and wild"; to Ponge, "Poetry, shit for this word."[115] According to Pleynet, the violent criticism that poetry attracts is directed at the irrational aspect of poetic creation as well as at the notion of divine inspiration. Is the poet an inspired being? If not, why has there been an unconditional acceptance of the sacred by poets? If we are unwilling to discard our artistic patrimony as one enormous bluff and yet refuse to

113. Pleynet, "Incipit Vita Nova," 225.
114. Kristeva, "The Ethics of Linguistics."
115. Pleynet, "La pensée contraire," *Tel Quel* 17 (Spring 1964): 55–56.

consider poems as objects of divine inspiration, perhaps we need to ask ourselves why we admire sublime poetic fables: What is so precious about them that has allowed us to justify the above-mentioned misunderstanding ("La pensée contraire" 56–57)?

Language is haunted by the sacred. Citing Vico and Tacitus, Pleynet notes that in creating fables and myths, man attempted to conquer his fear of the unknown through language: "When men are seized by fear, they invent at the same time that they believe" (Tacitus). A relationship exists between poetic creation and the birth of the great religious myths of Western culture, between the sacralization of poetry and the transcendence of fundamental human anguish ("La pensée contraire" 58–59). For Pleynet, it is this terror, which Vico attributes to ignorance, that justifies myths and other "phantas-magoria that weave with reality webs indissociable from dreams and appa-ritions" (Foucault) and that culture does not dissolve, for it would first have to dissolve ignorance, and in so doing would dissolve itself (59). Pleynet concludes that "this terror which the poet's verb has as its function to transcend, this eventual and barbaric death which language justifies and cultivates, is both at the source and at the center of all poetic inspiration, and constitutes its fundamental experience" (59). Death is at the heart of all writing: it is "the void towards which and from which we speak" or write.[116] Once the poetic experience ceases to be a profession of faith, once it abandons its incantations, it can reapprehend its essence in the movement that brought it into being.[117] Freed of all transcendence or mysticism, the poetic act has no other end but itself: all that remains is the human confrontation of fear, anguish, nonreason, death, the unknown. Only by considering the poetic experience outside of the notion of the sacred, concludes Pleynet, can one conserve what it has that is fundamental, and introduce it to its contemporaneousness. For if the poetic experience remains subject to the sacred, it ends up being integrated into an order that no longer uses the experience itself but the conclusions required by its integration. Consequently, the poetic experience is negated ("La pensée contraire" 59).

In order to comprehend both the proximity of the poetic experience to the sacred and the distance that it must maintain, a comparison between the Bataillian "inner experience," central to the poetics of *Tel Quel*, and the mys-

---

116. See Foucault, "Language to Infinity," in *Language, Counter-Memory, Practice*, trans. Donald Bouchard and Sherry Simon (Ithaca: Cornell University Press, 1977), 53. Originally published as "Le langage à l'infini," in *Tel Quel* 15 (Autumn 1963).

117. Pleynet, "La pensée contraire," 59, and Foucault, *The Order of Things*, 300.

tical experience is in order.[118] So close to and yet so distant from the mystical experience, the Bataillian (inner) experience, like the mystical one, implies the dispossession of identity, the loss of meaning, and the questioning of knowledge. Yet, unlike the mystical experience, there is no transcendence; the experience is for itself its own authority. If divine presence represents "the limit of the Limitless," Bataille's rejection of transcendence "does not restore us to a limited and positivistic world, but to a world exposed by the experience of its limits, made and unmade by that excess which transgresses it."[119] Without transcendence, there is no respite: in the absence of a center, origin, or foundation—a transcendental signified—language is condemned to eternal play, to an endless proliferation of meanings, and mankind to traveling the entire field of the possible, and to transgressing each limit encountered. Experience, contends Bataille, is "a voyage to the end of the possible of man."[120]

In the dream of deciphering a truth or an origin that escapes play and the order of the sign, man evidently lives the necessity of interpretation as an exile.[121] In the Bataillian inner experience, man is condemned to a more radical form of separation and loss associated with exile than the one

118. Widespread critical interest in Bataille only really began in 1963, a year after the author's death. Yet *Tel Quel*'s fifth issue (Spring 1961) already contained extracts from Bataille's last book, *Les Larmes d'Eros*. Published in June of the same year, the book was censored. In the summer of 1962 (no. 10), *Tel Quel* published "Conférences sur le non-savoir," lectures delivered by Bataille at the Collège Philosophique in 1952. It also published "The 'Old Mole' and the Prefix *Sur* in the Words *Surhomme* [Superman] and *Surrealist*" in no. 34, "Le berceau de l'humanité: la vallée de la Vézère" in no. 40, and "C'est une banalité" in no. 81. A special issue of *Tel Quel* is devoted to Bataille and Artaud (no. 52) and contains some of the presentations from the Artaud/Bataille colloquium that took place at Cerisy in July 1972. In the years following Bataille's death, and particularly in the 1970s, Bataille was recognized as a major author by both philosophers and literati. Sollers attributes a central place to him in *Logiques*. Bataille greatly influenced Sollers's notion of writing as an experience of limits and Kristeva's notion of poetic language. *Tel Quel* texts on Bataille include Derrida's "From Restricted to General Economy: A Hegelianism Without Reserve," in *Writing and Difference*; Kristeva's "L'expérience et la pratique," in *Polylogue*; Sollers's essays in *Logiques*; Hollier's "Le matérialisme dualiste de Georges Bataille," in *Tel Quel* 25; Jean-Michel Rey's "La figuration de la mort," in *Tel Quel* 40; Jean-Louis Baudry's "Bataille et l'expérience intérieure," in *Tel Quel* 55; Henric's review of Bataille's *Oeuvres Complètes*, vols. 8 and 9, in *Tel Quel*, 84; Sichère's "L'écriture souveraine de Georges Bataille"; and Michel Fardoulis-Lagranche's "Un art divin: L'Oubli" (a portion of which is devoted to Bataille) in *Tel Quel* 93.

119. Foucault, "A Preface to Transgression," in *Language, Counter-Memory, Practice*, 32. First published in *Critique*, nos. 195–96 (1963).

120. Georges Bataille, *Inner Experience*, trans. Leslie Anne Boldt (Albany: State University of New York Press, 1988), 7. Originally published as *L'Expérience intérieure* (Paris: Gallimard, 1954).

121. Derrida, "Structure, Sign and Play in the Discourse of the Human Sciences," in *Writing*

resulting from the ontology of presence underlying Western humanism. In his search for an origin or truth that escapes the play of language, man posits an end to his ontological exile, whereas Bataillian man does not seek to escape this play, which is at the heart of language and therefore of man. Inner experience neither points back to an origin nor leads "to some end point that would be given in advance."[122] It must lead where it will. Inner experience not only does not reveal anything—for it cannot found belief nor set out from it (*Inner Experience* 4)—it challenges the very presuppositions (meanings, values, beliefs, truths) of human existence. Knowledge is rest, argues Bataille: "he who already knows cannot go beyond a known horizon." Inner experience is "an experience laid bare, free of ties, even of an origin" (3). It responds to the necessity "of challenging everything (of putting everything into question) without permissible rest" (3). For Bataille, then, experience is synonymous with contestation (7).

"Experience is, in fever and anguish, the putting into question (to the test) of that which a man knows of being" (4). Bataille contends that "we have in fact only two certainties in this world—that we are not everything and that we will die" (xxxii). This is what we would rather not know, and so "we live in the false light of a dead language with narrow significations: we lack daylight to the extent that we lack the night that we are."[123] Thus, our abuse of language mirrors the abuse we make of our existence. In an effort to avoid suffering, we identify with the entirety of the universe; we judge each thing as if we were that thing. In the same way, we imagine that we will never die.[124] It is therefore only fitting to ask that language—the ultimate guaranty of meaning and identity—be "full of meaning, without void, without trial, without practice: therefore without a subject on trial."[125] According to Bataille, we harbor these illusions like a narcotic necessary to bear life (xxxii). To accept finally that these narcotics do no more than provide a temporary respite or sleep, a diversion from the human condition, is to begin a singular experience of disintoxication. "What happens to us when, disintoxicated, we learn what we are? Lost among babblers in a night in which we can only hate the appearance of light which comes from babbling" (xxxii).

---

and Difference, trans. Alan Bass (Chicago: University of Chicago Press, 1978), 292. Originally published in Collection Tel Quel as *L'Ecriture et la différence* (Paris: Seuil, 1967).

122. Bataille, *Inner Experience*, 3.
123. Sollers, "The Novel and the Experience of Limits," 197.
124. Bataille, *Inner Experience*, xxxii.
125. Kristeva, "Sujet dans le langage et pratique politique," 23.

Inner experience belongs to a "night of non-knowledge" after which comes the decision to "no longer wish oneself to be everything, therefore to be man rising above the need he had to turn away from himself" (25). Bataille contends that to "no longer wish oneself to be everything is for man the highest ambition, it is to want to be man" (25). Those who refuse to reach this limit where one rises above this need for complete self-actualization are servants or enemies of man: "He who does not 'die' from being merely a man will never be other than a man" (35).

Such an experience seeks to move beyond the traditional notion of man associated with humanism insofar as the name of man is "the name of that being who, throughout the history of metaphysics or of ontotheology—in other words, throughout his entire history—has dreamed of full presence, the reassuring foundation, the origin and the end of play."[126] According to Foucault: "From within language experienced and traversed as language, in the play of its possibilities extended to their furthest point, what emerges is that man has 'come to an end,' and that, by reaching the summit of all possible speech, he arrives not at the very heart of himself but at the brink of that which limits him; in that region where death prowls, where thought is extinguished, where the promise of the origin interminably recedes."[127] In "that formless, mute, unsignifying region where language can find its freedom," modern literature—to a degree with surrealism, but more so with authors such as Kafka, Bataille, and Blanchot—vertiginously situates itself, thereby positing itself as an experience of unthinkable thought, the impossible, madness, the unknown, or death (Foucault, *The Order of Things* 383–84). Kristeva can thus claim that poetic experience becomes "a certain position in language from which the meaning of the human adventure, bordering on the insane, is deciphered with an involvement that is decidedly risky (this has nothing to do with neutral 'scientific' description)."[128] Free of all transcendence and mysticism, with no other end but itself, the poetic act, like the Bataillian inner experience, forces man to confront the fundamental anguish or angst that he had called upon the gods, divine heroes, poetic fables and myths, and other phantasmagoria to dispel. If the unnameable and the unrepresentable are the source of such anguish, it is because our meanings or representations—Sollers would say our fictions—are the limits that determine a language marked by a void toward which and against

126. Derrida, "Structure, Sign, and Play in the Discourse of the Human Sciences," 292.
127. Foucault, *The Order of Things*, 383.
128. Kristeva, "My Memory's Hyperbole," 269.

which we address ourselves, and an existence harboring death as its ultimate end.

If Telquelians consider Hölderlin one of the first writers to have given the poetic experience its modernity, it is because he became aware "to the point of blindness, that he could only speak in the space marked by the disappearance of the gods and that language could only depend on its own power to keep death at a distance. Thus, an opening was traced on the horizon toward which our speech has ceaselessly advanced."[129] With Hölderlin and other writers of modernity, the poetic experience joins up with a contemporaneousness that is marked by the death or absence of God. Foucault writes: "More than simply an event that affected our emotions, that gave rise to the fear of nothingness, the death of God profoundly influenced our language: the silence that replaced its source remains unpenetrable to all but the most trivial works."[130] The poetic experience must now address this void inherent in language that a transcendental bounding had been asked to conceal. Without the assurance of an origin or center, a transcendental signified that escapes the infinite play of language and in which we can anchor an unquestionable meaning or truth, language can only direct itself toward this absence or void and seek to exhaust itself. That is why, according to Foucault, "eschatology has become of late a structure of literary experience" (86). The absence of a transcendental signified extends the domain and play of signification infinitely.[131] In order to move beyond the infinite play of signification, it has been necessary to make meaning contingent upon something that transcends language, something that would be external to it and therefore absent from it.

This has been the objective of Western thought, which in the guises of idealism and logocentrism bound up meaning and truth with an unquestionable foundation, origin, or absolute. Meaning, contends Kristeva, "necessarily guarantees a certain transcendence, if not a theology; this is precisely why all human knowledge, whether it be that of an individual subject or of a meaning structure, retains religion as its blind boundaries, or at least, as an internal limit."[132] For Derrida, "[t]he age of the sign is essentially theologi-

---

129. Foucault, "Language To Infinity," 59.

130. Foucault, "The Father's 'No,'" in *Language, Counter-Memory, Practice*, 85–86. Originally published in *Critique* 178 (1962).

131. Derrida, "Structure, Sign, and Play in the Discourse of the Human Sciences," 280.

132. Kristeva, "From One Identity to an Other," in *Desire in Language*, 124. Originally published as "D'une identité l'autre" in *Tel Quel* 62 (Summer 1975) and subsequently in *Polylogue*.

cal."[133] Insofar as the notion of God is intricately interwoven with an entire system of signification, it is not possible to question one without dismantling the other. Conversely, to tamper with this system of signification is eventually to call into question the existence of God. The poetic work of Hölderlin is exemplary because it manifests the link between the flight of the gods and the loss of language.[134] His merit was in discovering that "the gods had wandered off through a rift in language as it was in the process of losing its bearings."[135] Hölderlin thereby revealed not only how meaning is irremediably bound up with transcendence (how we have bound up meaning, that is, with something that escapes the play of language), but also how meaning is but a rift that we have sought to suture in a system calling for transcendental bounding. That is why Bataille could write that an act of impunity was committed by Western discourse when it added to language the word which transcends all words, the word "God."[136] The belief in an ultimate word goes hand in hand with the notion of a transcendental signified, a concept signified in and of itself, thus independently of language and, consequently, of man, for "language provides the very definition of man."[137]

For Derrida, "[t]here has to be a transcendental signified in order for the difference between signified and signifier to be somewhere absolute and irreducible."[138] As a result, it is possible to dissociate the intelligible from the sensible, speech from writing, the mind from the body, thought from language, and content from form. These dichotomies, which are central to Western idealism, necessarily imply a value judgment that is legitimated by the distinction between inside and outside. If over the centuries—from Plato to Saussure—Western culture has privileged speech over writing, it is because the voice has traditionally represented the illusion of absolute presence and transparency of meaning. We can thus pretend immediately to

133. Derrida, *Of Grammatology*, trans. Gayatri Chakravorty Spivak (Baltimore: Johns Hopkins University Press, 1974, 1976), 14. Originally published as *De la grammatologie* (Paris: Minuit, 1967).

134. Foucault, "The Father's 'No,' " 86.

135. Foucault, *The Thought From Outside*, trans. Brian Massumi (New York: Zone Books, 1987), 17. Originally published as *La Pensée du dehors* (Montpellier: Editions Fata Morgana, 1986). Written in 1966, this essay first appeared in a special issue of *Critique* (229) devoted to Blanchot.

136. Bataille, *Death and Sensuality* (New York: Walker, 1962), 269. Originally published as *L'Erotisme* (Paris: Minuit, 1957).

137. Benveniste, "Subjectivity in Language," in *Problems in General Linguistics*, 224.

138. Derrida, *Of Grammatology*, 20.

"know what we mean, mean what we say, say what we mean."[139] Spoken
language has been considered closer to pure thought (the traditional place
of truth), whereas written language has been viewed as a supplement,
"a decorative exteriority, a dangerous possibility of non-truth" (Sollers,
"L'Ecriture fonction 401). According to Derrida, "[t]he voice *is heard*
(understood) [*s'entend*]—which undoubtedly is what we call consciousness—
closest to the self as the absolute effacement of the signifier."[140] "This
experience of the effacement of the signifier in the voice is not merely one
illusion among many," contends Derrida; "it is the condition of the very idea
of truth" (*Of Grammatology* 20).

The quest for a transcendental signified—for a first, original, and absolute meaning freed from the material constraints of language—is fundamental to logocentrism, the matrix of Western idealism and to its sense of
truth.[141] Truth as we conceive it makes sense only within the logocentric
closure and the metaphysics of presence.[142] As a pivotal concept of logocentrism, the transcendental signified—and the dichotomies that it justifies
(signified/signifier, content/form, thought/language, mind/body)—makes it
possible to conceive of meaning independently of language and of truth prior
to discourse. So long as there is an original meaning, a final truth, language
remains an ornament, subordinate to a metaphysics. The speech act merely
serves to translate or actualize an a priori meaning.[143]

And what if meaning were but a mere effect of language? "To say 'there is
no a priori meaning; meaning is the result of language, of the reduplicated
practice of language, and the configurations of this practice,' is already to
subvert bourgeois idealism."[144] To acknowledge that there is language and
that it does not go without saying is to challenge, in effect, the fundamental
dichotomies and hierarchies of Western idealism: signified/signifier, meaning/
expression, content/form, mind/matter, soul/body. Clearly, if meaning does
not exist once and for all, if the notion of a privileged origin or center that
legitimates and perpetuates meaning is dispelled, then there is no point in
looking for the internal and hidden nucleus of discourse, the heart of a
thought or a meaning manifested in discourse, but rather for discourse's

139. Barbara Johnson, translator's introduction, to *Dissemination*, by Derrida (Chicago:
University of Chicago Press, 1981), viii.
140. Derrida, *Of Grammatology*, 20. I have altered the somewhat erroneous translation.
141. Derrida, *Positions*, 51.
142. See Derrida, *Of Grammatology* (e.g., "The Signifier and Truth").
143. Sollers, "L'Ecriture fonction de transformation sociale," 401.
144. *Tel Quel*, "Réponses à la Nouvelle Critique," 387.

external conditions of being: the source of the chance series of discursive events and the determinant of their limits.[145] What an idealist conception of language seeks to conceal is "that far from being 'first,' original or situated somewhere as an absolute beginning point, 'meaning' is derived in relation to an effect of trace, passage (*frayage*), of production dissimulated by the system of language invested as speech (*parole*), then as 'written' speech."[146]

If indeed meaning is contingent on the material constraints of language, it would behoove society to dissimulate the production of meaning, as it is a function of desire and power, instinctual drives and social law. Psychoanalysis has shown us, after all, "that speech [discourse] is not merely the medium which manifests—or dissembles—desire; it is also the object of desire."[147] Similarly, history continues to teach us that "discourse is no mere verbalization of struggles or systems of domination. It is both the means and the end of our struggles, the power we seek to usurp."[148] In "The System and the Speaking Subject," Kristeva maintains that the semiotic discovery lies in the realization "that there is a general social law, that this law is the symbolic dimension which is given in language and that every social practice offers a specific expression of that law."[149] Such a discovery deals a blow not only to the idealist notion of meaning as subordinate to itself and unaffected by external determinations, but also to a sociologizing dogmatism (for example, a mechanistic Marxism) that suppresses the specificity of the symbolic and its logic by reducing them to an external determinant such as ideology (25, 27). In both instances, the "semiotic logic of the sociality in which the (speaking, historical) subject is embedded" is neglected (25–26).

In establishing itself as a theory of social practices, conventional semiotics has tended to emphasize those practices that subserve social cohesion (26). In using language as its model, semiotics reflects a shortcoming of linguistics, which, as a science, "is still bathed in the aura of *systematics* that prevailed at the time of its inception."[150] By focusing on "the rules governing the coherence of our fundamental social code" ("The Ethics of Linguistics" 24),

---

145. Foucault, "The Discourse on Language," in *The Archaeology of Knowledge*, trans. A. M. Sheridan Smith (New York: Harper and Row, 1972), 229. Originally published as *L'Ordre du discours* (Paris: Gallimard, 1971).

146. Sollers, "L'Ecriture fonction de transformation sociale," 401.

147. Foucault, "The Discourse on Language," 216.

148. Ibid. I have altered the translation.

149. Kristeva, "The System and the Speaking Subject," in *The Kristeva Reader*, ed. Toril Moi (New York: Columbia University Press, 1986), 25. First published in the *Times Literary Supplement* (12 October 1973): 1249–52.

150. Kristeva, "The Ethics of Linguistics," 24.

linguistic theory is incapable of apprehending what belongs to the domain of play, pleasure, desire, or transgression, and which, in the best of instances, is relegated to aleatory forms of discourse devoid of empirical status.[151] And yet, beneath rhetoric and poetics, there is much to be rediscovered regarding humanity's "unchanging but always different polemic with the symbolic function."[152]

Kristeva argues that linguists, as "wardens of repression and rationalizers of the social contract in its most solid substratum (discourse)," are in a highly anachronistic position when it comes to accounting for contemporary crises in meaning, identity, structure, and sociality.[153] They remain oblivious to the ways in which this century's sociopolitical upheavals and cultural cataclysms have left their mark on the signifying function, thereby dismantling our established notions of meaning, identity, and truth. One cannot deny that our century, marked as much by historic regression as scientific progress, has produced a "monumental crisis in thought and word, a crisis in representation."[154] Where exactly does meaning lie in a wasteland overrun by camps and corpses? Auschwitz and Hiroshima totally defy any notion that we may have of reason or truth.

If "the diabolical couple of Fascism and Stalinism" (Lévy, *La Barbarie* 7) has begotten the most concentrated experiences of regression that history has known,[155] we cannot expect language and subjectivity to remain unaffected. Isn't it time to ask how these cataclysmic experiences are bound up with humanity's quest for meaning in a contemporary world that our philosophers and writers have qualified as "absurd," "nihilistic," and "apocalyptic"? Isn't it time to pay heed to "the nurturing horror that [civilizations] attend to pushing aside by purifying, systematizing and thinking"?[156] Hence the importance of literary practice: "far from being a minor, privileged activity in our culture, as a general consensus seems to have it," literature represents instead "the ultimate coding of our crises, of our most intimate and most serious apocalypses" (Kristeva, *Powers of Horror* 208). The "crisis of the verb" in the literary experiences of contemporary authors

151. Kristeva, "The System and the Speaking Subject," 26.
152. Kristeva, "From One Identity to an Other," 145.
153. Kristeva, "The Ethics of Linguistics," 24.
154. Kristeva, "The Pain of Sorrow in the Modern World: The Works of Marguerite Duras," *PMLA* 2 (March 1987): 138.
155. Sollers, "Folie: Mère-Ecran," *Tel Quel* 69 (Spring 1977): 97.
156. Kristeva, *The Powers of Horror*, trans. Leon Roudiez (New York: Columbia University Press, 1982), 210. Originally published in Collection Tel Quel as *Pouvoirs de l'horreur* (Paris: Seuil, 1980).

such as Kafka, Joyce, Céline, and Duras, reveals that the underside of our social codes, of our cultural or institutional lulls, displays, in fact, the nonidentity and horror that we do not care to acknowledge, and that can erupt in the form of a socialized, totalitarian horror.[157] Kristeva contends that an investigation of contemporary ideological upheavals hinges on a knowledge of the literary "machine."[158] If the *Tel Quel* group acknowledged Barthes as "the precursor and founder of modern literary studies," it was "precisely because he located literary practice at the intersection of subject and history; because he studied this practice as symptom of the ideological tearings in the social fabric; and because he sought, within texts, the precise mechanism that symbolically (semiotically) controls this tearing" (Kristeva, "How Does One Speak to Literature" 93). To the degree that literary practice "focuses on the *process* of meaning within language and ideology—from the "ego" to history—[it] remains the missing link in the socio-communicative or subjective-transcendental fabric of the so-called human sciences" (98). Kristeva nevertheless maintains that "the insertion of literary practice into the social science corpus necessitates a modification of the very notion of 'science,' so that an analogous dialectic may operate" (98).

By articulating semiotics with literature ("semio-criticism") and to psychoanalysis ("semanalysis"), Barthes and Kristeva no longer view language as a homogeneous structure or a static system, but rather as a signifying process characterized by heterogeneous forces. Central to their critical semiotics is the notion of language as a discourse enunciated by a speaking subject embedded in a sociopolitical context. The translinguistic and interdisciplinary work of Barthes and Kristeva, which would be fundamental for *Tel Quel* from the mid-1960s to early 1970s, attributes a fundamental place to the (speaking, historical) subject. For Kristeva, a critique of the semiology of systems is possible only if it starts from a theory of meaning bound up with a theory of the speaking subject.[159] *Tel Quel* became "the privileged link where the structuralist advance turned into an analysis of subjectivity"[160] because its collaborators realized that even structuralism would just

---

157. Kristeva, "Julia Kristeva: Pouvoirs de l'horreur" (from an interview with Henric and Scarpetta), *Tel Quel* 86 (Winter 1980): 53.

158. Kristeva, "How Does One Speak to Literature?" in *Desire in Language*, 93. Originally published as "Comment parler à la littérature?" in *Tel Quel* 47 (Autumn 1971) and subsequently in *Polylogue*.

159. Kristeva, "The System and the Speaking Subject," 27.

160. Kristeva, "My Memory's Hyperbole," 269.

be one more "science" if it continued to uphold the notion of a neutral (scientific) language, the product of a subject at sleep, disembedded from sociopolitical turmoil.

"Our philosophies of language," insists Kristeva, "are nothing more than the thoughts of archivists, archaeologists, and necrophiliacs. Fascinated by the remains of a process which is partly discursive, they substitute this fetish for what actually produced it."[161] Every theory of language suggests "a conception of the subject that it explicitly posits, implies, or tries to deny. Far from being an 'epistemological perversion,' a definite subject is present as soon as there is consciousness of signification."[162] For Kristeva:

> The theory of meaning now stands at a crossroad: either it will remain an attempt at formalizing meaning-systems by increasing sophistication of the logico-mathematical tools which enable it to formulate models on the basis of a conception (already rather dated) of meaning as the act of a *transcendental ego*, cut off from its body, its unconscious and also its history; or else it will attune itself to the theory of the speaking subject as a divided subject (conscious/unconscious).[163]

By bringing together semiotics and psychoanalysis, that is, the positivist notion of language as an object of scientific study and the Freudian decentered subject, Kristeva's work contests the semiology of systems, for meaning-systems provide the decentered subject with a sense of coherence. The "unary" subject, which is the subject implicitly posited by science, society, and most political theory and practice, and which views the self as a homogeneous, consistent whole, represents, in fact, a momentary stasis or damming up of instinctual drives and the transverbal process.[164] A theory of language upholding such a conception of the subject fails to recognize that there is a heterogeneity, known as the unconscious, that shapes the signifying function.[165]

161. Kristeva, *Revolution in Poetic Language*, trans. Margaret Waller (New York: Columbia University Press, 1984), 13. Originally published in Collection Tel Quel as *La Révolution du langage poétique* (Paris: Seuil, 1974).

162. Kristeva, "From One Identity to an Other," 124.

163. Kristeva, "The System and the Speaking Subject," 28.

164. Roudiez, introduction to *Desire in Language*, by Julia Kristeva, 19.

165. Kristeva, "From One Identity to an Other," 135.

By discovering that consciousness rests on the unconscious and that the latter is characterized by its capacity for displacement, Freud made it clear that it no longer was a question of being where I think I am. Lacan maintains that "the philosophical cogito is at the center of the mirage that renders modern man so sure of being himself even in his uncertainties about himself, and even in the mistrust he has learned to practise against the trap of self-love."[166] The reality denied by such a mirage is the one of language and the unconscious in structuring human subjectivity. In positing itself as the science of the unconscious, psychoanalysis teaches us that there is a fundamental gap between the subject, his language, and the knowledge that he has of himself. According to Lacan, "the slightest alteration in the relation between man and the signifier . . . changes the whole course of history by modifying the moorings that anchor his being" (174). Freud's revolutionary discovery of "the self's radical ex-centricity to itself" (171) "achieved the definitive displacement of the Western *épistémé* from its presumed centrality."[167] Freud thus dealt the third narcissistic blow to Western thought, after Copernicus and Darwin.[168] For the question now was, "Is the place that I occupy as the subject of a signifier concentric or excentric, in relation to the place I occupy as subject of the signified?"[169] For Lacan, "[i]t is not a question of knowing whether I speak of myself in a way that conforms to what I am, but rather of knowing whether I am the same as that of which I speak" ("The Agency of the Letter" 165). For "at the heart of my assent to my own identity," there is an other who agitates me (172).

Modern man, in his self-complacency, is certain of his identity only insofar as he denies the radical heteronomy within him that is bound up with the question of language. For that stranger who continues to remain more unknown than man and who is coextensive with his being, is none other than language itself.[170] If "the unconscious of the subject is the discourse of the other,"[171] it is because man's speech continually eludes him, leading him to

---

166. Lacan, "The Agency of the Letter in the Unconscious or Reason since Freud," in *Ecrits (A Selection)*, 165.

167. Kristeva, "The System and the Speaking Subject," 28.

168. Sigmund Freud cited in Michel Foucault, "Nietzsche, Freud, Marx," in *Nietzsche* (Royaumont Colloquium, July 1967) (Paris: Seuil, 1967), 185–86. See also Lacan, "The Freudian Thing, or the Meaning of the Return to Freud in Psychoanalysis," 114, and "The Agency of the Letter in the Unconscious or Reason since Freud," 165, in *Ecrits (A Selection)*.

169. Lacan, "The Agency of the Letter," 165.

170. Kristeva, *Language: The Unknown*, vii.

171. Lacan, "The Function and Field of Speech and Language in Psychoanalysis" in *Ecrits*

say something other than what he thinks he is saying in what he says.[172] To attribute one's fumbling with language to momentary inattention or absent-mindedness is to adhere to the notion that we know in advance what we will say, and that language is merely an instrument that we employ to transmit knowledge. The comparison of language to an instrument tends to dissociate the property of language from man,[173] thereby fostering the illusion that man is the cause—and not the effect—of his speech. It denies the constitutive role of language in defining human subjectivity, for "[i]t is in and through language that man constitutes himself as a *subject*" (Benveniste, "Subjectivity in Language" 224).

Psychoanalysis teaches us that it is as illusory to seek the reality of the subject beyond the language barrier as it is for the subject to believe that his truth is already known in advance.[174] It is speech alone that allows the truth of the subject to come to light.[175] The unconscious, writes Lacan, "is that chapter of my history that is marked by a blank or occupied by a falsehood: it is the censored chapter. But the truth can be rediscovered; usually it has already been written down elsewhere."[176] It is written down in "monuments" (my body); in "archival documents" (childhood memories); in "semantic evolution" ("this corresponds to the stock of words and acceptations of my own particular vocabulary, as it does to my style of life and to my character"); in "traditions" and in the "legends which, in a heroicized form, bear my history"; and finally in the "traces that are inevitably preserved by the distortions necessitated by the linking of the adulterated chapter to the chapters surrounding it, and whose meaning will be re-established by my exegesis" (50). Lacan reveals that "everything which has meaning for man is inscribed in him in the very archives of the unconscious

---

(A Selection), 55. Originally published as "Fonction et champ de la parole et du langage en psychanalyse," in *Ecrits*.

172. "Since Freud, the unconscious has been a chain of signifiers that somewhere (on another stage, in another scene, he wrote) is repeated, and insists on interfering in the breaks offered it by the effective discourse and the cogitation that it informs." Lacan, "The Subversion of the Subject and the Dialectic of Desire in the Freudian Unconscious," in *Ecrits (A Selection)*, 297. Originally published as "Subversion du sujet et dialectique du désir dans l'inconscient freudien" in *Ecrits*.

173. Benveniste, "Subjectivity in Language," 224.

174. Lacan, "The Function and Field," 94.

175. Antoine Vergote, foreword to *Jacques Lacan*, by Anika Lemaire, trans. David Macey (Boston: Routledge and Kegan Paul, 1977), xx. Originally published by Charles Denart in Belgium, 1970.

176. Lacan, "The Function and Field," 50.

by language, understood in the full extent of its semantic, rhetorical and formal structures."[177]

The unconscious represents, in effect, a certain detour through language of repressed thought or knowledge.[178] What is put into play by the structure of the unconscious is the scene of thought and its contestation: the profound and secret duel between a dominant disposition and its other, thanks to which and against which the former succeeds in instituting itself.[179] Each scene of thought is possible only at the cost of denying the struggle by which it establishes itself and which never ceases to disturb it secretly (76). Psychoanalysis reveals that the point of view of the triumphant unity is both illusory and repressive: it occults the more real view of the struggle that each domination precisely denies. Lacan writes, "The radical heteronomy that Freud's discovery shows gaping within man can never again be covered over without whatever is used to hide it being profoundly dishonest."[180]

If, in 1950, Natalie Sarraute could write that the French novel had entered "the age of suspicion," it was not merely because the contemporary reader distrusted the novelistic character and the outmoded literary apparatus that had assured its power.[181] At stake in the demise of the fictional character—a demise that Lucien Goldmann associated with the crisis of the individual in advanced capitalist society—was the notion of the unary subject as the last bastion of Western idealism. It was "now so necessary to think through fiction—while in the past it was a matter of thinking the truth"—because the "I speak" of contemporary writing ran counter to the "I think" of traditional thought.[182] For Foucault, " 'I think' led to the indubitable certainty of the 'I' and its existence; 'I speak,' on the other hand, distances, disperses, effaces that existence and lets only its empty emplacement appear" (13). According to *Tel Quel* collaborator Bernard Sichère, "The breakdown of philosophical subjectivity, its dispersion inside of a language that dispossesses it, yet multiplies it in the space of its lacunae, is probably one of the

---

177. Vergote, foreword to *Jacques Lacan*, xviii.

178. Sollers, interviewed by Monique Charvet and Ermanno Krumm in *Tel Quel: un'avanguardia per il materialismo*, 31.

179. Bernard Sichère, "L'Autre Histoire: A partir de Michel Foucault," *Tel Quel* 86 (Winter 1980): 76.

180. Lacan, "The Agency of the Letter," 172.

181. Natalie Sarraute, *L'ère du soupçon* (1956; Paris: Gallimard, 1972), 74, 94. "L'ère du soupçon" originally appeared in *Les Temps Modernes* (February 1950). Subsequently translated as *The Age of Suspicion*, trans. Maria Jolas (New York: G. Braziller, 1963).

182. Foucault, *The Thought From Outside*, 12–13.

fundamental structures of contemporary thought."[183] "No doubt," concludes Foucault, "that is why Western thought took so long to think the
being of language: as if it had a premonition of the danger that the naked
experience of language poses for the self-evidence of 'I think.' "[184] It is thus
no surprise to find the Nietzschean question "Who speaks?" reiterated with
such urgency in the novels of Blanchot, Beckett, Sarraute, Robbe-Grillet,
Duras, and Sollers. The novels of these writers are characterized by "a being
without contours, who is indefinable, elusive, and invisible; an anonymous
'I,' who is at once everything and nothing" and who has usurped the
assuring role of the traditional protagonist.[185] These works merely confirm
the Freudian discovery that "the position of the subject is not defined by
what he says, nor by what he talks *about*, but by the place—unknown to
him—*from which* he speaks."[186]

From this age of suspicion that characterizes the French novel of the 1950s
and 1960s, a new theoretical discourse on language as subjective experience
came into being with *Tel Quel*. Drawing both from the formalist experimentation of the new novel and from developments in semiotic theory, *Tel Quel's*
discourse on language in the mid- and late 1960s was also rooted in
psychoanalytical theory. With Foucault and Lacan, *Tel Quel* did not have to
bang its head against the walls of Sartre.[187] According to Kristeva, "The
labyrinths of the *speaking subject*—the microcosm of a complex logic
whose effects had only partially surfaced in society—led us directly toward
regions that were obscure but crucial, specific but universal, particular but
transhistorical, far from society's policed scenarios" ("My Memory's Hyperbole" 265).

In the midst of the structuralist advance, Telquelians like Barthes and
Kristeva sought to "dynamize" the prevailing notion of structure "by taking
into consideration the speaking subject and its unconscious experience on
the one hand, and on the other, the pressures of other social structures"
("My Memory's Hyperbole" 266–67). For Kristeva, language was not a
homogeneous structure or a static system, but rather a signifying process in
which "the heterogeneity of two separate modes should be distinguished: the
semiotic, emanating from instinctual drives and primary processes; and the
symbolic, assimilable to secondary processes, predicative syntheses and

183. Sichère, "Michel Foucault singulier," *L'Infini* 11 (Summer 1985): 124.
184. Foucault, *The Thought From Outside*, 13.
185. Sarraute, *L'ère du soupçon*, 72.
186. Felman, *Writing and Madness*, 50.
187. Kristeva, "My Memory's Hyperbole," 265.

judgement."[188] Language is bound up with the notion of practice: "To say language is a practice is to precisely see how the symbolic, and with it meaning, is displaced by the pressure of the semiotic."[189] Such a conception of language evidently requires "an analytical theory of signifying systems that [searches] within the signifying phenomenon for the *crisis* or the *unsettling process* of meaning and subject rather than for the coherence or identity of either *one* or a *multiplicity* of structures."[190] The merit of such a theory is that it does not confine itself, like traditional semiotics, to identifying the systematic constraint within a signifying practice, but instead attempts to specify "just what, within the practice, falls outside the system and characterizes the specificity of the practice as such."[191] It becomes a question of addressing "practice[s] of challenge, innovation or personal experiment," that is, of giving "a hearing to any or all of those efforts which, ever since the elaboration of a new position for the speaking subject, have been renewing and reshaping the status of meaning within social exchanges to a point where the very order of language is being renewed" ("The System and the Speaking Subject" 32). That is, after all, what the modernity of Kafka, Joyce, Artaud, Céline, and others represent.

In its "concern to make intelligible, and therefore socializable, what rocks the foundations of sociality," semanalysis or, for that matter, any critical semiotics "places itself at the service of the social law which requires systematization, communication, exchange" ("The System and the Speaking Subject" 33). It thereby encounters the dilemma of traditional semiotics, which, in establishing itself as a positive science, becomes a potential law insofar as it fails to recognize that it too is permeated by the symbolic, whose formal functioning it claims to merely observe from the outside.[192] As the science of discourse, semiology can at least have the following, albeit dangerous, advantage over the other sciences of man: to know the manner in which it articulates itself and the stakes of this articulation (Barthes, "L'aventure sémiologique" 28). Barthes maintains that two related systems can aid semiology in this self-critical task: Marxist and Freudian (Lacanian) analysis. The articulation of semiology with a theory of production and a

188. Kristeva, "Within the Microcosm of 'The Talking Cure,'" in *Interpreting Lacan*, ed. Joseph Smith and William Kerrigan, trans. Thomas Gora and Margaret Waller (New Haven: Yale University Press, 1983), 34.

189. Kristeva, "Sujet dans le langage et pratique politique," 23.

190. Kristeva, "From One Identity to an Other," 125.

191. Kristeva, "The System and the Speaking Subject," 26–27.

192. Barthes, "L'aventure sémiologique," 28.

theory of the subject leads to a critical (textual) semiotics, such as Kristeva's semanalysis, which is suspicious of all metalanguage (including the one of semiology), and which is characterized by the return of the semiologist to an activity of writing or textual production (Barthes, "L'aventure sémiologique" 28). The subject of the semiotic metalanguage, who is not "the phantom of 'pure science,'" must, "however briefly, call himself in question, must emerge from the protective shell of a transcendental ego within a logical system, and so restore his connection with that negativity—drive-governed, but also social, political and historical—which rends and renews the social code."[193]

In question in this critical theory and the literary practice it purports to analyze is a materialist gnoseology bound up with textual production and the subversion of the unary subject. Such a theory not only grounds literature back into the social context, from which Sartrean engagement maintained that it should never have been removed, but also frees language from an idealist framework that reduces it to an instrument or decor of a preexisting "reality," which it merely expresses. "Why is it," asks Tel Quel, "that viewed from a materialist or dialectic perspective, language no longer is an instrument, or a decoration?"[194] This question would be central to Tel Quel's critical theory and practice of writing from the mid-1960s to the early 1970s, consequently leading the Tel Quel group, like the avant-garde movements that had preceded it, to a confrontation with the French Left.

193. Kristeva, "The System and the Speaking Subject," 33.
194. Tel Quel, "Réponses à La Nouvelle Critique," 387.

CHAPTER THREE

THE COMMAND
OF THEORY

The hour belonged to theory . . . perhaps too much so.

—Philippe Sollers

In the preface to the 1980 edition of the *Tel Quel* manifesto *Théorie d'Ensemble*, Sollers felt compelled to explain the interval separating this edition from the one published in 1968: "Ten or twelve years, it's not much, but, in this case, one has the impression of a chasm. Everything went very quickly, and in every which way."[1] If in 1968 "[t]he hour belonged to theory, to the search for a synthesis" (7), by 1980, theory had lost its hold. But the *Tel Quel* mirage of the late 1960s, brought to light in *Théorie d'Ensemble*, was crucial to *Tel Quel*'s new aspirations. It was precisely this mirage that generated a unified reflection and consequently activated a generalized subversion of French intellectual thought. For Sollers, this unification had been facilitated by "an acute consciousness of the possible powers of literature that a habitual repression tended to minimize, check, or subordinate" (7).

Tel Quel's theoretico-formalist phase was a long one (1963–68). Even when the group considered Marxism an absolutely fundamental basis for

1. Sollers, preface to *Théorie d'Ensemble*, Collection Tel Quel (Paris: Seuil, 1968, 1980), 7.

considering the problems of an avant-garde that wanted to move forward, the question of Marxism was still posed in theorizing terms. Indeed, theory was in command.[2] If Kristeva wrote of *Tel Quel*'s exaggerated reverence for theory, it was because theory became the missing link between the essentially bourgeois class origins of the *Tel Quel* team, their elitist practice of writing, and the class struggle. *Tel Quel* came to the class struggle via theory. As preposterous as this action may seem, it is actually representative of Western Marxism in the 1960s and draws much of its legitimacy from Louis Althusser. *Tel Quel*'s cynicism in the late 1960s likewise derives from its overestimation of theory.[3] Kristeva maintains that *Tel Quel*'s political perversions in the late 1960s and early 1970s were governed by a theoretical "ideal," whereas others (such as the Resistance generation) had been motivated by a moral one (273). *Tel Quel*, however, equates "moral" engagement with sentimentality and a lack of theory.

Foucault took a most critical, retrospective view toward French writers' excessive deference to theory. In a 1977 interview, he claimed that "the whole relentless theorisation of writing which we saw in the 1960s was doubtless only a swansong. Through it, the writer was fighting for the preservation of his political privilege."[4] The search for scientific credentials in the disciplines of linguistics, semiology, and psychoanalysis and the production of mediocre literary products only proved that "the activity of the writer was no longer at the focus of things" (127).

In what could be interpreted as an attempt to preserve their political privilege, *Tel Quel* writers in the 1960s turned to theory and specifically to linguistics, psychoanalysis, and deconstructive philosophy. Was the theorization of writing to which Foucault refers and which *Tel Quel* perhaps best incarnates just a strategic ploy to salvage literature in the wake of Sartrean engagement? And yet, for *Tel Quel*, the activity of writing always came first. It had been central to the *Tel Quel* mission from the beginning. Not only did *Tel Quel* come to theory from its own practice of writing, it also made the *specific* practice of writing the basis for a comprehensive theory. The departure point for Sollers's politico-literary "Program" of 1967 (*Tel Quel* 30) was the following imperative: "A COMPREHENSIVE THEORY [THEORIE

2. Sollers, "Ebranler le système," 14.
3. Kristeva, "My Memory's Hyperbole," 273.
4. Foucault, "Truth and Power," in *Power/Knowledge: Selected Interviews and Other Writings (1972–1977)*, ed. Colin Gordon, trans. Colin Gordon, Leo Marshall, John Mepham, and Kate Soper (New York: Pantheon, 1980), 127.

D'ENSEMBLE] DERIVED FROM THE PRACTICE OF WRITING DEMANDS TO BE ELABO-
RATED."[5]

Foucault viewed the disappearance of the figure of the "great writer" as a function of the changing configuration of the French intellectual. As the "last writer," Sartre also brought to an end the line of universal intellectuals that had originated with Zola. New connections between theory and practice developed in the '60s that resulted in the notion of a nonuniversal, counterhegemonic, or "specific" intellectual, making it possible to rearticulate categories that had previously been kept separate. As "each individual's specific activity began to serve as the basis for politicisation, the threshold of *writing*, as the sacralising mark of the intellectual, disappear[ed]."[6] Just how accurate was Foucault's contention that the activity of the writer was no longer at the center of things? To what degree was his argument founded on a notion of writing ultimately linked to engagement? Couldn't Barthes's 1960 notion of the "écrivain," for whom writing was an intransitive activity, encapsulating the fusion of the creative and critical functions of language, be compatible with Foucault's notion of the specific intellectual?

In *Critique et vérité* [Criticism and truth], published in Collection Tel Quel in 1966, Barthes reflected on the changing intellectual scene and affirmed that the "journey across writing" (Sollers) was leaving its mark on the twentieth century as it challenged intellectual discourse as a whole.[7] If the writer was still a viable player on the intellectual scene, it was to the degree that he was defined less by a particular status than by the desire to exist in a certain way. He could no longer "be defined in terms of his role or his value but only by a certain *awareness of discourse*. A writer is someone for whom language constitutes a problem, who is aware of the depth of language, not its instrumentality or its beauty" (64). Before we dismiss Barthes's statement as having no concrete bearing, it is vital to contextualize it, for it ultimately disproves Foucault's contention of a decade later that as the writer tended to disappear as a figurehead, the university and the academic emerged. If this is true, it is because the upheaval of the university symbolized by May 1968 was the result of explosions that had taken place in institutional sites outside of and directly opposed to the university, such as the avant-garde as represented by Barthes and *Tel Quel*.

5. Sollers, "Program," in *Writing and the Experience of Limits*, 5. Originally published as "Programme" in *Tel Quel* 31 (Autumn 1967) and reprinted in *Logiques*.

6. Foucault, "Truth and Power," 127.

7. Barthes, *Criticism and Truth*, 65.

In a gesture reminiscent of the *Nouvelle Revue Française, Tel Quel* defined its strategic site in opposition to the university. In effect, what made *Tel Quel* unique in the early 1960s was that a group of writers came to theory from their own practice as writers, and not from an outside institution such as the university, which was still considered the traditional bastion of criticism. According to Sollers, *Tel Quel* did not work from a theory that it subsequently attempted to illustrate in its texts; rather:

> It is because a certain number of us decided to "write" in a certain manner that this theoretical articulation was made possible. There is thus no opposition between theory and practice but a dialectic that is made explicit and concrete by the *Tel Quel* issues and books. We never defined *Tel Quel* as a journal of purely theoretical knowledge, nor as an empirical one, that is, a pure and simple exposition of texts. This dialectic between a specific practice and a theorisation is what makes *Tel Quel Tel Quel*.[8]

This feature of *Tel Quel* would attract academics such as Gérard Genette and Tzvetan Todorov to the review at a time when criticism remained the monopoly of the university, and, to a lesser degree, the press. Unlike *Poétique*—founded by Genette, Todorov, and Hélène Cixous in 1968—the editorial committee of *Tel Quel* was never dominated by academics, an unusual situation for a review with theoretical responsibilities. For *Tel Quel*, which always strove to direct its own theoretical articulation, used its own practice of writing as the departure point for its theorization (Sollers, "Philippe Sollers décrit son action" 160), and in so doing, aimed not only at resisting the domination of outside institutions (such as the university, which remained one of the foremost citadels of conservatism in France until May 1968) but also at subverting knowledge. Telquelians wanted to dissociate themselves from academics formed from within the university philosophical tradition. Insofar as they continue to participate in the reproduction of university knowledge, academics have enormous difficulty in recognizing what subverts this knowledge.[9]

The subversion of knowledge by writers from outside the university was

---

8. Sollers, "Philippe Sollers décrit son action," in *Qui sont les contemporains*, ed. Jean Ristat (Paris: Gallimard, 1975), 163. Originally published in the *Gazette de Lausanne* (10–11 October 1970).

9. Sollers, "Philippe Sollers décrit son action," 161.

best highlighted by the vehement debate that took place between Barthes and Picard between 1963 and 1965. A great deal was at stake for *Tel Quel* in this contemporary variant of the "Querelle des Anciens et des Modernes." This polemic over the "new criticism" pitted the university—personified by Raymond Picard, whose scholarly work on Racine had earned him a chair in French literature at the Sorbonne—against Barthes, whom Picard dubbed the spokesperson for the avant-garde. Furthermore, the polemic clearly revealed how the question of intellectual discourse is irremediably linked to institutional power and, subsequently, to the monopoly of knowledge. The vocabulary of execution pervading the attacks on Barthes—the outsider who dared to challenge the intellectual legitimacy of the university—is indicative of the importance attributed to literature in ideological struggles: "It's an execution," wrote a journalist for *La Croix*; for the *Revue de Paris*, it was the "Pearl Harbor of new criticism." Summing up the remarks of critics and journalists, Barthes wrote, "People have dreamed of *wounding* new criticism, *pricking* its pretensions, *assaulting* it, *murdering* it, dragging it before the *criminal courts*, setting it in the *pillory* or putting it on the *scaffold*."[10]

What had led to Picard's aversion to New Criticism and conviction that it was "dangerous"? It was Barthes's book on none other than Racine that had set off the fire in 1963. *Sur Racine* [*On Racine*] was thoughtfully reviewed for *Tel Quel* (no. 15) by Jean-Louis Baudry, who acknowledged his debt to Barthes for articulating the social sciences (especially semiotics and psychoanalysis) through literary criticism. It nevertheless drew severe criticism from Picard in *Nouvelle Critique ou nouvelle imposture?* [New Criticism or new fraud?] (1965) for those very reasons that had attracted *Tel Quel* to it. In his review of Picard's book (*Tel Quel* 24), Sollers noted that Picard not only disallows the *sexualization* of a classical work, but also rejects the literary appropriation of the *unconscious*, which for him can only be conceived in clinical or medical terms.[11] Had Barthes written on a nonclassical author, such as Robbe-Grillet, he certainly would not have created the same uproar. He was clearly aware of what was at stake in his rereading of Racine when he wrote, "our [response] to Racine engages, beyond ourselves, the entire language by which our world expresses itself and which is an essential part of the history it calls its own."[12] The combined

---

10. Barthes, *Criticism and Truth*, 30–31.

11. Sollers, "Picard, cheval de bataille," *Tel Quel* 24 (Winter 1966): 92.

12. Barthes, foreword to *On Racine*, trans. Richard Howard (New York: Octagon Books/

influence of semiotics and psychoanalysis on literary criticism not only made for a new (sexualized) discourse on a classical author (object), it also made discourse (classical par excellence) the new object of desire and power. If for a long time classico-bourgeois society had viewed discourse as a mere instrument or decoration, the advent of structural linguistics and Lacanian psychoanalysis now permitted it to be seen as a sign and a truth,[13] which explains why the social sciences, in bringing a new dimension to texual analysis, appeared threatening to traditional (university) criticism. According to Barthes, "what is not tolerated is that language should talk about language" (33).

Barthes's work confirmed that any critique of knowledge must begin with a critique of the *language* that formulates it.[14] Indeed, it is less a question of knowing what is at stake when we talk about language than *who is at stake*, for we are the product of our language.[15] In reducing language to an instrument or a decoration, Western metaphysics denied us access to our bodies for centuries. The body is denied so that we may secure the sovereignty of a timeless idea.[16] Sovereign and timeless, our ideas supersede not only our body, but also our language; any disregard for language necessarily coincides with a rejection of the body: "We do not care to hear talk of [*entendre parler*] our body, because we do not want to hear it speak [*l'entendre parler*]—in other words: we do not want to talk of our language because we do not want to hear it speak."[17] When we deny our body and the language it speaks, we ultimately fail to recognize the historically specific conditions that underpin our knowledge and the sociopolitical forms that our truths take. But when language is no longer viewed as "merely the futile decor of humanity's more substantial interests" (Barthes), the revision of knowledge becomes inevitable. As a function of desire and power, language

---

Farrar, Straus and Giroux, 1977), x. I have substituted the word "response" for "answer." Originally published as *Sur Racine* (Paris: Seuil, 1963).

13. Barthes, *Criticism and Truth*, 66.

14. Jean-Louis Baudry, "La tragédie racinienne: une oeuvre ouverte," *Tel Quel* 15 (Autumn 1963): 65.

15. In "Literature and Totality," Sollers writes: "In truth, there is no subject in itself . . . since the subject is the *consequence* of its language. This language must therefore be pushed to its limits in order to know what is at stake, *who* is at stake in us. A most difficult enterprise, given the extent of the unconsciousness we immediately discover buried deep within us." In *Writing and the Experience of Limits*, 68–69.

16. Foucault, "Nietzsche, Genealogy, History," in *Language, Counter-Memory, Practice*, 158.

17. Sollers, "The Novel and the Experience of Limits," 202.

brings subjectivity and ideology back into the eternal quest for knowledge and language thus becomes a political stake (*enjeu*). This is exactly what Picard, in the name of objective, nonpartisan, university knowledge, rejected in the new criticism. The institution of the university itself was at stake: if all criticism were subjective and thus biased, criticism belonged to everyone and was no longer the prerogative of academics alone.

The political implications of the Barthes-Picard polemic were highlighted by an article entitled "M. Barthes et la 'critique universitaire' " directed to the general reading public in *Le Monde* (14 March 1964, 12). This essay was Picard's political response to Barthes and preceded his scholarly response, *Nouvelle Critique ou nouvelle imposture?* in 1965. His sense of obligation in bringing this intellectual disagreement to the attention of the general public enables us to understand the debate's political stakes. Picard essentially challenges Barthes's dichotomy between university and interpretative criticism, which Barthes had outlined in two essays, "The Two Criticisms" and "What is Criticism?" published respectively in *Modern Language Notes* and *The Times Literary Supplement* in 1963. The opening sentence in Picard's article is most revealing: "The University never responds, but perhaps you will understand why an academic reacts in his personal name to attacks which by their repetition—despite their scope or even their pertinence—end up becoming dangerous." Let us begin by nothing that Picard assumes that the University (with a capital *U*) is untouchable. Beyond reproach or appeal, it should not be involved in temporal disputes. Nevertheless, given the dangerous nature of the attacks against him, Picard is forced to respond. He seems particularly annoyed by the fact that Barthes published these articles abroad, "where among an ill-informed [that is, an ignorant British and American] public, this futile and irresponsible defamation [of the university] is more likely to succeed."

Picard disclaims Barthes's contention that despite all the upheavals of French society since World War I, the university, as a literary institution and a seat of knowledge, has remained unchanged (he would like to say, unchallenged). He also objects to Barthes's view of the university as a homogeneous entity. It is nonetheless significant that May 1968 immediately resulted in the decentralization of the University of Paris and consequently in its dehomogeneization (Paris IV or the Sorbonne was to remain the conservative faculty in the domain of literary studies). Picard nevertheless concedes that if a common aim exists in university (traditional) versus interpretative (ideological) criticism, it is precisely the desire that he and his colleagues share in their pursuit of objective, neutral, scientific truth—in other words, their refusal to be ideologically oriented. He concludes by stating that the attack on the University is part of an avant-garde conformism led by Barthes. Although a year later Picard opted for a more academic response in his rebuttal of Barthes's *On Racine* and new criticism in *Nouvelle Critique ou nouvelle imposture?*, Sollers qualified his response as reactionary and as personifying the moral order itself.[18]

For Barthes, literary criticism in and of itself did not exist: a critical method could not exist independently of a general philosophy, or Weltan-schauung. He believed that it is impossible to speak of literature without referring to psychology, sociology, aesthetics, or morality, and that criticism is always a function of ideology. Barthes was only willing to recognize a form of criticism that acknowledges its ideological basis, and was ready to contest any criticism claiming to be neutral and objective. In "Two Criticisms," Barthes in fact attacked university discourse for claiming to be neutral or objective, and thus quite one-sided. This claim, founded on a nineteenth-century positivist scientism, is diametrically opposed to the new criticism of the 1960s, which is grounded in the human sciences and acknowledges the ideological nature of its critical enterprise. Barthes was determined to show how much a scientific or positivist attitude represses ideology, and does so by not recognizing language and subjectivity (the speaking subject). For even positivism is ideological. By focusing only on the biographical or sociologi-cal circumstances surrounding the literary work, positivist criticism espouses a partial notion of literature in that it fails to question the being of literature itself. It is as though circumstances vary but literature remains untouched; such a perspective presupposes a timeless essence of literature. Furthermore, such criticism rests on a postulate of analogy: the literary work is seen in relation to *something else*, an *elsewhere* of literature.[19] Thus, to write is merely to reproduce, copy, or be inspired by. If there are any differences between the original model and the work, they are attributed to genius. Paradoxically, resemblances are seen as resulting from a rigorous positivism, whereas differences are attributed to magic ("The Two Criticisms" 251–52). In his review of Picard, Sollers corroborates Barthes in asserting that Picard not only rejects language and sexuality, but also continues to hold to a classical, creative conscience. Barthes argues that so-called positivist criti-cism continues to adhere to the muse, because the postulate of analogy allows it to dismiss the very being of literature that would explain the

18. Sollers, "Picard, cheval de bataille," 92.
19. Barthes, "The Two Criticisms," in *Critical Essays*, 250–51.

apparent differences between the literary work and its elsewhere (252). For Barthes and *Tel Quel*, the "alchemy of creation" can be dismissed only by a truly scientific approach that takes language seriously. Otherwise, essentialist, creative notions persist.

Academic criticism clings so strongly to the notion of analogy, because it posits an elsewhere of literature. It denies that interpretation can function in a purely internal realm within the work: it rejects immanent analysis. *Tel Quel*, on the other hand, always emphasized the immanent practice of the literary text. Perhaps, university criticism rejects immanence because of its belief in a "determinist ideology which holds that the work is the 'product' of a 'cause' and that external causes are more 'causal' than others" ("The Two Criticisms" 254). Such criticism is clearly underpinned by the notion that the author produces the text, rather than being its result. Perhaps too, notes Barthes, that outlook is maintained "because to shift from a criticism of determinations to a criticism of functions and significations would imply a profound conversion of the norms of knowledge, hence of technique, hence of the academic critic's very profession." Literary research is still linked to teaching: the university may conduct research but it also delivers diplomas. Consequently, it requires "an ideology articulated around a technique difficult enough to constitute an instrument of selection; positivism affords it the obligation of a vast, difficult, patient knowledge" (254).

In "What is Criticism?" Barthes concludes that by acknowledging itself as no more than a language, "criticism can be—paradoxically but authentically—both objective and subjective, historical and existential, totalitarian and liberal."[20] On the one hand, the language that each critic chooses to speak is "one of the various languages his age affords him, it is objectively the end product of a certain historical ripening of knowledge, ideas, intellectual passions—it is a *necessity*." On the other hand, "this necessary language is chosen by each critic as a consequence of a certain existential organization, as the exercise of an intellectual function which belongs to him in his own right, an exercise in which he puts all his 'profundity,' i.e., his choices, his pleasures, his resistances, his obsessions." There is thus at the heart of the critical work a "dialogue of two histories and two subjectivities, the author's and the critic's. But this dialogue is egoistically shifted toward the present: criticism is not an 'hommage' to the truth of the past or to the truth of 'others'—it is a construction of the intelligibility of our own time" (260).

20. Barthes, "What is Criticism?" in *Critical Essays*, 260.

In *Critique et vérité*, Barthes maintains that the critic confronts an object that is not the literary work, but his own language. By questioning the critic's relationship to language, Barthes places subjectivity and language at the heart of the critical enterprise. The reality of the new criticism resides in the belief that criticism is an act of writing. The critic must become a writer and vice versa. The distinctions between the creative and critical functions of language that used to make for separate operations are now incorporated into a new personage: "Formerly separated by the worn-out myth of the *'super' creator and the humble servant, both necessary, each in his place, etc.'*, the writer and the critic come together, working on the same difficult tasks and faced with the same object: language."[21]

In 1966, at a Johns Hopkins University symposium marking the impact of structuralist thought on critical methods in humanistic and social studies, Barthes stated that "literature and language [were] in the process of finding each other again."[22] Such a rapprochement should not be left unexamined if one recalls, with Barthes, that the notion of literature in relation to a theory of language (rhetoric) had been threatened since the sixteenth century by the advent of modern rationalism, and altogether ruined when rationalism was transformed into positivism at the end of the nineteenth century ("To Write: An Intransitive Verb?" 134). Barthes attributes the rapprochement to the radical exploration of writing by such avant-garde authors as Mallarmé, Proust, and Joyce, and to the development of linguistic theory, particularly in relation to poetics (134–35). He concludes that there exists a new perspective of reflection common "to literature and to linguistics, to the creator and the critic, whose tasks, hitherto absolutely self-contained, are beginning to communicate, perhaps even to converge, at least on the level of the writer, whose action can increasingly be defined as a critique of language."[23]

Tel Quel's conception of writing, supported by the great poetic revolutions of the century, was also incontestably molded by the theoretical advances in semiotic theory in the 1960s. Yet it was precisely the contradictory status of language as a "problem and a model" (Barthes) that would interest *Tel Quel*. For *Tel Quel* would become "the privileged link where the structuralist advance turned into an analysis of subjectivity."[24] In fact, the question of

21. Barthes, *Criticism and Truth*, 64.
22. Barthes, "To Write: An Intransitive Verb?" 134.
23. Ibid., 135. I have used the translation in *The Rustle of Language*, 11–12.
24. Kristeva, "My Memory's Hyperbole," 269.

subjectivity would be irremediably linked to the notion of poetic language as envisioned by the Russian formalists and, particularly, by Roman Jakobson, who had several pioneering essays published in *Tel Quel*.[25]

Situated on "the dividing line between linguistics and poetics,"[26] Roman Jakobson's work was fundamental to the *Tel Quel* group. For them—most particularly Barthes, Kristeva, Faye, Genette, and Todorov—he was a prominent figure, one who "shoved *into the past* some highly respected things to which we were attached: he converted prejudice into anachronism."[27] In "Linguistics and Poetics," Jakobson noted:

> If there are some critics who still doubt the competence of linguistics to embrace the field of poetics, I believe that the poetic incompetence of some bigoted linguists has been mistaken for an inadequacy of the linguistic science itself. All of us here, however, definitely realize that a linguist deaf to the poetic function of language and a literary scholar indifferent to linguistic problems and unconversant with linguistic methods are equally flagrant anachronisms.[28]

Jacobson's articulation of science with literature was a reaction to the positivist separation between science, reason, and fact, on the one hand, and art, sensibility, and impression, on the other.[29] By establishing poetics as a special realm of linguistics, he succeeded in freeing linguistics of its technocratic intent, and poetry of its purely aesthetic status (160). Unlike his predecessors, Jakobson did not define poetics from the perspective of literature, as if it depended on the "poetic" or on "poetry," but rather from an analysis of the functions of language. For him, any speech act that accentuates the form of a message is poetic. Jakobson was thus able, "*starting from a linguistic position,* to join the vital (and often the most emancipated) forms of Literature" (159).

That an anthology of the Russian formalists' writings would come out of the very ideological climate that gave rise to the Barthes-Picard polemic is

25. *Tel Quel* published Jakobson's "Du réalisme artistique" (no. 24), "Glossolalie" (no. 26), "Une microscopie du dernier Spleen dans Les Fleurs du Mal" (no. 29), "Un exemple de termes migratoires et de modèles institutionnels à propos du cinquantième anniversaire du Cercle Linguistique de Moscou" (no. 41).

26. Roman Jakobson, "Glossolalie," *Tel Quel* 26 (Summer 1966): 3.

27. Barthes, "A Magnificent Gift," in *The Rustle of Language*, 160–61. Originally published in *Le Monde* (1971).

28. Roman Jakobson, "Linguistics and Poetics" in *Language in Literature*, 93–94.

29. Barthes, "A Magnificent Gift," 159.

certainly understandable. Moreover, given the university climate, it is clear why the Russian formalists were not translated in France until 1965.[30] Finally, it is not surprising that a publication devoted to their writings would be disseminated by *Tel Quel*. The project was conceived by Genette, who early on brought to *Tel Quel* a formalist slant reflected in his work on Valéry, a precursor of formalism. Genette encouraged Todorov to translate a selection of the fundamental texts of the Russian formalists, which was published in 1965 in Collection Tel Quel under the title *Théorie de la littérature*.

The publication of *Théorie de la littérature* was viewed as nothing less than a major event, and it gave *Tel Quel* a new "scientific" status (the subtitle "Science/Literature" was added to the review in the spring of 1967) on the French cultural scene, at a time when the structural analysis of literary texts had become the new intellectual trend. Furthermore, the publication of the anthology greatly contributed to the establishment of a new working relationship between the literary avant-garde and the Communist Left. Indeed, the rediscovery of the Russian formalists generated great interest among Marxists and non-Marxists alike. Even the Communist Left considered the *Tel Quel* publication a major catalyst for cultural renewal. In *Les Lettres Françaises* of 7–13 July 1966, the Communist intellectual Pierre Daix wrote: "The big event for us French of 1966, is the discovery of the Formalists of the '20s" (12). That same year was highlighted by the appearance in *Les Lettres Françaises* of a number of articles on the formalists and on related linguistic questions. These included Jean-Pierre Faye's "La lettre du formaliste" (11 August 1966) and his interview with Jakobson entitled "Questionner Jakobson" (17 November 1966). A year later, *Les Lettres Françaises* published "Littérature et linguistique: la collaboration entre littéraires et linguistes est-elle possible?" [Literature and linguistics: is collaboration between literati and linguists possible?] (20 April 1967). Furthermore, in 1967–68, the Communist theoretical journal *La Nouvelle Critique* published such texts as "Deuxième révolution linguistique?" (no. 12); Sollers's "L'Ecriture fonction de transformation sociale" [Writing as a function of social transformation] (no. 12); Jean-Louis Houdebine's "Texte, structure, histoire" (no. 11); and Kristeva's "La sémiologie: science critique

---

30. Jakobson's *Essais de linguistique générale*, translated from the English by Ruwet, came out in 1963; Propp's *Morphologie du conte*, published in French in 1958, was the first text by a Russian formalist to be translated in France.

et/ou critique de la science?" [Semiotics: A critical science and/or a critique of science] (no. 16).

Such an array of publications clearly reveals the Communist intellectuals' interest in the formalists of the 1920s and the structural linguistics of the 1920s and 1960s. This new interest in language stirred a dialogue between the Communist organs and *Tel Quel*, with a number of meetings between Communist intellectuals and Telquelians taking place at the headquarters of *La Nouvelle Critique* in 1967.[31] These meetings were attended by the Telquelians Baudry, Faye, Pleynet, and Sollers; and the Communists Antoine Casanova, Claude Prévost, André Gisselbrecht, Christine Glucksmann, and Houdebine.[32] Although discussions tended to be dominated by the question of linguistics and its relation to literature, these gatherings nevertheless resulted in *Tel Quel*'s political initiation. The common interest in language led to the April 1968 Cluny colloquium on "Linguistique et littérature," which brought together the Communist Left and the avant-garde (*Tel Quel*).

French intellectuals disinterred the formalists with considerable delay. After all, Americans had discovered them a decade earlier with Victor Erlich's *Russian Formalism* (1955). But a number of reasons can be advanced for the delayed reception and endorsement of Russian formalism in France. As Marxist orthodoxy gained prominence in the 1930s, it led to the stifling of formalism, which had become a heresy in antiformalist Russia. Ensnared in socialist realism until the late 1950s and early 1960s, the PCF, which did not officially undergo cultural de-Stalinization until the Argenteuil Central Committee hearings of 1966, had inevitably supported the Soviet antiformalist purges. But the French university tradition remained the greatest bastion of resistance to Russian formalism. Why would the university have taken an interest in Russian formalism when it had kept its distance from Anglo-American New Criticism, German stylistics, and the Italian Crocean tradition? No wonder Barthes accused university criticism of

31. Jean-Louis Houdebine, who had been on the staff of *La Nouvelle Critique* since 1961, played an important role in establishing a dialogue between the Communist journal and *Tel Quel*. The initial idea for an encounter dates back to 1965–66. Houdebine met with Sollers at the *Nouvelle Critique* quarters in February 1967. Together, they decided to organize encounters, which took place every two to three months at *La Nouvelle Critique*. Approximately ten people participated in the presentations and discussions, a number of which were subsequently published in the Communist journal. From an interview with Houdebine, Paris, 23 June 1987.

32. Interview with Houdebine and "Tel Quel nous répond," *La Nouvelle Critique*, nos. 8–9 (1967): 50. Subsequently published as "Réponses à *La Nouvelle Critique*" in *Théorie d'Ensemble*.

being nationalistic.[33] In effect, in contrast to the United States, comparative literature was still an embryonic discipline in France in the 1950s. Moreover, university criticism was suspicious of any critical approach that dared to use conceptual tools tied to linguistics, that dared to return to what Paul Valéry, the French formalist precursor, had called "the verbal condition of literature."[34] At the conference "Language and Literature" held in Belgium in 1960, Leo Spitzer expressed his enormous surprise at the quasi-inexistence of stylistic research in France, which he defined as the "bridge between linguistics and literary history" ("La lente percée" 39). This bridge had been built by the formalists. Another reason for the late translation of the Russian formalists into French is that they wrote in a language few intellectuals practiced in France: thus the strategic importance of Todorov, and later Kristeva, for *Tel Quel*. As we can see, there was clearly no welcome mat set out for the formalists in France, most particularly in the domain of literary criticism at the university. The breakthrough was, in fact, facilitated by the human sciences. It was only in 1960, thanks to the influence of structuralism in linguistics and ethnology, that structural linguistics came into being. Yet the interest in Russian formalism, albeit delayed, profoundly transformed French literary theory for more than a decade.

In her preface to the French translation of Mikhail Bakhtin's work on Dostoevsky (1929) published in 1973, Kristeva remarked that presenting a work to foreign readers after a lapse of forty years poses both theoretical and ideological problems: "How does one interpret a work when it is taken out of its place, time and language and then revived beyond a gap which is temporal, geographical, historical and social?"[35] Clearly *Tel Quel*'s publication of *Théorie de la littérature* was a strategic gesture with both theoretical and ideological ramifications. In a text on the "Formalists and Futurists" that appeared in a special issue of *Tel Quel* entitled "Semiology in the Soviet Union Today" and guest-edited by Kristeva,[36] Todorov noted that the 1960s renaissance of the Russian formalists, who had been repressed and forgotten during the 1930s and 1940s, raises two types of questions: one on the

33. Barthes, "What is Criticism?" 256.

34. Philippe Hamon, "La lente percée des formalistes-structuralistes," *Magazine Littéraire* 192 (February 1983): 38–39.

35. Kristeva, "The Ruin of a Poetics," in *Russian Formalism*, ed. Stephen Bann and John E. Bowlt (New York: Harper and Row, 1973), 102.

36. In her presentation, "Linguistique et sémiologie aujourd'hui en U.R.S.S.," Kristeva contends that the work of these semiologists and the interest in them "indicate the trace on which our culture renews with its repressed." *Tel Quel* 35 (Autumn 1968): 8.

possible "proximity" of the two periods—a question we know is central to the *Tel Quel* experience, the other on the very status of criticism—a central question of the mid-1960s in France, as revealed by the Barthes-Picard polemic. As a general rule—and this was certainly the case in France until the 1960s when the status of criticism changed—one does not read the critics of the past:

> Unless one is a cultural historian, one only considers a text of the past if it has an autonomous status. The text as means or tool comes into being to accomplish a precise function; once accomplished, it no longer exists. The critical study always oscillates between two poles: to be a text, to speak of another text. The more it approaches the latter, the shorter its life span, the further it goes away from it, the less it is critical. The critical enterprise is, so to speak, a self-sacrifice.[37]

If one reads the critical texts of the past, it is less for their critical than their textual dimension. One reads Baudelaire's criticism to read Baudelaire, the author, not the critic (42).

How, then, does one account for this intense and converging interest on the part of the intellectual avant-garde and the Communist Left in the critical texts of the formalists in 1965–66? To answer this question, Todorov turns to Krystyna Pomorska (Jakobson)'s influential book, *Russian Formalist Theory and its Poetic Ambiance* (1968). Pomorska argues that every critical method is a generalization of its contemporary literary practice. She also emphasizes the vital relationship between futurist poetry and formalist criticism. Thus, one explanation for renewed interest in the formalists lies perhaps in their relation to futurism, and in the manner in which this relation is fundamental to their enterprise. But Todorov favors another explanation. In fact, he reverses Pomorska's thesis: contrary to other critical movements that could only consider the literature of which they were, in a sense, the product, the formalists elaborated an approach that applies to all literature. If the formalists continue to be popular forty years later, it is because they are not merely literary critics, but the precursors—if not the creators—of a science of literature. For the most part, they succeed in going beyond the individual text whose analysis constitutes their departure point for the consideration of theoretical problems,[38] thereby laying the foundations for a

---

37. Todorov, "Formalistes et futuristes," *Tel Quel* 35 (Autumn 1968): 42.
38. Ibid., 45.

scientific study of literature—or poetics—that has the notion of literariness (*literaturnost*) as its cornerstone.

Influenced by Saussurean (structural) linguistics, the work of Jakobson and the formalists made literature, like language, a system or structure analyzable in and of itself. The object of this science of literature was not the individual work or body of works (literature), which had been the focus of traditional literary history, but the formal specificity of the literary. As Jakobson noted in 1919, "The object of a science of literature is not literature but literariness, that is, what makes a given work a work of literature."[39] Russian formalism was revolutionary to the degree that it was one of the first critical movements to focus on the specifically literary nature of the text. By formulating the question of literariness, Russian formalism freed the study of literature from mysticism, psychologism, and sociologism. In "Settling Accounts with the Russian Formalists," the Italian Marxist philosopher Galvano Della Volpe argues that the historical merit of the formalists was twofold. Russian formalism was as much opposed to the sociological contentism of the epigones of Hegelian idealism as it was to the mystical formalism of the symbolists. It was precisely this twofold plan of literary battle that made the program of the formalists an aesthetically revolutionary one accounting for the fascination of their revival in the 1960s.[40]

Greatly influenced by the impact of structuralist analysis on literary criticism, Genette and Todorov's interest in the formalists essentially lay in their contribution to establishing poetics as an autonomous theoretical discipline. Although the futurist connection would be important to Telquelians such as Faye, Kristeva, and Sollers, Todorov, like Genette, was less interested in the "avant-garde" nature of Russian formalism. In effect, Todorov downplayed the central thesis of Pomorska's book: the impact of futurism and the revolutionary cultural and political context surrounding the birth and development of Russian formalism. As academics, Tororov and Genette were a minority at *Tel Quel*, and it is not surprising that they would leave *Tel Quel* as it embarked on its ("terrorist") avant-garde course a few years later, in order to found a theoretical, university journal, *Poétique*, with Cixous in 1968. *Poétique* would be everything *Tel Quel* had struggled not to be: it was not a "group" review; it published only critical texts (and not

39. Jakobson cited in Todorov, *Théorie de la littérature* (Paris: Seuil, 1965), 106.
40. Galvano Della Volpe, "Settling Accounts with the Russian Formalists," trans. John Mathews, *New Left Review* 113–14 (January–April 1979): 134–35.

poetry and fiction); and its objective was to give the French university a review—to introduce a type of criticism that had heretofore been restricted to extrauniversity Parisian life. *Poétique* aimed to bring the separation of New Criticism and the university to an end: "Criticism has the right to enter the University," declared Todorov in an interview of October 1970.[41] Nevertheless, New Criticism only entered the university after May 1968. Much of the groundwork for this realization had been laid in the deliberately extrauniversity and purely literary realm of *Tel Quel*. This recuperation of formalist theory by the university also retrospectively explains why Genette and Todorov downplayed the avant-garde dimension of Russian formalism.

By deemphasizing the avant-garde dimension of formalism, Todorov ended up displacing the central axis of Pomorska's work. For Pomorska, the radical complicity between linguistic theory and the practice of literature that defined the originality of the formalist movement resulted from its strong links to futurism and from the impact of other artistic currents such as cubism. Although the formalists favored a theory of literature founded on the science of linguistics, they were not about to privilege science over literature. In effect, they disarmed the epistemological bases of structural linguistics by reintegrating the study of poetic language into linguistic theory. Furthermore, their analysis of poetic language drew from such revolutionary poets as Velimir Khlebnikov and Vladimir Mayakovsky. Insofar as futurism was an avant-garde movement that challenged the literary canon of its times, any critical theory related to this avant-garde practice had to be critical of the science it depended on: linguistics. Futurism was linked to revolutionary aesthetic changes (it modeled its poetry on cubism) and sociopolitical changes (the Revolution of 1917). For the futurists, poetic revolution and political revolution went hand in hand. It was with the utmost sincerity that they called themselves "Communists-Futurists" in 1918.[42] These poetic watchwords of the futurists became the working hypotheses of the formalists.[43]

If *Tel Quel* was attracted to Russian formalism, at a very critical phase of its enterprise, it was first of all because the formalists gave *Tel Quel* theoretical ammunition from the "scientific" realm of linguistics to develop further its critique of literature. Yet the formalists did not subsequently

41. Todorov interviewed by Ristat in *Qui sont les contemporains*, 200.
42. Krystyna Pomorska, *Russian Theory and Its Poetic Ambiance* (The Hague: Mouton, 1968), 118.
43. Todorov, "Formalistes et futuristes," 45.

subsume literature within a scientific metalanguage. They viewed linguistic theory in relation to poetic language and, as a result, established a new relationship between the two that challenged traditional dichotomies such as theory and practice, linguistics and literature. It is precisely this dimension that Todorov and Genette had slighted in their depreciation of the avant-garde dimension of Russian formalism. They had overlooked the contestation of science by literature that was fundamental to *Tel Quel* and its avant-garde project in the mid- and late 1960s. With the formalists as their precursors, Telquelians were not about to let a scientific metalanguage take control of literature. Thanks essentially to the work of Kristeva and Faye, *Tel Quel* developed the avant-garde implications of the formalists and used their notions of poetic language and literariness to develop, along with Barthes, a theory of the text and a critical semiotics that challenged the dominant mode of structuralist thought and eventually linked up the study of literary texts to Freudianism and Marxism.

"Bearing essentially on a certain way of taking language—in the former case dodged and in the latter assumed—the opposition between science and literature" was central to structuralism in the 1960s.[44] While language can unite science and literature, it can also divide them. For science

> language is merely an instrument, which it chooses to make as transparent and neutral as possible; and subjugated to scientific matters (operations, hypotheses, results) said to exist outside it and to precede it: on one side and *first of all*, the contents of the scientific message, which are everything; and on the other and *afterwards*, the verbal form entrusted with expressing these contents, which is nothing. (Barthes, "From Science to Literature" 4)

For literature, on the other hand, language is everything. It is the very being of literature, as Telquelians argued in the 1960s. The "role of literature is to *represent* actively to the scientific institution just what it rejects, i.e., the sovereignty of language" (10). Barthes maintained that structuralism could either "keep the distance of a science in relation to its object" or "compromise and [spoil] the analysis it wields in that infinitude of language of which literature is today the conduit—in a word, depending on whether it seeks to be science or writing" (5–6).

Tel Quel's bridging of literature and science had a subversive intention,

---

44. Barthes, "From Science to Literature," 5.

one that already resided in structuralism. With its focus on the linguistic nature of human works, structuralism was capable of playing an important role in reopening the linguistic status of science. With all languages as its object, structuralism had very quickly become the metalanguage of the 1960s. However, for Barthes, this stage had to be transcended, as the opposition of language-objects and their metalanguage remained ultimately subject to the model of a science without language. Structural discourse had to make itself entirely homogeneous to its object. This could only be accomplished by two radical methods: either an exhaustive formalization, or an integral writing (*écriture*, text, critical semiotics).[45] Barthes would favor the latter method, which would underlie not only his textual semiotics but Kristeva's semanalysis. It would ultimately lead to a critique of the epistemological bases of structural linguistics and of science in general.

Barthes argued that structuralism would merely be one more "science" if it did not make the subversion of scientific language its central enterprise; that is, if it did not call into question the very language by which it knows language.[46] To "resort to scientific discourse as an instrument of thought is to postulate that a neutral state of language exists, from which would branch off, like so many gaps and ornaments, a certain number of special languages such as literary or poetic language." Such a neutral state "would be, it is assumed, the code of reference for all the 'eccentric' languages which would be only so many sub-codes." By "identifying with this referential code, basis of all normality, scientific discourse arrogates to itself the very authority which writing must contest." Writing implies that "language is a vast system of which no single code is privileged" (8–9).

This was, in fact, Jakobson's great discovery when he made the poetic a function of language. For what happens to linguistics when it decides to account for such "eccentric" languages or "deviations" from the norm? Linguistics has traditionally failed to consider literary or poetic language. In response to the question "Why does a linguist want a definition of poetry or literature?" the linguist Sol Saporta stated that "a partial answer seems to be that, as a writer of grammars, a linguist wants to be able to identify poetry for the same reason that he needs to identify unassimilated loan words or slips of the tongue, namely, as justification for not including them in his

45. Ibid., 10.
46. Ibid., 7.

grammar."[47] With poetic language as an essential dimension of their language theory, Russian formalists prompted the science of linguistics to account for a certain functioning of language that was traditionally relegated to an eccentric or irrelevant, literary realm. Contrary to traditional linguists who separated poetic language from that of everyday communication, Jakobson established the poetic as a function of language. He considered the poetic not something specific to poetry and thus easily dismissed by linguistics as a science, but rather one function of language among others, including the heretofore dominant function of communication in structural linguistics. Accordingly, Russian formalism challenged the epistemological bases of linguistics as a science.

The functions of communication and expression are characteristic not only of everyday speech but of theoretical language (i.e., scientific metalanguage) as well. In communicative language, the referential (or denotative, cognitive) function predominates, directing the linguistic message toward the context (or referent). Communication, at the basis of structural linguistics, "implies a transmission charged with making pass, from one subject to another, the identity of a signified object, of a meaning or of a concept rightfully separable from the process of passage and from the signifying operation."[48] The problem with the notion of communication is that it "presupposes subjects (whose identity and presence are constituted before the signifying operation) and objects (signified concepts, a thought meaning that the passage of communication will have neither to constitute, nor, by all rights to transform)" (Derrida, *Positions* 23). Implicit in communication and the theory of the sign that it sustains is "the possibility of thinking a *concept signified in and of itself*, a concept simply present for thought, independent of a relationship to language, that is of a relationship to a system of signifiers" (Derrida, *Positions* 19). In poetic language, on the other hand, the focus shifts to the autonomous value of the sign. According to Jakobson: "The distinctive feature of poetry lies in the fact that a word is perceived as a word and not merely a proxy for the denoted object or an outburst of emotion, that words and their arrangement, their meaning, their outward and inward form acquire weight and value of their own."[49]

Boris Eichenbaum tells us that the aim of poetry is to "make perceptible

47. Sol Saporta, "The Application of Linguistics to the Study of Poetic Language," in *Style in Language*, ed. Thomas A. Sebeok (Cambridge: M.I.T. Press, 1960), 85.

48. Derrida, *Positions*, 23.

49. Jakobson cited in Victor Erlich, *Russian Formalism* (The Hague: Mouton, 1955, 1980), 183.

the texture of the word in *all* its aspects."[50] The phonetic quality of words, of little importance to communication, is essential to the poetic function. Phonology, that is, the relation of sounds and meaning, underlies Jakobson's structural linguistics. By accentuating both the phonetic and semantic texture of the word, by "promoting the palpability of signs," the poetic function further accentuates the fundamental dichotomy of signs and their objects.[51] The emphasis on the phonetic aspect of language brings into focus the organization of the signifier: "Similar sounds, rhymes, intonation, the rhythmics of different types of verses, etc. have a function which, far from being purely ornamental, is the vehicle of a new signified that is superimposed on the explicit signified."[52] The application of phonology to poetry helps rid literary analysis of its metaphysical overtones. Meaning can no longer be considered independently of language. If the phonetic aspect of words is not ornamental and in fact contributes to engendering/transforming meaning, then the study of language and literature cannot be limited to the practical functions of communication, expression, or representation. No longer confined to its mimetic dimension, literature allows us to explore what is at work in what has traditionally been viewed as a means of contact and comprehension: "The literary act, by not allowing for an *ideal* distance with respect to *what* signifies, instills the radical strangeness of what language is supposed to be: a bearer of meaning. Strangely near, intimately foreign to the matter of our discourses and our dreams, literature, today, seems to be the very act that grasps how language works and indicates what it is capable of transforming tomorrow."[53]

This emphasis on the materiality of language would have important consequences not only for the study of literature, but also for linguistic theory. The focus on the formal nature of the literary text (literariness) and the reintegration of the poetic into a theory of language enabled the formalists to challenge a science of linguistics founded on communication and the sign. In her first piece to be published in *Tel Quel* (no. 29), "Pour une sémiologie des paragrammes" [For a semiology of paragrammes], Kristeva acknowledged the importance of both Jakobson's work on poetic language and Saussure's "Anagrammes" for the notion of the text bound up with language as productivity that would mark *Tel Quel* in the late 1960s. By

50. Eichenbaum cited in Erlich, 185.
51. Jakobson, "Linguistics and Poetics" in *Language in Literature*, 70.
52. Kristeva, *Language: The Unknown*, 289.
53. Kristeva, "Le texte et sa science," 7.

emphasizing the nonlinear functioning of the poetic signifier and thus a textual logic different from the one of the sign, the formalists, along with Saussure, were the first to open up linguistics to a semiotics of literary texts. In so doing, they challenged the very bases of structural linguistics. In effect, remarks Kristeva, the text is precisely what cannot be considered by a certain conceptual system whose limits it marks.[54]

The ignorance of the text is the very basis for linguistics.[55] As a science of textual production, the critical semiotics envisioned by Kristeva and other Telquelians paved the way for a cultural materialism. In opposition to the idealism of a meaning anterior to what expresses it, *Tel Quel* emphasized the materiality and productivity of language brought into play by literary texts. Guided by the pioneering work of the formalists, *Tel Quel* lay the bases for a materialist gnoseology bound up with the production and transformation of meaning. *Tel Quel*'s theory and practice of textual production also called upon the work of Marx, Freud, and Derrida.

Derrida contends that the explicit formulation of the question of literarity, initiated by the formalists and further developed in the 1960s by *Tel Quel*, revolutionizes not only the practice of literature but also an entire philosophical tradition founded on mimesis.[56] Derrida developed the tremendous importance of this new accent on literarity not only for the study of literature, but also for Western philosophical thought. In an era marked by the discovery of space and language, his philosophical project challenged Western metaphysics and the logocentric basis that sustained it. Deconstruction brought the irreductibility of writing to the forefront of philosophical interrogation. It is clear why such a project would constitute the launching pad for *Tel Quel*'s "Step on the Moon."[57] Indeed, from 1965 to 1969, the work of Derrida and *Tel Quel* intersected. The journal published several of Derrida's most important pieces: "La parole soufflée" (no. 20); "Freud et la

54. Kristeva, 24.

55. Kristeva, "Littérature, sémiotique, marxisme" (interview with Christine Glucksmann and Jean Peytard) *La Nouvelle Critique* 38 (November 1970): 30.

56. Derrida, *Positions*, 70.

57. In 1966, Barthes wrote: "The present emphasis on problems of language irritates some, who regard it as an excessive fashion. Yet they will have to resign themselves to the inevitable: we are probably only beginning to speak of language: along with other sciences which tend, today, to be attached to it, linguistics is entering the dawn of its history: we have yet to discover language, as we are in the process of discovering space: our century will perhaps be marked by these two explorations." In "Why I love Benveniste" in *The Rustle of Language*, 162. Sollers entitled his review essay on Derrida's *De la grammatologie* "Un pas sur la lune" [A step on the moon] (*Tel Quel*, no. 39, Autumn 1969). Also published in the *Times Literary Supplement* (25 September 1969).

scène de l'écriture" [Freud and the scene of writing] (no. 26); "La pharmacie de Platon" [Plato's pharmacy] (nos. 32, 33); and "La double séance" [The double session] (nos. 41, 42). "La Différance" was published in *Théorie d'Ensemble* and *L'Ecriture et la différance* [Writing and difference] (1967) appeared in Collection Tel Quel. With the notion of grammatology, a new relation between literary practice and philosophy became possible. In substituting the term "grammatology" for "semiology," Derrida sought to free the semiological project from a linguistics founded on logocentrism or phonocentrism. This gesture constituted the first philosophical challenge to the use of linguistics in the human sciences.[58] This challenge would be integrated into the literary sphere by *Tel Quel*'s conception of the text or textual production.

Of particular interest to *Tel Quel* was the fact that Derrida's philosophical deconstruction was necessarily a function of a practice of writing, of a textual activity called "literature." In an interview with Houdebine and Scarpetta conducted in June 1971 and subsequently published in *Promesse*, *Tel Quel*'s satellite journal, Derrida acknowledged that the texts of Mallarmé, Artaud, Bataille, Sollers, and others appeared to "organize a structure of resistance to the philosophical conceptuality that allegedly dominated or comprehended them, whether directly, or whether through categories derived from this philosophical fund, the categories of esthetics, rhetoric, or traditional criticism."[59] Consequently, the traditional values of meaning or content, of form or signifier, of representation and truth no longer account for certain textually (and ideologically) subversive operations inherent in the "texts of rupture" of the late nineteenth and twentieth centuries (Derrida, *Positions* 69–70). In fact, such texts compel us to address the question of truth in relation to the contemporary notion of "literariness" (70). The limit-texts of modernity reveal not only that philosophical questions are a function of linguistic and rhetorical strategies, but also that so-called literary texts manifest "powerful philosophical deconstructions once the importance of their special logics . . . is recognized."[60] If a writer is someone who does not want to skip over language, the signifier, and writing; that is, someone

58. Elisabeth Roudinesco, *Jacques Lacan & Co. (A History of Psychoanalysis in France, 1925–1985)*, trans. Jeffrey Mehlman (Chicago: University of Chicago Press, 1990), 385. Originally published as *La Bataille de cent ans: Histoire de la psychanalyse en France*, vol. 2 (Paris: Seuil, 1986).

59. Derrida, *Positions*, 69.

60. Jonathan Culler, "Jacques Derrida," in *Structuralism and Since*, ed. John Sturrock (New York: Oxford University Press, 1981), 178.

who continually questions the matter to which he is subjected and the constraints this matter imposes on him; then philosophers like Nietzsche and Derrida are always in the position of a writer even when their discourse is apparently philosophical.[61] True literature questions its origins, limits, presuppositions, in the way that true philosophy questions its signifiers, their history, and those of its text and its rhetoric. That is the work of writing (17).

Derrida's interrogation of philosophical discourse by means of literary texts not only erased the boundaries between literature and philosophy, but also attributed a new status to literary practice. In bypassing disciplinary boundaries, Derrida formulated questions that had been systematically occulted by Western metaphysics—questions that transformed the status of literature itself in the 1960s. He contributed to freeing the literary arts from the presuppositions of metaphysics. In the wake of formalism, he renewed the debate on the literary object on the basis of its signifying forms[62] and brought to it a philosophical dimension that allowed *Tel Quel* to situate its practice of writing in relation to the contestation of Western idealist thought. The deconstruction of logocentrism at the heart of *De la grammatologie*, along with the pioneering work of the Russian formalists, provided *Tel Quel* with the basis for the formulation of a materialist gnoseology. Derrida's extension of the notion of idealism to the broader one of logocentrism permitted *Tel Quel* to approach the question of dialectical and historical materialism through the bias of language.

Language thereby became the missing link that made possible all previously incompatible associations or unlikely reconciliations. Not only did language bring together such disparate disciplines as literature, semiotics, psychoanalysis, anthropology, and philosophy in a fruitful interdisciplinary dialogue, but it also gave the literary avant-garde (*Tel Quel*) and the political Left (the PCF) a common platform for the renewal of avant-garde practice and Marxist thought. In effect, *Tel Quel*'s rapprochement with the PCF, highlighted by the Cluny Colloquium of 16–17 April 1968, was described by the Communist writer Raymond Jean as "nuptials—extremely mood-elevating—that took place thanks to the sciences of language."[63]

The Cluny Conference "Linguistics and Literature" inaugurated a new era not only for *Tel Quel*, but also for the Communist Party. As the official

---

61. Catherine Clément, "A l'écoute de Derrida," *L'Arc* 54 (1973): 17.
62. Roudinesco, *Jacques Lacan & Co.*, 388.
63. Raymond Jean, "Trajet politique et romanesque," *Magazine Littéraire* 166 (November 1980): 13. See also "Linguistique et Littérature" in *Le Monde des Livres*, 27 April 1968: II.

coming together of the avant-garde and the political Left, the conference played a "historical role, and one that [was] not limited to the development of theory."[64] Organized by *La Nouvelle Critique*, the Cluny conference had a significant impact on Communist intellectuals who referred to it, for years, as a "key ideological event." Jean hailed it as a "great ideological moment" that benefited everyone. Thanks to Cluny, "the Party was less stiff and dogmatic, the avant-garde more responsible and militant" (13).

What magical power allowed the sciences of language to bring together two long-term foes? How could a dialogue taking place in the name of language possibly result in a more militant avant-garde and a less dogmatic PCF? Just what exactly was *Tel Quel* doing at Cluny? What did Communist intellectuals hope to gain from *Tel Quel* and from the sciences of language that dominated the French intellectual scene of the '60s? Even if Kristeva subsequently maintained that the Communist Party "was the best mouthpiece for experimental literary or theoretical work,"[65] the encounter cannot be dismissed simply in the name of opportunism. If opportunism was, indeed, a guiding motive, then we need to examine what the PCF hoped to gain from *Tel Quel* and vice versa.

We have already seen how French Communist intellectuals welcomed *Tel Quel*'s translation of the Russian formalists in 1965, and how this welcome had been made possible by a changing intellectual climate characterized by the de-Stalinization of Marxist thought after 1956. This process of de-Stalinization was, nevertheless, a slow and painful one whose impact on philosophy and the arts would not be discerned until the mid- and late 1960s. Indeed, cultural de-Stalinization had to wait for the official resolution of the PCF at Argenteuil in 1966. On 11–13 March, the Central Committee met for three (instead of the customary two) days in order to discuss "ideological and cultural concerns." As a result of these discussions, the Committee decreed that the arts and sciences could henceforth develop free of party intervention. With respect to literature, de-Stalinization permitted Communist intellectuals to forgo the heretofore dominant notion of socialist realism, based, for the most part, on extraliterary (ideological) considerations. As a result, Communist writers and academics were more willing to consider the specificity of the literary text and to shift their attention to formal concerns. The impact of linguistics and the other human

64. Kristeva, response in "Linguistique et Littérature" (Colloque de Cluny I, 16–17 April 1968), *La Nouvelle Critique*, special issue (1968): 170.
65. Kristeva, "My Memory's Hyperbole," 272.

sciences on Communist intellectuals was particularly evident in *La Nouvelle Critique* after February 1967. A number of Communists viewed the human sciences as a potential catalyst for the renewal of Marxist thought. The widespread use of linguistic procedures by researchers, whose theoretical fields and orientations were often far apart, especially interested *La Nouvelle Critique*, as demonstrated by the questions addressed at the Cluny encounter. Eighty academics and writers convened to discuss linguistics and its relation to literature: What could the science of linguistics bring to the study of literature? How did contemporary linguistics view literature? How did literary analysis use linguistic methods? How did writers react to linguistics?[66] Four Telquelians—Sollers, Kristeva, Pleynet, and Jean-Louis Baudry—joined such academics and Communist intellectuals as Michel Arrivé, Raymond Jean, Henri Mitterand, Jean-Louis Houdebine, Jean Peytard, Henri Meschonnic, and Philippe Bonnefis.

Sollers claimed that the PCF had come to them for non-Marxist reasons, whereas they had approached the PCF for Marxist ones. To a degree, this is true. Driven by a desire to regain the intellectual hegemony it had lost as a result of Stalinism, the party was characterized by a spirit of proselytism after Argenteuil. It wished to bring together all "specialists working for the progress of knowledge—Communists and non-Communists."[67] Thus, among the party's numerous new intellectual endeavors were the two Cluny colloquia of April 1968 and 1970 ("Literature and Ideologies"). Although clearly a minority at these gatherings, the Telquelians succeeded in upstaging the Communist hegemonic enterprise. How could a handful of avant-grade writers dominate a colloquium where they were outnumbered twenty-to-one by party intellectuals and academics? This question was answered, years later, by one of the Communist participants at Cluny who confessed that they—the Communists—had been theoretically incompetent with respect to questions of ideology, literature, and art. It was thus not surprising that the Telquelians were treated like royalty and that Kristeva became the diva of the intellectual gathering. As for the Communist intellectuals, they "were left to grovel": "I told myself, it serves us right, we never worked on these questions, we don't dare to, we base ourselves on completely false things."[68] The encounter with *Tel Quel* brutally reminded party intellectuals how

---

66. Introduction to "Linguistique et Littérature," *La Nouvelle Critique*, 6–7.
67. Ibid., 6.
68. See Jeannine Verdès-Leroux, *Le Réveil des Somnambules: Le Parti communiste, les intellectuels et la culture, 1956–1985* (Paris: Fayard, 1987), 124–25.

culturally retrograde they were in the wake of Stalinism. Referring to Cluny a decade later, many spoke of acculturation.

Despite attempts by some Party militants to downplay *Tel Quel*'s role in this acculturation by claiming that the Telquelians had approached the party and not the contrary, *La Nouvelle Critique* had had a sustained interest in the group since the publication of *Théorie de la littérature* in 1965. The Communist journal published articles by Telquelians or devoted to *Tel Quel*, as a result of encounters between the two editorial teams in 1967. Moreover, that same year, *La Nouvelle Critique* published *Tel Quel*'s responses to a questionnaire they had sent them. In introducing *Tel Quel* to their Communist constituents, *La Nouvelle Critique* not only emphasized *Tel Quel*'s premier position in contemporary literature, but also their ideological evolution, both on a political and a theoretical level. *La Nouvelle Critique* stressed the importance of *Tel Quel*'s theoretical activity and emphasized how much Communists stood to gain from it. It acknowledged that the time was ripe for confronting new theses that had emanated from syntheses in the human sciences—particularly those focusing on language—and for integrating them into a new theory of literature.[69] Because party intellectuals were clearly looking for a theoretical enrichment from their encounter with the avant-garde, a working relationship between the avant-garde and the party now seemed possible.

While Houdebine played a central role—he refers to himself as a "kingpin"—in instituting relations between *La Nouvelle Critique* and *Tel Quel*, which ultimately led to the Cluny encounters of 1968 and 1970, two other Communist militants, Scarpetta and Henric, were also vital in the dissemination of *Tel Quel*'s work in other Communist publications. Scarpetta (b. 1946), who was ten years younger than the Telquelians, belonged to the Union of Communist Students (UEC) and published articles on *Tel Quel* for their journal, *Clarté*, as well as for *La Nouvelle Critique*. Henric, on the other hand, wrote for Aragon's *Les Lettres Françaises* and took over the literary section of *France Nouvelle* (the ancestor of *Révolution*) in 1964–65, where he was free to defend *Tel Quel* and the avant-garde.[70] On 31 May 1967, Henric published an interview in *France Nouvelle* that he had conducted with Baudry, Faye, Pleynet, and Sollers.

69. "Introductory note to "Réponses à la *Nouvelle Critique*," in *Théorie d'Ensemble*, 385.
70. The information in this and the following paragraphs has been taken from personal interviews with Henric (24 June 1987), Houdebine (23 June 1987), and Scarpetta (23 June 1987) in Paris.

What immediately becomes apparent from these publications and from discussions that I had in 1987 with these former Communist militants—all three of whom abandoned the party for *Tel Quel* in 1971–72—is the tremendous importance they accorded to both the PCF and *Tel Quel* for their politico-intellectual formation of the 1960s. In order to understand the role that both played in their formation, Houdebine claims that it is vital to realize how very different the period 1964–66 was from, say, the late 1980s. At the time of the Cluny 1968 encounter, the PCF still exerted considerable influence on its intellectuals and on French intellectual life in general. In the March 1967 legislative elections, the PCF had obtained 22.4 percent of the vote; the Gaullists barely won the elections with a 37.7 percent majority through a coalition (Comité d'Action pour la Vième République). By March 1986, the PCF had only 9.78 percent of the legislative vote, the same as Jean-Marie Le Pen's National Front (9.65 percent).

Tel Quel, on the other hand, was the avant-garde or modernist review par excellence for Houdebine. For Scarpetta, a university student majoring in literature in 1964–66, *Tel Quel* was *the* leading literary review. Scarpetta saw *Tel Quel* as the literary realm's equivalent of the great explosion that shook French intellectual thought in 1965–66. *Tel Quel* had begun to take an interest in political concerns in 1964–65, just about the time that the PCF was to undergo cultural de-Stalinization. Houdebine, Scarpetta, and Henric claim that as Communist militants in the 1960s, they believed that the French Left could be revolutionized from within—from within the party, that is. They were, nevertheless, left with the belief—handed down by Aragon and the surrealists, on the one hand, and Sartre and engagement, on the other—that it was not possible to articulate art and politics; that the two had nothing whatsoever to do with one another. The avant-garde dream belonged to the past. Raymond Jean, who was so enthusiastic about the Cluny 1968 gathering, maintains that when he came to literature in the late 1950s, an entire generation had come to distrust greatly all forms of the prostration of literature to engaged thought. Socialist realism was at the origin of the worst deceptions in both Eastern Europe and France.[71]

Tel Quel's presence at Cluny was crucial. Not only did it signal the possibility of a dialogue between the avant-garde and the party, it also symbolized a coming to terms with the inflation of linguistics that had permeated all domains of French thought by 1968. The Cluny gathering was meant to facilitate discussion among writers, linguists, and critics on the

---

71. Jean, "Trajet politique et romanesque," 12.

nature of the literary object. Although by now linguistics was a hegemonic discipline, was it necessarily the best vantage point from which to discuss literature? Posed by Telquelians, such a question shifted the emphasis of the gathering (which, incidentally, did not take place in a neutral, ideological climate). Just a few weeks before the outbreak of May, a mutual reconciliation of Marxist thought and modernist writing finally seemed possible. This convergence very quickly became the real focus of the gathering, subsequently resulting in the destitution of the hegemonic position of linguistics with respect to literature.

Tel Quel managed to become the most important force at Cluny. Although only four of the presentations were by Telquelians, many of the other presentations and the group discussions made references to *Tel Quel's* textual production. This was clearly advantageous for *Tel Quel* in that the focus (and power) shifted from linguistics back to literature. But it was also propitious for the PCF, as *Tel Quel's* conception of literary practice, which had begun to incorporate Marxist notions, undermined the dominant structural linguistics. The systematic valorization of structural linguistics had resulted in structuralism's supplanting of dialectical materialism. The Marxist edifice was barely standing. Here was a chance to prop it up a bit.

We have already seen how a number of Communists and fellow travelers viewed structuralism as the ideology of a technocratic, postindustrial society. *Tel Quel* would, in fact, join up with the PCF by contesting structural linguistics and its relation to capitalism. It would do so by challenging the ideological girdings of linguistics through its alternative practice of textual production. Inspired by the futurists and formalists and armed with a Derridian critique of the logocentric basis of linguistics and philosophy, *Tel Quel's* theory of the text had now joined up with Marx and Freud through the concept of production. In "La Sémiologie: Science critique et/ou critique de la science?" initially published in *La Nouvelle Critique* (no. 16, 1968) and subsequently in *Théorie d'Ensemble*, Kristeva argued that the concept of production could become the crucial connection among Marx, Freud, and semiotics. Coined by Kristeva, the concept of the text as "production" or "productivity" (as opposed to creativity or representation) gave *Tel Quel's* semiotic theory and scriptural practice its Marxist slant.

The theory and practice of textual production became the landmark of *Tel Quel* in the late 1960s. It allowed for the intersection of the work of writers, linguists, critics, and philosophers such as Sollers, Kristeva, Derrida, Baudry, and Jean-Joseph Goux. By bringing Marxism and psychoanalysis to bear on its textual theory, *Tel Quel* would not only—in the wake of Derridian deconstruction—continue to challenge the idealist underpinnings of philosophical thought and literary practice in the West, but would also contribute to the expansion of Marxist thought. The notion of the text as production dismantles both an aestheticizing ideology and the conception of literature as a reflection of the real (or as "a servant of the economy").

In the opening presentation at Cluny entitled "Relations et interférences entre la linguistique et la littérature" [Relations and interferences between linguistics and literature], the Communist Jean Peytard affirmed: "The vogue of linguistics is an epistemological and ideological problem. We must focus our attention on those works that attempt to situate linguistics within the context of our capitalist society, that show how certain founding concepts of linguistics are tinged by idealist mists."[72] Peytard and a number of Communist intellectuals acknowledged the importance of Derrida's work on the sign. They were particularly interested in the way his philosophical deconstruction of Western idealism fed into a critique of meaning that also underpinned textual production, as an alternative practice to structural linguistics. For the Telquelians and a number of Marxist intellectuals at Cluny, the notion of the sign was problematic not only because it had theological overtones—"The age of the sign is essentially theological"[73]— but also because it appeared linked to a capitalist society of circulation and exchange. For Sollers, the linguistic and philosophical tradition of the sign belonged to an era of meaning as divinity and capital.[74] Baudry went so far as to say, "It's not by chance that linguistics developed in the West, whereas semiotics, as a science of translinguistic practices, developed in the Soviet Union or in zones marked by Marxism."[75] Hence, noted Peytard, it was no coincidence that *Tel Quel*'s defiance toward structural linguistics was inscribed in the prolongation of Russian formalism and postformalism.[76] Expanding on the analogy, Baudry concluded: "Perhaps we could say that with respect to textual theory, linguistics has played the role and is in the same position as classical economics with respect to historical materialism."

72. Jean Peytard, "Rapports et interférences de la linguistique et de la littérature" ("Linguistique et Littérature"), *La Nouvelle Critique*, 14.

73. Derrida, *Of Grammatology*, 14.

74. Sollers, "The Novel and the Experience of Limits," 207.

75. Jean-Louis Baudry, "Linguistique et production textuelle" ("Linguistique et Littérature"), *La Nouvelle Critique*, 54. Reprinted in *Théorie d'Ensemble*.

76. Peytard, "Rapports et interférences," 14. See also Kristeva's presentation to *Tel Quel*'s special issue (no. 35) on "Semiology in the U.R.S.S. Today" (Autumn 1968).

Semiology, as the science of textual production, would thus replace linguistics, the science of the sign and exchange.[77]

Undoubtedly, a theory of the text could only be constituted insofar as it remained bound up with scriptural practice itself (Baudry, "Linguistique et production textuelle" 54). Herein lies the strategic importance of *Tel Quel*. Peytard, in fact, devoted the final section of his presentation to the revolutionary implications of *Tel Quel*'s "textual writing." He remarked that textual writing had detached itself from linguistics and represented a literary practice attempting to theorize itself against linguistics. Peytard concluded that it was "reassuring to see that the questioning of linguistics [came] from the best of contemporary literature"; that is, from *Tel Quel*.[78]

Was there a union or a rupture between linguistics and a theorization resulting from the textual production promoted by *Tel Quel*? Baudry addressed this question in his presentation entitled "Linguistique et production textuelle." Textual production is obviously restricted to a small group of writers reflecting on their own practice, whereas linguistics is a constituted science that has left its mark on various domains.[79] *Tel Quel* is obviously the underdog. By shifting the question underlying Cluny—the possible relations between linguistics and literature—to the possible interactions between linguistics and the theorization resulting from textual production, Baudry touches on the strategic ploy of *Tel Quel* at this meeting: not only to join up with the PCF against the university, but also to accord literature once again a key role in the advancement of knowledge, one that would challenge the hegemonic position of structural linguistics and, ultimately, theory.

In an interview with Sollers published in *Tel Quel*, the Communist Jacques Henric contended that a materialist practice of writing had to question radically the notion of expression, which claims that a text must be the putting into form of a preexisting meaning. Derrida had shown how any representative conception of writing admits the existence of a transcendental signified and thus rests on presuppositions belonging to an absolute philosophical idealism. In conjunction with the work of Derrida, dialectical materialism could bring out all the implications of the notion of *écriture*, by accentuating its productive aspect and the mode of production of the literary text.[80] Like other Telquelians, Henric believed that literature had to be

77. Baudry, "Linguistique et production textuelle," 54.
78. Peytard, "Rapports et interférences, 14.
79. Baudry, "Linguistique et production textuelle," 48.
80. Jacques Henric, "Pour une avant-garde révolutionnaire," *Tel Quel* 40 (Winter 1970): 64.

analyzed from a new theoretical perspective: one that emphasized the productivity of the text, rather than the circulation of meaning and the consumption of a product (*oeuvre*). The writings of Kristeva, Goux, Baudry, Sollers, Pleynet, and Houdebine—a number of which are brought together in *Théorie d'Ensemble*—would shed light on what Henric called "the decisive homology and profound complicity between the discourse of bourgeois political economy and the one of the representative system which founds 'literature': the valorization of exchange or communication (of values, meanings); the camouflage of the productive gesture or trace" ("Pour une avant-garde révolutionnaire" 64). In effect, by articulating Derrida, Marx, and Freud with semiotic theory, *Tel Quel* sought to show how the concealment of the work of the trace or "differance" in *écriture* and the production of meaning were homologous with the negation of work in pre-Marxist theory. In an interview accorded to *Les Lettres Françaises* in 1968, Sollers boldly declared: "With respect to 'literature,' what we propose aims to be as subversive as Marx's critique of classical economics."[81]

The emphasis on productivity instead of creativity, on the text or signifying activity instead of literary genres, eliminates both an aestheticizing approach to literature characteristic of art for art's sake, and a notion of literature as a reflection of the real that has marked *engagé* and Marxist approaches to literature. Although apparently diametrically opposed to one another, both approaches view the literary work as "oeuvre," that is, as a definitive result referring back to a singular cause, be it the author as creator, or economic and class determinations. Whether one focuses on divine inspiration or the economy, the perspective that one has of literature is not all that different. For Derrida, idealism, realism, and mechanistic Marxism are equivalent insofar as they are all marked by a reference to something absolutely prior to the work of language or the text. These three currents merely serve to reinforce the belief that there is always something that preexists what represents it; consequently, representations and their material forms are merely instrumental and derived.

For *Tel Quel*, the text is not just a derived product. Its texture manifests the process of its own production (*écriture*), which cannot merely be described in terms of expression or reflection. If the text itself produces meaning, then meaning can no longer be conceived as the "origin" of the text (that is, a work would express a meaning), nor as its "end" (definitive, achieved). Meaning must now be posited in relation to the process of textual

---

81. Sollers, "Ecriture et révolution," in *Théorie d'Ensemble*, 68.

production.[82] The functions of representation and communication cannot account for the production of meaning. We have already seen, with Derrida, how communication, which is at the basis of structural linguistics, implies that the identity of meaning and the subject can be separated from the signifying operation. By continuing to view language as a mere instrument that can lead us to an ultimate signified, to an original meaning, or a last, true text, we remain oblivious to the productive and transformational aspects of scriptural work. Language can be reduced to an instrument of communication only if we bypass not what it expresses (the circulation of a given meaning) but what determines it (the processes governing the production of meaning). Kristeva contends that "Marx's critical reflections on the system of exchange resemble the contemporary critique of the sign and the circulation of meaning."[83]

According to Kristeva, the problem of contemporary semiotics is either to formalize semiotic systems from the point of view of communication (in the same way, she notes, that Ricardo regarded surplus-value from the point of view of distribution and consumption), or to "ope[n] up to the internal problematics of communication (inevitably offered by all social problematics) the 'other scene' of the production of meaning prior to meaning" (84). This calls for a critical semiotics based on work instead of exchange. For Kristeva, a fundamental distinction exists between discourse (*parole*) and text: the former is based on the spoken language and is thus sustained by phonocentric or logocentric biases; the latter places semiotic theory in a Marxist perspective in that the accent is on the production rather than on the exchange or circulation of meaning.[84] Marxist thought is important to the development of semiotic theory, then, because it is "the first to pose the problematics of productive work as a major element in the definition of a semiotic system."[85]

The notion of productivity implies that the text makes work a fundamental dimension of language. To work in/on language (*travailler la langue*) is to

---

82. Jean-Louis Houdebine, "Première approche de la notion de texte," in *Théorie d'Ensemble*, 284. Originally published as "Texte, structure, histoire" in *La Nouvelle Critique* 11 (February 1968).

83. Kristeva, "Semiotics: A Critical Science and/or a Critique of Science," in *The Kristeva Reader*, trans. Seán Hand, 83. Originally published as "La sémiologie: Science critique et/ou critique de la science" in *La Nouvelle Critique* 16 (1968) and subsequently in *Théorie d'Ensemble*.

84. Kristeva, "Problèmes de la structuration du texte" ("Linguistique et Littérature"), *La Nouvelle Critique*, 56. Reprinted in *Théorie d'Ensemble*.

85. Kristeva, "Semiotics: A Critical Science and/or a Critique of Science," 81.

explore the engendering of meaning and the subject. According to Marx, production means objectifying; that is, expressing one's individuality and its particularity, which differs from the social agreement and contract implied by exchange value.[86] The text opens up the language of communication and representation—what Kristeva calls the "pheno-text" (a structured surface whose literary function has traditionally been to represent reality or express an innermost subjectivity)—to an underlying volume of signifying activity (the "geno-text"). Obviously, we cannot consider what surfaces as meaning and what operates beneath the surface in quite the same manner. To analyze the text as a production of meaning requires the reversal of structural linguistics. We move from the description of a static, ahistoric structure to the analysis of a signifying practice viewed as a dynamic process of engendering. The text is not just a structure but rather a structuration, an apparatus that produces and transforms meaning before it is circulated. The concept of the text opens semiotics, as a science of signification, to *signifiance*, which studies the production and transformation of meaning in a text. With textual practice, we are in an "other" semiotics, appropriately termed "semanalysis" by Kristeva, bringing together semiotics and psychoanalysis.

The Marxist notion of work suggests "a scene where work does not yet *represent* any value or *mean* anything," where "the relation of a *body* to *expenditure*" is in question.[87] Kristeva maintains that "Marx had neither the wish nor the means to tackle this notion of productive labour prior to value or meaning" (Kristeva, "Semiotics: A Critical Science" 82). To the Marxist notions of work and production must be added Freud's "dream-work." By distinguishing between the logics of the dream-work and of conscious thought (The dream-work "does not think, calculate or judge in any way at all; it restricts itself to giving things a new form"), Freud was "the first to think of the work involved in the process of signification as anterior to the meaning produced and/or the representative discourse." As a theoretical concept, the dream-work "triggers off a new research, one that touches on pre-representative production, and the development of thinking before *thought*" (83–84). Freudian psychoanalysis provides *Tel Quel* with a theory and practice of textual production that can now account for that

---

86. Karl Marx, "Excerpt-Notes of 1844," in *Writings of the Young Marx on Philosophy and Society*, ed. and trans. Lloyd Easton and Kurt Guddat (Garden City, N.Y.: Anchor Books, 1967), 281.

87. Kristeva, "Semiotics: A Critical Science," 82.

other scene where desire is played out before being subsumed by the linguistic functions of communication and expression.

It is no coincidence that processes of production—be they socioeconomic or scriptural—have been dissimulated in favor of circulation and exchange, communication and expression. The reasons for this dissimulation cannot be understood if Western thought and its entire socioeconomic apparatus remain unaccounted for. That is why *Tel Quel*, by 1968, was so interested in shedding light upon the economy—a word, remarks Henric, that the dominant class or social group does not like to hear and for good reason whether this economy is political, scriptural, or sexual.[88] The exploration of these three economies, and their possible convergence, is at the heart of *Tel Quel*'s work in the late 1960s: culminating in *Théorie d'Ensemble* and marking the beginning of a major theoretical project: that of producing a "new human relation" by bringing together the two great *epistemes* of modernity—materialist and Freudian dialectics.[89] What relation exists between production and desire? Between class determination and the unconscious? For *Tel Quel*, it was precisely this relation that was missing from Marxism and needed to be established by a new semiotic theory and practice of writing that accounted for what had traditionally been excluded from Western idealism: matter, work, the body, and writing.

Freud would give Kristeva's semanalysis and *Tel Quel*'s work on the text a theoretical edge. Freudian psychoanalysis would enable *Tel Quel* to rethink Marxism from the perspective of the subject and language. Marxism, argues Kristeva, has traditionally viewed contradiction in terms of the class struggle. It places Hegelian negativity (bound up with the dissolution of structure) outside of the speaking subject: in relations of production. It thus fails to address contradiction as inherent in the signifying process and in each speaking subject within a class.[90] For Kristeva, contradiction is the matrix of all *signifiance*. *Tel Quel* would reexamine the question of class struggle in light of what happens to the subject, insofar as he/she is the subject of a practice or an experience. To Althusser's "process without a subject," *Tel Quel* would contrapose a "subject in process/on trial." This eccentric subject

88. Henric, "Pour une avant-garde révolutionnaire," 65.

89. Barthes asks: "How can the two great *epistemes* of modernity, i.e., materialist and Freudian dialectics, be made to converge, intersect, and produce a new human relation (nor is it to be excluded that a third term lurks in the inter-diction of the first two)?" "Writers, Intellectuals, Teachers," in *The Rustle of Language*, 328. Originally published in *Tel Quel* 47 (Autumn 1971).

90. Kristeva, "Sujet dans le langage et pratique politique," 24.

has traditionally been relegated to art and literature. Could such a subject become the basis for theoretical reflection or social change? Is it coincidental that a theory of social change, which only viewed language in terms of reflection and subjects in relation to classes, could not tolerate modernist art and psychoanalysis? *Tel Quel* would define its new theoretical and political project in relation to the following question posed by Barthes in 1971: "how to assist the inter-action of these two desires: to change the economy of the relations of production and to change the economy of the subject?"[91] Guided by this question in its political venture from 1968 to the early 1970s, *Tel Quel* would assume its place alongside the masses in the class struggle against the bourgeoisie. Several weeks after the theoretical discussions with the PCF at Cluny, May 1968 erupted, and *Tel Quel* found itself not with "a foot on the barricades" as Kristeva would later claim, but instead embarked on the Communist "galley."[92]

91. Barthes, "Writers, Intellectuals, and Teachers," 328.
92. Kristeva, "My Memory's Hyperbole," 272, 273.

CHAPTER FOUR

THE SEDUCTION
OF POLITICS

". . . my idiocy in thinking that it was possible to overtake him [Aragon]
on the extreme Left with the aid of the other Louis, who received
no decorations, Althusser . . ."

—Philippe Sollers

In the late 1960s, *Tel Quel* sought a political interlocutor—in the form of a collective movement or party—for its program of cultural renewal, defined, on the one hand, by the latest theoretical advances in semiotics, philosophy, and psychoanalysis, and, on the other, by the "poetic revolutions" of the nineteenth- and twentieth-century avant-gardes. *Tel Quel* would thus briefly associate itself with "the only French political party to have a cultural politics,"[1] namely, the PCF. *Tel Quel*'s dialogue with Communist Party intellectuals, a number of whom (Henric, Houdebine, Scarpetta) became closely associated with the journal, led to the 1968 and 1970 ("Literature and Ideologies") Cluny colloquia, organized by *La Nouvelle Critique*. Despite certain divergences of opinion, these colloquia were important in that they reaffirmed the key position occupied by literature in ideological debates, and revealed how both literary theory and traditional Marxist thought could benefit from textual semiotics, deconstructive philosophy, and Lacanian psychoanalysis.

1. Kristeva, "My Memory's Hyperbole," 272.

In 1967–68, *Tel Quel* took on the avant-garde wager of revolutionizing literature and transforming society. Like its predecessor, surrealism, *Tel Quel* temporarily fostered the illusion that only a "Socialist revolution would create a social climate propitious for the writing of the avant-garde."[2] And so it relived the "old adventure" of the twentieth-century avant-gardes, namely "the contradiction between art and political engagement."[3] On the one hand, *Tel Quel* wanted the revolutionary specificity of its literary practice to be recognized, which did not imply, however, that the review advocated the idealist notion of the autonomy of art, as epitomized by "art for art's sake." On the other hand, in contending that literature and politics were inevitably bound up with one another—"It is not possible to bring about an economic and social revolution without, at the same time, realizing, on another level, a symbolic revolution"[4]—*Tel Quel* was, nevertheless, adamantly opposed to the political saturation of literature and culture as caricatured by Zhdanovism.

In light of its program of cultural materialism and of events of the mid- and late 1960s such as the Chinese Cultural Revolution and the uprisings of May 1968, it followed that *Tel Quel* would seek to articulate its theory and practice of writing in terms of the class struggle. *Tel Quel* adopted Marxist theory not only to formulate a materialist conception of the literary text and its subject, but also to associate its scriptural theory and cultural practice with the class struggle. In introducing *Tel Quel* to the Communist Left in 1967, *La Nouvelle Critique* claimed that *Tel Quel* had undergone an ideological evolution that manifested itself not only at a theoretical level (by more and more resolute attempts to place itself in a Marxist perspective) but also at a political level (by the taking of marked political positions).[5] In the summer of 1968 (no. 34), *Tel Quel* published several political manifestos pertaining to May 1968. Although this was not the first issue of *Tel Quel* to have political overtones—previous issues contained brief statements against anti-imperalism in Vietnam (nos. 28, 30),[6] in support of the Chinese

2. Sollers cited by Kristeva in "My Memory's Hyperbole," 270.
3. Sollers, "On n'a encore rien vu," 25.
4. Sollers, "Réponses," *Tel Quel* 43 (Autumn 1970): 76.
5. Introductory note to "Réponses à la *Nouvelle Critique*," in *Théorie d'Ensemble*, 385. In 1970 (no. 43), *Tel Quel* adopted a new subtitle: "Littérature/Philosophie/Science/Politique."
6. Vietnam was a rallying point of many PCF militants in the mid- and late 1960s. In addition to the notices appearing in *Tel Quel*, Baudry, Faye, and Sollers had also expressed their opposition to the war in Vietnam in a number of open letters written between August and December 1966; one such letter was addressed by them to *Le Nouvel Observateur* in August 1966. Cited in Faye, "Interphone," *Tel Quel* 30 (Summer 1967): 93. Faye had also signed

Cultural Revolution and antifascist struggles in Spain (nos. 22, 28, 31),[7] and in endorsement of Edouardo Sanguineti's Communist candidacy in Italy (no. 33)—this issue was distinct from previous ones. In prior issues, political positions appeared as short notices interjected at the end of the issue, with no apparent connection to the aesthetic and theoretical pieces of the review. This was clearly not the case for the summer 1968 number, where manifestos drew explicit parallels between *Tel Quel's* aesthetic program and the socio-political reality of 1968.

The opening piece was an ostentatious and aggressive seven-point program entitled "La Révolution ici maintenant" [The revolution here and now], signed by Pierre Boulez, Hubert Damisch, Denis Hollier, Jean-Louis Schefer, Paule Thévenin, Denis Roche, Claude Cabantous, Jean-Joseph Goux, Baudry, Kristeva, Pleynet, Devade, Ricardou, Risset, Rottenberg, Sollers, and Thibaudeau. The manifesto emphasized the theoretical focus of *Tel Quel* and the decisive nature of signifying activity in social transformation. It insisted on the necessity of constructing a theory derived from textual practice in order to bypass engaged discourse—"that model of teleologico-transcendental, humanist and psychologist mystification, complicit with the definitive obscurantism of the bourgeois state."[8] It was understood that textual theory had to be bound up with Marxism-Leninism, "the only revolutionary theory of our time." The manifesto concluded: "Any ideological undertaking which does not today present itself in an advanced theoretical form and settles instead for bringing together under eclectic or sentimental headings individual and under-politicised activities, seems to us counter-revolutionary, inasmuch as it fails to recognize the process of the class-struggle, which has objectively to be carried on and reactivated."[9]

In conjunction with the program outlined in "La Révolution ici maintenant," *Tel Quel* subsequently founded a "Groupe d'Etudes Théoriques" [Theoretical Studies Group] that met weekly from October 1968 to June

---

manifestos against the war in Vietnam that were published in *Le Monde* on 14 May 1966, 9–10 July 1972, and 26–27 January 1975. The latter two were also signed by Sollers, and Kristeva signed the last one. See Jean-François Sirinelli, *Intellectuels et passions françaises: Manifestes et pétitions au XXe siècle* (Paris: Fayard, 1990), 250–51, 256–57.

7. Even though *Tel Quel* did not officially support the Chinese Cultural Revolution until 1971, when it broke with the PCF, subtle notices indicating interest in China began appearing in the mid- and late 1960s. One of the notices against oppression in Franco's Spain was signed by Faye; Houdebine maintains, however, that Sollers, who is fluent in Spanish, has always been interested in the history of Spain. Interview with Houdebine, Paris, 23 June 1987.

8. "La Révolution ici maintenant," trans. Keith Reader, *Tel Quel* 34 (Summer 1968): 4.

9. Ibid.

1969. The guiding theme for the presentations and discussions was the "Elaboration and Transformation of the Concept of Text." The presentations by Thévenin, Damisch, Schefer, Kristeva, Derrida, Sollers, Houdebine, Pleynet, Goux, Ricardou, Rottenberg, Risset, and Baudry—the majority of which were published in *Tel Quel*—focused on textual production and ideological confrontation. According to the explanatory notice published in *Tel Quel* 38 (Summer 1969)—that is, when the enterprise was over—the Group had been founded in opposition to "the reactionary politics of teaching in France."[10] Once again *Tel Quel* positioned itself against the university, founding its own autonomous site for the production and diffusion of knowledge.

The other "May 1968" manifesto, appearing at the end of the same issue as "La Révolution ici maintenant," severely criticized the student movement. More political than "La Révolution ici maintenant," which emphasized the central place of theory in revolutionary struggle, this second text underscored the essential and impassable role of the working-class party and criticized the petit bourgeois contestation of the students that had been substituted for the class struggle. Furthermore, these two political pieces pertaining to the events of May were complemented by three texts associating *Tel Quel*'s avant-garde wager with that of its predecessor of the 1920s and 1930s: surrealism. These texts include Sollers's "La Grande Méthode" [The great method], a piece devoted to intellectuals and the revolution; Bataille's unpublished text, dating from 1929 to 1930, "La 'vieille taupe' et le préfixe *sur* dans les mots *surhomme* et *surréaliste*" [The "Old Mole" and the prefix *sur* in the words *surhomme* (Superman) and *surrealist*], and Hollier's introduction to this piece, "Le savoir formel" [Formal knowledge]. In these texts, and in a later issue on surrealism (no. 46), *Tel Quel* attempted to show how a stronger grounding in both Marxist and Freudian theory enabled them to avoid the idealist or anarchic deviations of surrealism. *Tel Quel*, in fact, picked up where surrealism left off; it reactivated the avant-garde venture just as surrealism disintegrated as a movement. In 1966, Breton died; three years later in "Le Quatrième Chant" published in *Le Monde* of 4 October 1969, Jean Schuster officially proclaimed the end of surrealism.

To better understand how *Tel Quel* articulated its aesthetic project with the revolution in 1968, let us consider for a moment how a young graduate

10. For a list of the presentations of the Theoretical Studies Group, see *Tel Quel* 38 (Summer 1969): 103.

student of semiotics and literature, who had just left Marxism and socialism behind in her native Bulgaria, was seduced by *Tel Quel* at the very moment of its own political seduction. Looking back on the *Tel Quel* years, Kristeva wrote: "*Clarté*, the journal of Communist students, had published, at the end of 1965, I think, a large picture of Sollers along with a text in which he explained, in essence, that only the socialist Revolution could provide a social setting propitious to avant-garde writing. This was, before the mediation of Genette, my first encounter with *Tel Quel*. And the first seduction."[11] How could an academic who had just turned her back on a socialist regime possibly be captivated by *Tel Quel* precisely at that moment when *Tel Quel* was lured by revolutionary politics? At precisely the time when other academics, such as Genette and Todorov, were forsaking *Tel Quel* as the review embarked on a "terrorist" course, abandoning its "formalist" and "scientific" phase for Derridian deconstruction, Althusserian Marxism, Lacanian psychoanalysis, and PCF politics? As a Bulgarian émigré, shouldn't Kristeva have known better? And conversely, being well acquainted with the misadventures of the twentieth-century avant-gardes, and particularly the surrealist experience whose shadow overcasts this entire phase of *Tel Quel*, shouldn't Sollers have known better than to let himself be seduced by the political wager? Kristeva does not deny, however, the quixotic quality of Sollers's wager:

> [I]t seemed to me completely unrealistic from the standpoint of the socialism I had experienced. I knew to what extent a regime born of a Marxist social mutation rejected not merely all aesthetic formalism deemed individualistic or antisocial, but also all individual stylistic experience that could question or explore the common code and its stereotypes in which ideology must seek shelter in order to dominate. ("My Memory's Hyperbole" 270)

Nevertheless, Kristeva and her associates at *Tel Quel* were led to believe that "in France, it would be different." Hadn't Louis Althusser "taken the toughest (for [Kristeva], the most 'Stalinist') points of Marxism in order to instill new hope in the French Communist Party and all of French society, the harbinger of a worldwide Marxist spring?" Kristeva, however, remained "less sensitive to the arguments of the director of studies of the rue d'Ulm than to the revolutionary aestheticism of *Tel Quel*, which seemed after all, to

11. Kristeva, "My Memory's Hyperbole," 270.

bode well for the success of the futurist utopia" (270). By stating that "in France, it would be different," Kristeva was alluding to a changing cultural climate—paving the way for May 1968—and to an intellectual thaw on the part of the PCF, which took place predominantly after the Argenteuil conference of March 1966. After decades of severe conflict with their intellectuals, why had the French Communist Party leaders decided to devote an extra day to ideological and cultural concerns at Argenteuil? Why did the need arise for an emphasis on ideology and culture rather than on politics and economics? One answer lies in Althusser's theoretical approach to de-Stalinization in the party.

With respect to literature, de-Stalinization implied not merely abandoning socialist realism but, more important, its underpinnings: economic determinism and cultural interventionism. Socialist realism was synonymous with Zhdanovism or cultural Stalinism. A central tenet of Stalinism was the Marxist notion that the economic base directly and totally determines the superstructure of society: its political institutions, its ideology, and its art and literature. From this perspective, bourgeois culture could only be rejected on the grounds that it necessarily reflected bourgeois society; that is, a capitalist economy based on human exploitation. The notion of economic determinism necessarily implies that form reflects content, and thus presupposes the absolute subordination of art and literature to political ends. Art, therefore, has no autonomy.

Stalin had, in fact, professed that content precedes form. Thus, Picasso's 1948 portrait of Stalin could only be interpreted negatively by Communists as an alteration of Stalin's person and thought. The lack of resemblance was less an issue than the artistic attitude behind the portrait, which attested to the intimidating power of art as soon as it strays from what the party wants to see (form reflecting content); that is, as soon as it is seen as having a reality of its own. In "Le Refus d'hériter" [The refusal to inherit], published in *Le Nouvel Observateur* of 30 April 1968, Barthes asserted that Sollers had broken with the political language of his fathers: "the fathers being, in this instance, the left-wing writers and intellectuals who have been absorbed for the last ten years by the anti-Stalinist struggle."[12] "A Communist in 'Tel Quel'?" Why not? questions Barthes, if this means "unwriting the traditional distaste for formalism among Communist intellectuals" (70). Barthes argues thus:

12. Barthes, "The Refusal to Inherit," reprinted in *Writer Sollers*, 70.

Confronted with a new historical situation, Sollers profits from it. He exploits the principle—which has long been repressed—according to which the relationship between the revolution and literature cannot be analogical, only homological. What is the point of copying the real, even from a revolutionary point of view, since this would be to have recourse to the essence of bourgeois language, which is, above all else, a language which copies? (73–74)

If, during the 1950s, Communist writers and artists were considered important by the Central Committee, it was only insofar as they adhered to the party line and subordinated their artistic expression to party ends—the class struggle at whose vertex was the party. In what appeared to be a liberating gesture, the PCF Central Committee officially proclaimed, at Argenteuil, that it would no longer intervene in scientific and artistic matters. Many militants interpreted this gesture as a desertion: "It wasn't the passage to correct positions, as they claimed, but simply a jilting; nothing else was said about painting, it just was no longer discussed."[13] In the late 1940s and 1950s, artists wielded a certain power at the expense of the subordination of their craft to party ideology, that is, insofar as they abandoned their specificity. These years were marked by literature as a reflection of the real, art subordinate to politics, and intellectual activity as a function of party militantism. Politics remained firmly in command.

Conversely, in the mid- and late 1960s, with the recognition of artistic specificity by the party, the separation between culture and politics ensued. This led to a hands-off approach: Do what you will in the cultural sphere but leave politics alone. Did this split imply a loss of power for intellectuals? Or was it the trade-off of one lack of power for another? Houdebine maintains that the political apparatus of the PCF was not the least bit interested in the intellectual discussions of the 1960s: Central Committee politicians certainly could not fathom what an avant-garde current like *Tel Quel* could contribute to Communism. However, if having Telquelians as fellow travelers meant influencing French youth and getting their vote, then the party was in favor of encounters with avant-garde writers and intellectuals. Divergences of opinion expressed in *Nouvelle Critique*–*Tel Quel* gatherings did not matter: it was merely a question of getting the vote.[14]

In the 1940s and 1950s, Communist intellectuals had subordinated their

13. Anonymous Communist cited in Verdès-Leroux, *Le Réveil des somnambules*, 316.
14. Houdebine, interview of 23 June 1987.

artistic freedom in exchange for a measure of political power. Did they then regain their artistic freedom at the cost of losing their political power in the party in the mid- and late 1960s? For someone like Althusser, this appears to have been the case. The Communist Party could ill afford to dismiss Althusser at a time when it was haunted by the specters of Stalinist repression and yet claimed to be taking de-Stalinization seriously. The party was in a particularly vulnerable position. Yet with his excessive regard for theory, Althusser was more of a solution than a threat. In order to maintain the freedom he desired in the philosophical realm, Althusser agreed not to counter publicly the official political lines of the party. Althusser would provide the party with the intellectual credibility it so desperately sought. After the cult of Stalin, what better way to fill the immense theoretical void left in French Marxism than by an excessive regard for theory? The French Communist Party sorely needed a theoretician and Althusser was the perfect answer for avoiding the repression to which the cult of Stalin had led. What better theoretician than Althusser, for whom theory was a theoretical practice? What may have initially appeared to be potentially threatening and destabilizing for the party—the break with economism, the autonomy of the superstructure—was, in effect, the perfect solution. Althusser himself had created the distinction between theory and politics. At a time when the party was seeking credibility and trying to open up to a broader constituency, Althusser was its comeback. He was regarded as an important theoretician outside the party, a Marxist who could stand on his own alongside such important figures as Foucault, Lacan, Derrida, and Barthes, who had brought about the intellectual explosion of 1965–66. Althusser succeeded in taking his place in this intellectual explosion by showing that Marxism could be comfortably synthesized with the structuralist recasting and with such disciplines as semiotics and psychoanalysis.

The command of theory and the relative autonomy of the superstructure espoused by Althusser was appealing to non-Marxist intellectuals, including the *Tel Quel* group, who were looking for an articulation between literature and politics that would allow them to maintain their avant-garde aesthetic program. Althusser's work marked the decisive break with economism in the party. In distancing Marxist thought from economic determinism by placing the emphasis on theory as a form of (theoretical) practice and recognizing the importance of philosophy in the class struggle, Althusser gave non-Marxists, such as Telquelians, the possibility of becoming Marxists without so much as modifying their non-Marxist positions. If Kristeva writes of an exaggerated regard for theory on the part of *Tel Quel*, it is because theory led the *Tel Quel* group to a rapprochement with the PCF and, as a result, prompted them to articulate their revolutionary aestheticism with the class struggle. The key issue for *Tel Quel* in making this articulation was to avoid sacrificing the specificity of its literary practice. This became feasible with the new distinctions among theoretical (or textual), ideological, and political practice made possible by Althusser, which enabled *Tel Quel* to articulate easily its avant-garde work with the class struggle.

One Telquelian who comfortably assimilated Althusser's distinctions was Henric. He was one of several Communist militants who had been drawn to *Tel Quel* in the early 1960s; in reading its pages he had foreseen the eventuality of being militant in politics while remaining modern in literature. His interview with Sollers, refused by *Les Lettres Françaises* and published instead in *Tel Quel* in 1970, enables us to understand *Tel Quel*'s avant-garde articulation in 1968. Henric recognizes that a central problem is posed by the relationship between political action and literary activity, which has typically been the site of misunderstanding. If one does not engage in a theoretical reflection to account for these two modes of action—politics and writing in their structural correlations, similarities, and irreducible differences—the result is an obscurantist discourse.[15] We are thus led to the conclusion that literature is one thing, and politics another. Hence, the flourishing of decadent aestheticism, in complicity with political disengagement, or its opposite, which is the result of a moral reaction and is identical in essence to the former: literature and politics are the same thing (58). In one instance, the choice is between literature and life—writing and the revolution—in the other, textual activity is simply assimilated to an ideology that must be of service to the immediate political combat. Both situations ignore the dialectical articulation of theory with practice (59).

Henric claims that Stalinism greatly contributed to the production and perpetuation of these two discourses. Its effects are felt even in its opposite: right-wing revisionism, whose characteristics are opportunism on a political level, and unbridled eclecticism on an ideological level. To avoid the pitfalls of Stalinism and revisionism, one needs to differentiate clearly the political from the theoretical. Revisionism runs counter to Marxism since it does not theoretically demarcate itself from surrounding ideologies; it thereby reduces historical and dialectical materialism to preexisting idealist philosophies. We are thus left with a transcendental humanism, precisely what Althusser was combating along with economism. Revisionism makes no real

15. Henric, "Pour une avant-garde révolutionnaire," 58.

distinction between the political and theoretical. In line with Althusser, Henric insists on the importance of this distinction, without which we run the risk of bringing back idealism into the philosophical and scientific realm, and run the danger of supporting social democracy ("Pour une avant-garde révolutionnaire" 59).

In the "Mai '68" manifesto, *Tel Quel* adopts a strict Leninist interpretation of the events. It insists on the necessity of the party, and on the observation of party discipline, without which the proletariat would be disarmed to the profit of the bourgeoisie. For *Tel Quel*, the May movement is not a revolution, but an attempt to demobilize the proletariat. It is a question of contestation as opposed to class struggle, affecting only the most peripheral superstructures, and not the essential infrastructure or relations of production. What disturbs *Tel Quel* even more is the lack of theoretical foundation underpinning the movement: "What is challenged by this pseudo-revolutionary lexicography [for example, "power to the imagination," "the creative imagination of the masses"] is a coherent political practice founded on theory" (95).

Although Leninist in inspiration, the emphasis on theory takes on Althusserian dimensions that become conspicuous in the other *Tel Quel* manifesto, "La Révolution ici maintenant." This manifesto departs from the hard-line (infrastructural) focus of "Mai '68"; instead, it attributes strategic importance to theory and the work of the avant-garde. Given its opening position ("Mai '68" is at the very end of the issue), this text is obviously more central to the *Tel Quel* mission. In many respects, "Mai '68" reads like a piece written after the fact to convince the party of their adhesion during May. On the other hand, "La Révolution ici maintenant" underscores *Tel Quel*'s action as being textual, with its own particular laws, which cannot be suspended or neglected. This textual action has its own efficacy, even though it is linked to the social struggle, whose primacy is not contested and to which *Tel Quel* adheres without any ambiguity (3). The repetition of the expression "here and now," in reference to its textual action, reveals *Tel Quel*'s avid desire to establish an immediate analogy with the revolution, in order to strengthen the relationship of its avant-garde work to the class struggle. But the specificity of its avant-garde work must not be overlooked.

Tel Quel was accused of adopting quasi-Stalinist stances during May 1968, which resulted from trying to protect the specificity of their practice as writers, while at the same time remaining attuned to the sociopolitical reality. Why, in effect, did they side with the PCF against the May movement? Why did *Tel Quel* attempt to adhere to seasoned Marxist-Leninist paradigms? In an interview with former Telquelian Jean-Edern Hallier, which appeared in the September 1970 issue of *L'Idiot International*, Sartre noted that many writers "thought that May was the occasion to realize ideas they had held in the past."[16] For Sartre, these were individuals "who were on the sidelines (they were often former Communist militants). They unavailingly tried to make May correspond to their preconceived notions." Sartre argued that many intellectuals were hostile toward the May movement because it contested their role *as* intellectuals and demanded a radical conversion on their part (15). The May movement denied intellectuals the possibility of leading the masses. Their preconceived ideas could not account for the reality of May, which made each individual an active possessor of language, thereby dispensing the intellectual from his need to guide. The intellectual could no longer "speak" to the proletariat, that is, make theory, which would then be supported by the action of the masses (19). The intellectual was no longer at the forefront of social change. That is why, Sartre contends, many intellectuals endeavored to make May correspond to preconceived notions.

The pre-1968 intellectual was, in many respects, the universal intellectual who, on the one hand, believed in the universality of knowledge and, on the other hand, realized that all knowledge is class-determined. Even though knowledge may strive to be universal, it will never concurrently serve all people. In a country such as France where social barriers subsist, knowledge essentially serves the ruling class. Intellectuals belong to this class: they work *for* the privileged; they are, in effect, *on their side*. They are perpetually in contradiction.[17] As a result, they must contend with a "guilty conscience." The contradictory status of universal intellectuals enables them to be useful to others, for they are led to criticize society and its oppressive institutions. They thereby find a certain comfort in their discomfort. Although, *in principle*, they are not at peace with themselves, intellectuals, nevertheless, continue to labor for the society that accords them the privilege of being intellectuals, while at the same time condemning (at meetings, in petitions, articles, etc.) the repression this privilege entails (Pingaud, "Faut-il 'rééduq-

16. Sartre, "L'Ami du peuple," in Sartre, Pingaud, and Mascolo, *Du rôle de l'intellectuel dans le mouvement révolutionnaire* (Paris: Eric Losfeld, 1971), 19.

17. Bernard Pingaud, "Faut-il 'rééduquer' l'intellectuel?" in *Du rôle de l'intellectuel dans le mouvement révolutionnaire*, 34. Pingaud, a collaborator of *Les Temps Modernes* criticized *Tel Quel*'s cultural politics in "Où va 'Tel Quel'?" *La Quinzaine Littéraire* 42 (1–15 January 1968): 8–9.

uer' l'intellectuel?" 34). Intellectuals thus recapture a "clear conscience" from this "guilty" one.

May 1968 forced many intellectuals, such as Sartre, to recognize that their "guilty conscience" did not justify their status as intellectuals. They had to place their knowledge directly in the service of the masses: they had to acknowledge the universal that was desired by the masses, in the immediate moment, that is, the *concrete universal* (Sartre, "L'Ami du peuple" 21). Working for *Libération*, distributing the newspaper in the streets, was only a beginning for Sartre. Yet Sartre made it clear that he was not ready to abandon the *Flaubert* project, even if it situated him in the pre-1968 context.[18] Telquelians would circumvent Sartre's dilemma by continuing to defend their practice as writers.

Clearly, Telquelians did not assume the "guilty conscience" of the intellectual. We have seen how *Tel Quel* demarcated itself from the onset from this engagé impasse. For *Tel Quel*, the writer did not have to feel guilty about being a writer; the writer's raison d'être was in his or her writing. The relationship to writing, and to language in general, determined the relationship to society at large. Writing incorporated the knowledge of its time, whether it was linguistic, philosophical, psychoanalytical, or political. Engagement had subordinated the writer to something exterior to the practice of writing. From the very beginning, *Tel Quel* had refused this subordination by incorporating the various upheavals of knowledge into the practice of writing. In being compelled, as a progressive journal, to move forward with the times, *Tel Quel* could not remain untouched by sociopolitical events. It certainly could not remain silent about an event that made an impact on France on all levels—cultural, social, and political. *Tel Quel* had to take a position, and so it chose the PCF over the movement. For PCF militants like Houdebine, *Tel Quel* had become, by the mid-1960s, a highly topical journal. It had an incredible knack for projecting current events onto its own work.[19] *Tel Quel* clearly could not afford to ignore a portentous event like May 1968. Nonetheless, it was not about to put its literary practice in question. Once again, literature had to be defended, and this time—

18. In her critique of engagement in *Pour Gramsci*, the Italian ex-Communist militant Maria-Antonietta Macciocchi analyzes the split between theory and practice among engaged French intellectuals. Of Sartre, she writes: "Even Sartre, who is the most engagé intellectual in France, the philosopher of engagement, did not cease to further his immense essay on Flaubert, volume after volume, even in the course of the hot years, around 1968, during the great tempest that shook up intellectual France." *Pour Gramsci* (Paris: Seuil, 1974), 264–65.

19. Houdebine, interview of 23 June 1987.

paradoxical as it may now seem—*Tel Quel* used the PCF to ward off the perils of May.

In accordance with Althusser's notion of theoretical practice, Telquelians may have felt that it was not necessary to engage in a confused and apparently ephemeral movement. Its avant-garde work was such that it did not need to follow an agitation whose political lines and ideological beliefs were diffuse and multiple,[20] as the enormous post-May interpretations have confirmed. *Tel Quel* had repeatedly underscored that *écriture* was a specific practice; as such, there was no need to become entangled in a pragmatic struggle. Telquelians were not about to follow Sartre out into the streets, megaphone in hand. The fact that Sartre supported the movement was a further incentive for them to take another route, for they had always done exactly the opposite of their major rival. *Tel Quel* continued to defend the revolutionary specificity of its own work, which did not need to take to the streets. In order to avoid assimilating literature with politics, *Tel Quel* persisted in accentuating the theoretical moment. By emphasizing the strategic importance of theory, *Tel Quel* could claim that its avant-garde work was bound up with the revolution, while at the same time keeping its distance from the political realm. And yet *Tel Quel* was only too happy to find an interlocutor for its experimental work in the PCF. Kristeva claimed that during May 1968, they kept "an eye in search of something that could ensure cultural transmission, something in the party that could be useful to [them]."[21]

What was the danger in supporting the PCF? After all, what did *Tel Quel* stand to lose? They had more to lose with the May movement, which threatened their prerogative as writers and intellectuals. They were not about to abandon the hegemonic position they had achieved in the theoretical domain of literature, which even the PCF had officially recognized at Cluny just a few weeks before May. Thanks to the cultural de-Stalinization of the party and, particularly, Althusser's Marxism, *Tel Quel* could separate its avant-garde work from party politics and still claim, in good faith, to associate its work with the class struggle. Unlike the surrealists, they were not being asked to give up their specificity as artists and writers in the name of the party: to choose like Breton and Aragon between surrealism and Communism. In a sense, Kristeva had correctly concluded that in France it might be different.

---

20. Patrick Combes, *La Littérature et le mouvement de Mai 68* (Paris: Seghers, 1984), 231.
21. Kristeva, "My Memory's Hyperbole," 273.

If the situation in the late 1960s was indeed different from the one in the late 1920s, why then did *Tel Quel* devote so much energy to attacking the surrealist enterprise as it sought to win over and remain in the good graces of the PCF from 1968 to 1970? Why did Telquelians assume hard-line stances with respect to the PCF, coupled with virulent attacks on surrealist ideology? To understand how *Tel Quel* managed to be pro-PCF during the May events and then break with the PCF during the so-called June 1971 movement (no. 47), it is essential to consider *Tel Quel*'s curious relationship to its avant-garde predecessor in France: surrealism. The relationship to surrealism inevitably appears in all introductory studies on *Tel Quel*.[22] Susan Suleiman has aptly noted that the more *Tel Quel* became politicized, the more it sought to separate itself from the surrealist movement.[23] Attacks were aimed for the most part at Breton, who had struggled to keep surrealism free of political subservience.

Tel Quel certainly could not ignore the legacy of surrealism and its impact on cultural life in France. As one reason—but not the determining one—for *Tel Quel*'s relentless attacks on mainstream surrealism, Suleiman invokes Harold Bloom's notion of the "anxiety of influence." *Tel Quel* had to "overcome" its precursor in France ("As Is" 1014). Jean-François Fourny further develops this hypothesis in his analysis of *Tel Quel* as a "second wave." The relationship between the tactical and the theoretical, alluded to by both critics in their essays, needs to be further analyzed in conjunction with May 1968.

Tel Quel's relationship to surrealism was an important and long-standing one. It is one that took three directions: via Breton and mainstream surrealism; Aragon and the Communist Party; and the "dissident" surrealists Artaud, Bataille, and Ponge. *Tel Quel* ended up breaking its ties with Breton and Aragon; however, it remained faithful to Artaud, Bataille, and even Ponge. We have already seen how Sollers did what he could to rid himself of

22. For the theoretical differences between *Tel Quel* and surrealism, see Susan Suleiman, "As Is," in *A New History of French Literature*, ed. Denis Hollier (Cambridge: Harvard University Press, 1989): 1011–18; for the relationship between the theoretical and the ideological, see Robert Hefner, "The *Tel Quel* Ideology: Material Practice upon Material Practice," *Sub-Stance* 8 (Winter 1974): 127–38; for a study concerning the theoretical and the tactical, from a Bourdieu perspective, see Jean-François Fourny, "La Deuxième Vague: *Tel Quel* et le Surréalisme," *French Forum* (1987): 229–38, and on the psychological motivations of envy and ambition, see his "A Propos de la Querelle Breton-Bataille," *Revue d'Histoire Littéraire de la France* 84, no. 3 (May–June 1984): 432–38. See also Stephen Bann, "The Career of *Tel Quel*: *Tel Quel* becomes *L'Infini*," *Comparative Criticism* 6 (1984): 327–29.

23. Suleiman, "As Is," 1013.

the initial patronage of Aragon—one of his two godfathers—even if that meant repudiating his early works, which he subsequently judged too bourgeois. But no matter how hard he tried, Sollers could not deny that Aragon and his *Lettres Françaises* had played a capital role in launching both him and his review. *Tel Quel*'s presence on the French Communist scene went way back. Suffice it to say that Sollers only attacked Aragon after 1971, that is, after *Tel Quel* "officially" broke with the party.[24] During the pro-PCF years, that is, 1966–70, Sollers and *Tel Quel* did not touch Aragon: they were too busy assaulting Breton. This was no time, obviously, to be tampering with the (albeit outmoded) image of one of the PCF icons!

Before addressing *Tel Quel*'s attacks on Breton, let us first trace the evolution of this relationship, which started out positively. Sollers's debt to Breton and surrealism is visible in his first fictional piece, "Le Défi," and his first important theoretical essay, "Logique de la fiction."[25] Sollers also acknowledges his debt to surrealism in a number of interviews, such as those published in *Le Figaro Littéraire* (22 September 1962) and *Les Lettres Françaises* (28 March 1963). *Tel Quel* repeatedly announced an interview with Breton that never materialized. Several short notices on surrealism appeared in numbers 6, 9, 10, and 13. In *Tel Quel* 10 (Summer 1962), Boisrouvray critically reviewed the surrealist Jean-Louis Bédouin's *Vingt ans de surréalisme (1939–59)*, published by Denoël in 1961. Boisrouvray refutes Bédouin's excessive claims that surrealism was alive and well in the late 1950s and early 1960s, while nonetheless acknowledging the importance of such Breton texts of the 1920s as *Nadja* and the *Manifestos*.[26] In no. 13 (Spring 1963), *Tel Quel* published the text of a 1962 radio broadcast on Antenne 2 by Sollers and Thibaudeau devoted to surrealism. In *Mes Années "Tel Quel,"* Thibaudeau cleverly juxtaposed certain portions of this text with subsequent statements pronounced by Sollers at Cluny II (1970), where

24. See the criticism addressed against Aragon in "Positions du movement de Juin 71," *Tel Quel* 47 (Autumn 1971). See also Sollers's caustic eulogy to Aragon, "Traité du style," published in *Le Nouvel Observateur*, 1 January 1983, 50–52, which also appeared in *L'Infini* 1 (Winter 1983): 121–22. In the "Traité," Sollers writes: "my idiocy is thinking that it was possible to overtake him [Aragon] on the extreme left with the aid of the other Louis, who received no decorations, Althusser" (trans. Stephen Bann), 50.

25. Sollers received the Fénéon Prize for his first short novel "despite the violent opposition of Aragon," remarks Paulhan in a letter of 11 March 1958 to Ponge. See Jean Paulhan and Francis Ponge, *Correspondance II (1946–1968)* (Paris: Gallimard, 1986), 249.

26. Maurice Nadeau also criticizes Bédouin's enterprise in the 1963 postscript to *Histoire du surréalisme* (Paris: Seuil, 1964, 1970), 190.

he takes very different positions from those of 1962.[27] "André Breton à la radio" contains nothing but the most positive praise for the surrealist leader, and implicitly situates the work of *Tel Quel* in its wake. According to the broadcast, Breton's main objective was to find the "point" that would resolve all contradictions between the mind and the real. If Breton is a man of *oppositions*, it is because his enterprise touches on such apparently different activities as politics, art, philosophy, and psychoanalysis. Breton's genius lies precisely in an *investigation* that is simultaneously conducted in all domains. If others opted for either a political party or art for art's sake, Breton, always endeavored, without compromising with immediate *actualité*, to clear a path where knowledge would never cease to adorn itself with the profusion of the imaginary, yet where the imaginary was subject to the critique of the knowledge of the times (61). Breton's contribution is essentially in the theoretical definition of experiences, as well as in those works where poetry and criticism alternate. This is why Breton's work is current (62). His entire work is defined with respect to surrealism's absolute contestation of language, a contestation that was also carried out in the realm of thought (63). In addition to these remarks that obviously situate *Tel Quel*'s ambitions in relationship to those of Breton, Sollers and Thibaudeau also refer to Breton as a somber revolutionary and a theoretician (61), and praise his sense of fidelity, evident in his relationship to Trotsky (63). They also acknowledge that Freud was introduced in France essentially thanks to the surrealists (62).

Several of the above remarks are juxtaposed in Thibaudeau's book with excerpts from Sollers's Cluny II presentation "La lutte idéologique dans l'écriture d'avant-garde" [The ideological struggle in avant-garde writing] where he states, for example, that "the surrealist movement, in effect, at once posited and misunderstood all the problems necessarily confronting a Western avant-garde." These problems include the relationship between the unconscious and language, the Orient, and Marxism, which Sollers claims are lumped together in a "phantasmatic synthesis."[28] The criticism directed at Breton is less political—that is, he is not directly reproached for defending surrealism over Communism or for his Trotskyist deviation—than theoretical. Instead Breton is criticized for opting for the Hegelian dialectic rather than for dialectical materialism and for abandoning Freud for Jung, and

27. Thibaudeau, *Mes Années "Tel Quel,"* 189–90.
28. Sollers, "La lutte idéologique dans l'écriture d'avant-garde," 75. A summary of Sollers's positions "Thèses générales" appeared in *Tel Quel* 44 (Winter 1971): 96–98.

Marxism for utopian socialism. In short, for being an idealist. Suleiman rightly states that "idealism became the password in *Tel Quel*'s critique of surrealism" ("As Is" 1015). Now that the group had seduced PCF intellectuals at Cluny I with its synthesis of textual semiotics, deconstructive philosophy, Lacanian psychoanalysis, and Althusserian Marxism, it certainly did not want to be accused of the "phantasmatic synthesis" for which it reproached Breton and mainstream surrealism. Nor was an analogy with Breton and surrealism opportune as it sought to convince the party of its Marxist qualifications both on a theoretical and pragmatic level. But since the theoretical level was the only one on which it could feasibly arm itself, it was there that it had to combat surrealism. *Tel Quel* set out to convince the PCF and the French press (which continued to compare its enterprise to the failure of the surrealists) that it was more Marxist than the surrealists, and it did so by means of theory.

Such a strategy became essential at Cluny II, the second gathering organized by *La Nouvelle Critique* on 2–4 April 1970, where *Tel Quel* no longer enjoyed the hegemonic position it had held two years earlier. The second Cluny encounter, "Literature and Ideologies," brought together representatives of *La Nouvelle Critique, Tel Quel, Change,* and *Action Poétique* with other intellectuals and academics. In contrast with the first gathering, *Tel Quel* was contending with *Change* and *Action Poétique* for the good graces of the PCF intellectuals. Elisabeth Roudinesco—who participated in the colloquium with a critical examination of Derrida's notion of *écriture* (the very notion *Tel Quel* was exploiting in its avant-garde stances)—claims that Cluny II led to *Tel Quel*'s break with the PCF and with Derrida.[29] Faye had left *Tel Quel* at the end of 1967 to found his own journal, *Change* (1968–85). After the polemics between the two journals concurrently published by Seuil became too heated, Faye was forced to take his journal elsewhere (to the publisher Seghers/Laffont). Roudinesco writes that "[t]he struggle between the two journals was violent and pivoted on the imaginary conquest of the proletarian fortress" (536). After being played out in the

29. Roudinesco had published in *Action Poétique*. Her affinities were more with the *Change-Action Poétique* group than *Tel Quel*. She is one of several to claim that *Tel Quel* broke with Derrida because he did not distance himself from *La Nouvelle Critique* when *Tel Quel* severed ties with the PCF in 1971. Furthermore, Lacan, whose expulsion from ENS (Ecole Normale Supérieure) in 1969 had been criticized by *Tel Quel*, insinuated that even Derrida had not opposed the expulsion. Derrida's increasing critique of Lacan's work at this time did not go over well with *Tel Quel*, for it had more and more recourse to the Lacanian subject as it turned to China and broke with the PCF. See Roudinesco, *Jacques Lacan & Co.*, 540–42.

respective journals and in the French and foreign press, it reached a climax at Cluny II, where *Change* was joined by *Action Poétique*, edited by Henri Deluy.

A heated polemic, which began in none other than *L'Humanité*, had taken place between *Tel Quel* and Faye in the winter of 1969. In an article entitled "Le camarade 'Mallarmé'" [Comrade Mallarmé], Faye criticized Derrida's theses on the degradation (*abaissement*) of writing in the light of Heidegger and the German extreme-right wing. He also objected to *Tel Quel*'s analogy between the debasing of *écriture* by *parole* and the repression of the proletariat by the bourgeoisie.[30] This "caricature of *Tel Quel*" was refuted by both Sollers and PCF militant Claude Prévost, who came to the rescue of *Tel Quel*, which he claimed was being accused of Nazi leanings just as it was forming an alliance with the Communist Party.[31] Obviously at stake in this polemic was intellectual hegemony on the Left. Both *Tel Quel* and *Change* were vying for the attention of the PCF. *Tel Quel*, which had been attacked in the "bourgeois press" for its adherence to the PCF, was now also the target of defamation in *L'Humanité*.[32] By virtue of their publication in the PCF daily, Faye's statements were "vested with a political authority" (100). The attacks on Derrida inevitably touched the heart of *Tel Quel*; as we saw in Chapter 3, Derridian deconstruction became an essential ingredient of *Tel Quel*'s materialist gnoseology. The polemic over Derrida continued at Cluny II. As for "Comrade Mallarmé," who had served as the pretext for Faye's criticism of Derrida and *Tel Quel*, he too was one of the stakes of the *Change–Tel Quel* controversy. Faye repeatedly claimed that he had joined *Tel Quel* because of a common passion for Mallarmé (positioned against Sartre), a passion shared by Sollers, Derrida, and Kristeva. Faye supposedly left *Tel Quel* because he did not get along with Kristeva (this assertion was

30. Faye, "Le camarade 'Mallarmé,'" *L'Humanité*, 12 September 1969, 5. See also his "Mise à point" in the October 10 issue of the same paper. In an interview I conducted with him on 30 May 1979, Faye maintained that the first time the Telquelians met with the *Nouvelle Critique* intellectuals in 1967, who had used the naive and consenting Houdebine to initiate a dialogue with the bourgeois avant-garde, Sollers adopted the most hard-line Marxist line, in an effort to dispel the bourgeois nature of *Tel Quel*. Faye was amused when Sollers supposedly made the following analogy that overcast the *Tel Quel–Nouvelle Critique* encounters from Cluny I to II: the debasing of *écriture* by *parole* is analogous with the repression of the proletariat by the bourgeoisie!

31. See the responses of Prévost and Sollers in "*L'Humanité* 19-9-1969: 'Camarade' et Camarade," *Tel Quel* 39 (Autumn 1969): 100–103. See also "Tel Quel," *Tel Quel* 40 (Winter 1970): 100–104 and "Vérité d'une marchandise: le bluff 'Change,'" *Tel Quel* 43 (Autumn 1970): 77–93.

32. Sollers, "*L'Humanité*, 19-9-1969," 100.

made by a number of Telquelians whom I interviewed); in any case, he thought very little of her linguistic expertise and did not share her negative appraisal of Noam Chomsky's work. At Cluny II, Mitsou Ronat and Roudinesco—both of the *Change–Action Poétique* group—attacked the linguistic and philosophical work of Kristeva and Derrida respectively. Faye claims that *Tel Quel* subsequently broke with *La Nouvelle Critique* because it failed to censor Ronat for her polemic against Kristeva.[33] Roudinesco supports this view. According to her account, the *Nouvelle Critique* agreed to censor Ronat (in effect, they did not, as Ronat's presentation was published in *La Nouvelle Critique*) after Sollers threatened to "withdraw his troops" from the colloquium. Roudinesco contends that the editors of *La Nouvelle Critique* then decided to sever relations with *Tel Quel*.[34] *Tel Quel*'s position at Cluny II certainly was no longer the enviable one it had held two years prior.

The opening presentation by Francis Cohen, the editor of *La Nouvelle Critique*, clearly revealed what was at stake for *Tel Quel* at Cluny II. Feeling compelled to justify the privileged position once again occupied by literature at the gathering, Cohen stated that "literature . . . is becoming more than ever the key sector of ideological debates. The themes encountered in literature, its capacity for affecting a broad and decisive public, the intersection it represents more and more for various disciplines, these are no doubt a few reasons for its social impact."[35] These opening remarks could not have pleased *Tel Quel* more as it set its eyes on the prize: the conquest of intellectual hegemony. Cohen's remarks were right in line with the premises of *Théorie d'Ensemble*. Cohen also implicitly acknowledged the strategic position *Tel Quel* had held at Cluny I when he stated that the former gathering on "Linguistics and Literature" had been organized "in a period of systematic—even inflationist—valorization of the processes of structural linguistics, at a moment when an alleged structuralism was readily proposed as the relay of dialectical materialism which was supposedly historically surpassed" ("Le sens d'un colloque" 7).

In an attempt to preserve its already precarious position at the vanguard of revolutionary aesthetic practice, *Tel Quel* kept attacking surrealism at Cluny. In fact, the presentations by Sollers, Houdebine ("Le 'Concept'

33. Interview with Faye, Paris, 30 May 1979.
34. Roudinesco, *Jacques Lacan & Co.*, 540.
35. Francis Cohen, "Le sens d'un colloque," Paper presented at the colloquium "*Littérature et idéologies*" (Cluny II, 2–4 April 1970), *La Nouvelle Critique*, special number 39a (1970): 7.

d'écriture automatique: sa signification et sa fonction dans le discours idéologique d'André Breton"), and Pierre Rottenberg ("Breton et le spiritualisme de Valéry"), and the discussions that ensued were so antisurrealist that Henri Deluy, the editor of *Action Poétique*, was prompted to ask why there was such a need on the part of *Tel Quel* and its supporters (for example, Houdebine, Scarpetta) to attack surrealism—and particularly surrealism reduced to a mere ideology. Perhaps because, as Robert Hefner perceptively notes, *Tel Quel*'s own ideology at this time depended on its critique of surrealism.[36]

In a very general presentation, inspired by Houdebine's "André Breton et la double ascendance du signe," published in *La Nouvelle Critique* (February 1970), Sollers claims that it is not necessary to dispense with the notion of the avant-garde. Having said this, he immediately begins to criticize Breton for his Hegelianism, his Jungian deviation from Freud, and his notion of automatic writing. In his Cluny presentation, Houdebine does a Derridian deconstruction of Breton's notion of automatic writing, showing how he failed to grasp the materialist subject operating in the Freudian relationship between language and the unconscious. As for Scarpetta ("Brecht et la Chine"), he attempts to show how Artaud had a more materialist slant on the Orient than Brecht. What is making its way into these presentations by Telquelians—in addition to their obvious attacks on Breton's idealism—is the notion of a materialist subject and the connection with China that allowed *Tel Quel* to break with the PCF a year later. In fact, at the Cerisy Colloquium of 29 June–9 July 1972, entitled "Towards A Cultural Revolution: Artaud and Bataille" and organized by *Tel Quel*, the works of these dissident surrealists were read in the light of the Chinese Cultural Revolution.

Although both Sollers and Houdebine criticize Breton for failing to relinquish his idealist "flightiness," they nevertheless recognize a materialist gnoseology at work in Artaud and Bataille. In fact, in the issue (no. 34) devoted to May 1968, *Tel Quel* strategically positions Bataille against Breton. Sollers's offensive against Breton in "La grande méthode" is supported by Bataille's hitherto unpublished response to Breton's attacks against him in the *Second Manifesto*, which appears in the same issue. Suleiman claims that by promoting Bataille as a counterexample to Breton in no. 34, *Tel Quel* "may already have inscribed its individualistic turn of 1980, with its insistence on the 'experience of writing' [she refers to inner experi-

---

36. See Hefner, "The *Tel Quel* Ideology."

ence] onto its revolutionary Marxist politics of the late 1960s and early 1970s."[37] While she is correct about the direction *Tel Quel* was taking, her statement does not account for the fact that both Bataille and Artaud were with *Tel Quel* from the beginning—as were Aragon and Breton. As Foucault had pointed out at Cerisy, Bataille was already at the heart of the *Tel Quel* experience in 1962. Artaud's "Chiote à l'esprit" [Shit to the spirit], a brilliant attack on Western idealism, and particularly its traces in surrealism and Marxism, appeared in the third issue of *Tel Quel*. The text not only prefigures *Tel Quel*'s political positions of 1971, but also allows us to understand how Artaud would be set against the mainstream surrealists (especially Breton), in the same way that Maoism would be used against the PCF.[38]

Faye claims that Sollers was trying to assume all the contradictory surrealist roles: he wanted to be the avant-garde pope (Breton), the intellectual at the head of a mass movement serving as a resonance chamber (Aragon), and the dissident who refuses to play the game (Bataille).[39] Whether or not we agree with Faye's characterization of Sollers—situated in the wake of his break with *Tel Quel*—it becomes apparent, if we look at the *Tel Quel* texts of these years, that Sollers and other Telquelians were trying to avoid the gridlock represented by Breton and Aragon.

Theory became a tactical arm for *Tel Quel* and its affiliates in its attempt to distinguish its enterprise from that of surrealism. The theoretical attacks against surrealism came not only from Telquelians such as Sollers, Pleynet, and Rottenberg, but also from PCF militants like Houdebine and Scarpetta. In fact, Houdebine became one of the most outspoken critics of surrealism in both *La Nouvelle Critique* and *Tel Quel*. Years later, Houdebine admitted that he had been too hard on Breton, even though he did not think highly of him—after all, Joyce was a thousand times more important—but this had been necessary because of the historical moment. *Tel Quel*'s enemies kept bringing up surrealism to discredit their avant-garde enterprise:

> It was like for the trains of the SNCF [Société nationale des chemins de fer français (National Society of French Railroads)]. One avant-garde can hide another. At level crossings, you see, "Warning! One train can hide another." They kept sticking this old avant-garde under

37. Suleiman, "As Is," 1015–16.
38. Texts by and on Artaud were published in *Tel Quel* 3, 15, 22, 30, 35, 39, 40, 46, and 81. Two special issues were devoted to Artaud: 20 (which contained Derrida's first essay to be published in *Tel Quel*, "La parole soufflée") and 52 (with Kristeva's "Le sujet en procès").
39. Interview with Faye, 30 May 1979.

us. We kept saying the avant-garde isn't them; it's us. It was a way of clearing the track. That's why we kept bringing up Breton, Aragon.[40]

Tel Quel had to keep proving to everyone that it was not repeating an experience that had not only failed in its attempts to be both aesthetically and politically revolutionary, but had also come "to be regarded as an 'elitist' artistic movement that owed its continued existence to the support of the very bourgeoisie it claimed to detest."[41] *Tel Quel* did not want to appear as an elitist literary current just as it was setting up an alliance with Communist intellectuals and their cultural apparati. This could explain to some degree the hard-line language—Faye calls it Stalinist—they adopted in their manifestos and texts during this period. It could also explain their "unconditional" support of the party during and after May: "Once again we manifest here our support of the working-class party line."[42]

In the issue devoted to May 1968 where *Tel Quel* professes its support for the party while nonetheless affirming the importance of its textual activity, Sollers's text, "La grande méthode," analyzes the relationship between intellectuals and the revolution from the 1920s to the 1960s, that is, from surrealism to *Tel Quel*. Sollers quotes Brecht to define the "great method" as the practical knowledge that is gained from alliances and ruptures, formations, and dissociations of groups, and that makes action possible. Given the historical moment, *Tel Quel* must act. And it must form alliances: it sides with the PCF instead of the student movement. In so doing, once again it stands opposed not only to its old rival in the intellectual field—Sartre—but also to surrealism. Much has already been said on the surrealist dimensions of the situationists and the May movement, which we shall not enter into here.[43] *Tel Quel* contests the spiritualistic deviation of surrealism along with the "teleologico-transcendental, humanist and psychologist mystification" ("La Révolution ici maintenant") of engagement, and does so by means of a "real, theoretical depth: the complex, differentiated, mortal war between idealism and materialism."[44] Citing Althusser, Sollers states, "The entire class struggle can sometimes be summarized in the struggle of one word for another" ("La grande méthode" 27). For Sollers, "the historical necessity of

---

40. Houdebine, interview of 23 June 1987.
41. Suleiman, "As Is," 1016.
42. "Remarques," *Tel Quel* 37 (Spring 1969): 103.
43. Even Houdebine acknowledges the impact of surrealism on May 1968. See "André Breton et la double ascendance du signe," *La Nouvelle Critique* 31 (February 1970): 43.
44. Sollers, "La grande méthode," *Tel Quel* 34 (Summer 1968): 22.

the connection between revolutionary intellectual practice and the struggle of the proletariat has to be thought out at this real, theoretical depth: the complex, differentiated, mortal war between idealism and materialism" (22). Before we dismiss Sollers's remarks as ludicrous, let us see what he is attempting to do here. Sollers has to justify why *Tel Quel* is not pro-May and why it is pro-Communist (not that Sollers ever joined the party!). But even more important, he has to show how the revolutionary textual practice of the *Tel Quel* group is involved with the class struggle. The word "action" is crucial here. The seven-point program of "La Révolution ici maintenant" begins with the following phrase:

> The action which is exercised by and through us being here and now textual, that is, having its own particular rules which it is not a question of suspending or neglecting; this action having its own efficacy, even though bound up with the social struggle whose primacy is not, for that matter, questioned (we politically participate without ambiguities) . . . (3)

Although this phrase establishes a link between *Tel Quel*'s textual action and the class struggle, it clearly favors the former. In "La grande méthode," Sollers establishes a relationship between textual action and the class struggle via the theoretical contest between idealism and materialism. In fact, Sollers's attacks on the idealism of Breton are judiciously reinforced by Bataille's claims in "La 'vieille taupe' et le préfixe *sur* dans les mots *surhomme* et *surréaliste*" that Breton's idealism lies in the fact that he thinks he can be independent of the class struggle. Now Sollers claims that *Tel Quel* is active in the class struggle, even though he defends the specificity (and thus autonomy) of its theory and practice of writing.

To justify the tenuous position of the group in 1968, Sollers symptomatically denigrates Breton's *Légitime Défense* [Legitimate defense], published in September 1926 in response to Pierre Naville's attacks against surrealism in *La Révolution et les Intellectuels. Que peuvent faire les surréalistes?* [Revolution and intellectuals: What can surrealists do?] The previous year, the surrealists had signed a common declaration with the *Clarté* group entitled "The Revolution First and Always." Should there be any doubt about the quasi-identical wording of this declaration and *Tel Quel*'s, let us also note in passing that Sollers quotes heavily from Marx's *Eighteenth Brumaire*, as though he were desperately trying to convince himself that if the first time had been a tragedy, the second time would not be a farce. With his critique from within, Naville was not exactly facilitating the alliance with the Communists, even though he was forcing the surrealists to take a position, that is, encouraging them to forgo individual liberation in the name of revolutionary class struggle. Although Breton reiterates his adhesion in principle to the party, he minimizes its importance by stating that the Communists do not have a monopoly on revolution. The materialistic orientation of the party is not necessarily the only path to liberation. Breton nevertheless states that he supports the proletariat and hopes that they come to power. But in the meantime, "It is no less necessary that the experiences of inner life be pursued and, of course, without any external control even Marxist."[45] Sollers criticizes Breton for his desire ultimately to defend the autonomy of the surrealist experience and to keep it free of Marxist control. It would appear that *Tel Quel*, on the other hand, is unconditionally in support of the party. In a sense, it is. But, like Breton, it firmly believes in the revolutionary potential of its own practice. *Tel Quel* can afford to take strong positions with respect to the party; in effect, it has nothing to lose, for it has only gambled on a theoretical terrain. In fact, *Tel Quel*'s positions are not substantially different from Breton's except that *Tel Quel* has the bias of theory to demarcate itself from him.

The "detour through theory," provided by Althusser, placed the Telquelians in an advantageous position. They could thus claim that their struggle was on two fronts: "the specific front of artistic, theoretical and scientific practice: utilization of 'the organizational autonomy' of the avant-garde; the political front: assuming our place *at the side of* the masses in the struggle they lead against the bourgeois order and its accomplices."[46] To assimilate these fronts would be, as Henric had pointed out, to adopt Stalinist or revisionist stances. The emphasis on the autonomy of the superstructure empowered intellectuals into believing that their work against the bourgeois order was effective in cultural renewal and social change. Bourgeois society was a complex, structured entity that should be attacked at all levels.[47] *Tel Quel*'s work was at the level of signifying practice, and, particularly, textual practice that ran counter to the representative bias of both (realist) bourgeois literature and traditional (economist) Marxism. If literature did not necessarily reflect the exploitative nature of relations of production in advanced

---

45. André Breton, "Légitime Défense," in *Oeuvres Complètes* (Paris: Gallimard, 1992), 2:292.
46. "Le dogmatisme à la rescousse du révisionnisme," *Tel Quel* 48–49 (Spring 1972): 190.
47. Henric, "Pour une avant-garde révolutionnaire," 59.

capitalist society and thus had a transformational potential of its own, Telquelians could, in good faith, claim that they were working against the bourgeois order and, consequently, that they were supporting the masses in the class struggle. To support this belief, it was essential for them to emphasize the autonomy of the superstructure and the importance of theory in the class struggle. While defending the "organizational autonomy of the avant-garde," their interest in Marxism was guided by the importance of the intellectual in social change and the revolutionary specificity of his work. This explains *Tel Quel*'s attraction to the Marxism of Althusser, Antonio Gramsci, and Mao Tse-tung.

Tel Quel published two texts on Gramsci: Jacqueline Risset's "Lecture de Gramsci" [A reading of Gramsci] (no. 42) and Maria-Antonietta Macciocchi's "Pour Gramsci" (no. 54), excerpted from the book *Pour Gramsci* [For Gramsci] published in Collection Tel Quel in 1974. Macciocchi permitted *Tel Quel* to read Gramsci from the perspective of May 1968 and the Chinese Cultural Revolution. She played a strategic role in *Tel Quel*'s break with the PCF in 1971 when her book, *De La Chine* [On/Of China], was banned at the annual Communist cultural festival, "La Fête de l'Humanité," held in September of that year. Sollers was one of the first to defend her in a letter published in *Le Monde* on 11 September 1971, in which he indicated that the book was not only important for its account of the Chinese Cultural Revolution, but also for its theoretical analysis (of Marxism). Sollers refused to attend the festival as he had in previous years as an invited guest of the PCF, now that the party had banned the Italian Communist's book. Macciocchi later claimed that had it not been for Sollers's immediate denunciation in *Le Monde*, the affair would have been suffocated.[48] Instead, an incredible polemic took place in France. Letters and commentary by leading intellectuals appeared in such newspapers and journals as *Le Monde*, *L'Humanité*, *La Nouvelle Critique*, *Tel Quel*, *France Nouvelle*, *Promesse*, and *Cahiers du Cinema*.[49] The publication of the book created an uproar in both the French and Italian Communist parties. The Italian left-wing publisher Feltrinelli, judging the affair to be an important one for what it had to say about repression in European Communist parties, published the key

48. Maria-Antonietta Macciocchi, "Réponse à 'La Nouvelle Critique': De la Nouvelle Critique ou des racines de la sinophobie occidentale," *Tel Quel* 48–49 (Spring 1972): 85.

49. For a summary of the polemic, see Macciocchi's "Réponse à 'la Nouvelle Critique,'" 71–101. See also Macciocchi, *Polemiche sulla Cina* (Milan: Feltinelli, 1972).

texts of the controversy in *Polemiche sulla Cina* [Polemics on China] in its Libelli collection in 1972.

Although the clamor in France was greater, the PCI (Italian Communist Party) did take its own measures: in 1972, it did not allow Macciocchi to run for reelection as a Communist deputy of Naples-Caserta. Macciocchi left for France to assume a teaching post in the Department of Sociology at the University of Paris VIII (Vincennes), where from 1972 to 1973 she taught a seminar on Gramsci. Sollers once again defended her in 1973 when, under orders from the minister of the interior (Macciocchi was a foreigner!), the Department of Sociology at Vincennes refused to renew her teaching appointment because of a seminar that she had taught on Gramsci. Macciocchi was once again the target of xenophobia, this time not because of Sinophobia (although she did make connections between the Chinese Cultural Revolution and Gramsci in her seminars and in *Pour Gramsci*), but because of her already problematic status as a dissident Communist emphasizing the relevance of Gramscian theory for a socialist revolution in Western Europe at the experimental Vincennes in the wake of May! And the revolution she was promoting was one that both the French and Italian Communist Parties had failed to achieve in their revisionist turn toward "the common program" and "the historic compromise."[50] This heretical Communist was a brilliant journalist: she had edited two journals, *Noi Donne* and *Vie nuove* of the PCI, of which she had been a militant member since 1942. For years, she insisted on renewing her PCI card while nonetheless continuing to protest from within. She had already created a stir in 1969 with the publication of her *Lettere dall'interno del PCI* [Letters from within the PCI], where she attacked the incompetence and corruption of the party that she witnessed as deputy-elect of Naples-Caserta (she served from 1968 to 1972).[51] In 1977, Macciocchi was excluded from the PCI for her outspoken criticism of the historical compromise that led her to sign the 4 July 1977 Manifesto Against Repression in Italy, along with Félix Guattari, Deleuze, Sartre, and other French intellectuals, and to participate in the National Convention Against Repression, which took place 23–25 September 1977 in the Communist-run city of Bologna.[52] Macciocchi played a key role in getting Sollers and other

50. After another polemic, she was reinstated at Vincennes. The polemic is detailed in the concluding chapter of her *Pour Gramsci* (Paris: Seuil, 1974).

51. For an interesting account of Macciocchi's life, see Guido Quaranta's "Quell'eretica di Maria" in *Panorama* (16 August 1977): 38.

52. She describes her break with the PCI in *Après Marx, Avril*, which had a preface by Leonardo Sciascia and was published by Seuil in 1978.

Telquelians to break first with the PCF, and then (along with the new philosophers) with Eurocommunism in the mid- and late 1970s.

Macciocchi's *De La Chine* was published by Seuil one month after the Italian *Dalla Cina* (May 1971) appeared. The French title has a "striking bivalence"[53] that is lacking in the original Italian, which begins to account for the immediate uproar the book provoked in France. Macciocchi is not only writing a book about her trip to China in October–December 1970 (although she went to China on a personal invitation, as a Communist deputy-elect her trip was approved by the PCI); she is also expressing her views on the Chinese Cultural Revolution and its implications for Western Europe at a time when Eurocommunism is still operating in the shadows of the Soviet Union. Macciocchi was criticized by both the PCF and PCI for her pro-China positions (in response to pressure from the PCUS [Communist Party of the Soviet Union]; even the PCI judged her book on the Chinese Cultural Revolution too enthusiastic and acritical), but the polemic in France reached dramatic proportions as the PCF revealed itself to be as intransigent as ever. The Chinese Cultural Revolution had ben plaguing the pro-Soviet PCF for a number of years, particularly in 1968 when the conflict between the Soviet Union and China was at its peak and when many participants in the May movement were pro-China.[54] Little wonder that the PCF had kept its distance from the May movement. Or that *Tel Quel* had downplayed its interest in China.

Tel Quel's fascination with the Chinese Cultural Revolution began prior to May 1968. In the Fall 1967 issue (no. 31) of *Tel Quel*, a brief note read: "China disturbs the West. Godard produces *La Chinoise*, where one can see Francis Jeanson overlook a remark of the type: '*L'Humanité* and *Le Figaro* are now one and the same'" (94). Nevertheless, *Tel Quel* did not heed the implications of this remark until 1970–71. As fellow travelers of the PCF until 1971, Telquelians for the most part suppressed their interest in the Chinese Cultural Revolution. *Tel Quel*'s Maoist positions were only proclaimed in June 1971, when it violently broke with the PCF, accusing the latter of revisionism.[55] Kristeva maintained that a major consequence of May 1968 was to accelerate the revisionism of the PCF, leading to a general social-democratization of French society.[56] But May also prompted *Tel Quel*

53. See "Nota dell'Editore," in Macciocchi's *Polemiche sulla Cina*, 6.
54. Massimo Teodori, *Storia delle nuove sinistre in Europa (1956–1976)* (Bologna: Il Mulino, 1976), 385.
55. See "Positions du Movement de Juin 71," *Tel Quel* 47 (Fall 1971).
56. Kristeva, "My Memory's Hyperbole," 273.

to recognize the revisionism of the party during the events of 1968, and thus the enigmatic positions they themselves had held at that time.

On a cultural level, *Tel Quel* fully grasped the implications of May. For their work prior to 1968 was, in many respects, what May epitomized. Patrick Rotman, one of the two authors of *Génération, les années de rêve*, contended, "Anti-Communism was the most solid acquisition of 68! That generation ended up discovering that life is not changed by politics but by culture."[57] May confirmed what *Tel Quel* had known all along. And yet, for a brief moment, *Tel Quel* was led astray by theory and let politics attain the upper hand. Thus Sollers's and Kristeva's retrospective regrets about the excessive importance they had attributed to theory during the late 1960s, and the problematic mirage that had ensued.

Tel Quel's "official" break with the PCF was declared in an ultra hard-line declaration entitled "Positions du Mouvement de Juin 71," published in a special issue devoted to fellow traveler and mentor, Roland Barthes (no. 47).[58] The declaration was supposedly made in response to the PCF's censoring of Macciocchi's *De La Chine*, which had come out in June. The tone of the declaration is already revealed in the *Tel Quel* epigraph taken from Mao Tse-tung: "A mortal combat has been declared between the new culture and reactionary cultures" (2). Apparently, *Tel Quel* mimicked the Chinese Cultural Revolution to the hilt: there were "dazibaos" posted all over the walls of the *Tel Quel* premises at Rue Jacob.[59] There was much tension among the editorial board members, evident in the declaration that continually refers to "two lines" in conflict at *Tel Quel*: one, dogmatic-revisionist (pro-PCF), and the other, revolutionary (pro-China). The "Positions" are followed by a "Chronology" of the *Tel Quel* years 1960–71 retrospectively—and opportunistically—viewed in terms of this conflict. The excessive tone of these two texts clearly reveals that there is an ideologico-tactical struggle taking place and that the editorial board is anything but unanimous in its positions. Furthermore, *Tel Quel* is under attack from both the "bourgeois" and the Communist press. It must find a theoretical means to combat this double-headed (capitalist-revisionist) en-

57. Patrick Rotman interviewed by Chantal De Rudder in "Une seule solution la révolution," *Le Nouvel Observateur* (6–12 March 1987): 47.

58. *Tel Quel* even published four issues of *Tel Quel–Mouvement de Juin 71—Informations* from 15 March to 1 October 1972. The *Bulletin* was edited by Pleynet.

59. From interviews with Thibaudeau (19 May 1979) and Faye (30 May 1979). See also Thibaudeau's *Mes années "Tel Quel."* For a critique of *Tel Quel*'s revolutionary jargon, see Henri Meschonnic's *Pour la poétique II* (Paris: Gallimard, 1973).

emy. It is no longer supported by any external political institution that can legitimate its so-called revolutionary "turn to the left." Placed in a vulnerable position, it must consolidate and defend itself. The statements justifying *Tel Quel*'s alliance with the PCF during May 1968 seem tame compared to the excessive sloganism needed for the break:

> Down with the corrupt bourgeoisie! Down with filthy revisionism! Down with the binarism of the super-powers! Long live *De la Chine*! Long live revolutionary China! Long live the thought of Mao Tsetung!" (135)

Outraged by the excessive nature of the "movement" and for being excluded, as editorial committee members, from the decision-making process (which they claimed was essentially in the hands of Pleynet and Sollers), Ricardou and Thibaudeau left *Tel Quel* at this time.[60] Thibaudeau decided to join the PCF (which he apparently failed to tell *Tel Quel*), to the dismay of Houdebine, Henric, and Scarpetta, who were abandoning it for *Tel Quel*. A few months earlier (March 1971), the controversial writer and Communist Pierre Guyotat, whose novel *Eden Eden Eden* had been censored on obscenity charges by the minister of the interior in October 1970 (a decision subsequently appealed by hundreds of writers, artists, politicians, and teachers), had declared in *La Nouvelle Critique* that "*Tel Quel* and the party are the two sites where for the first time I found interlocutors."[61] The

60. See Ricardou's letters of explanation in *La Quinzaine Littéraire*, 1 December 1971, 31, and 1 January 1972, 31, and *Les Lettres Françaises*, 15 December 1971. In his letter of resignation, Ricardou claims that beginning with an internal crisis in 1967, the editorial committee of *Tel Quel* met less and less regularly (two or three times a year by 1971) and that decisions were essentially made by the two appointed "permanents" at Seuil, Sollers and Pleynet. In Thibaudeau, *Mes Années "Tel Quel,"* 212–13. Thibaudeau's letters are reprinted in *Mes Années "Tel Quel."* Both objected to what they conceived to be ideological justifications for tactical measures.

61. *Eden. Eden, Eden* had been prefaced by Barthes, Sollers, and Michel Leiris. Among those who denounced the act of censorship were then Prime Minister François Mitterand in *Le Monde* of 26 November 1970, Aragon's *Les Lettres Françaises* of 4 November 1970, Christine Glucksmann in *L'Humanité* of 19 November 1970, Claude Simon in *Le Monde* of 2 December (who had even resigned from the Médicis jury where he was severely criticized after expressing his wish to vote for Guyotat). A petition in favor of Guyotat was initiated by Jérôme Lindon who compared the censoring of *Eden, Eden, Eden* to the ones of *Madame Bovary* and *Les Fleurs du mal*. The petition was initially signed by twenty-four writers and intellectuals, including Barthes, Beauvoir, Sartre, Simon, Derrida, Duras, Foucault, Pleynet, Robbe-Grillet, Sollers, Thibaudeau, François Wahl, and Kateb Yacine. Hundreds of others subsequently signed the petition (e.g., Aragon, Blanchot, Bertrand Blier, *Cahiers du Cinema*, Italo Calvino, Antoine

possibility of being militant in the party and modern in art, envisioned briefly also by Houdebine, Scarpetta, and Henric, was over; it was an either-or (the Party or *Tel Quel*) situation now. Guyotat, Henric, Houdebine, and Scarpetta left the PCF in 1972. Party dogmatico-revisionism was being abandoned for a Parisian "literal" revolution: *Tel Quel*, in fact, equated its "great proletarian literal revolution" (no. 38) with the Chinese Cultural Revolution!

Tel Quel positions its avant-garde struggle in relation to the Chinese Cultural Revolution, Maoist thought, and May 1968 in France. In its June 1971 Declaration, it seeks to rectify its previous misreading of May—in accordance with Macciocchi, for whom "May '68 confirms Gramsci's thesis according to which a massive ideological struggle which breaches the hegemonic bloc of the bourgeoisie is not only possible but also victorious even if the bourgeoisie remains in power."[62] Insofar as it constitutes a moment of the cultural revolution, intellectual and moral transformation takes place at two different times: not only after the working class is in power, but also during the preparatory phase that will bring it to power. Given the importance that Gramsci gives to superstructures, it is possible, Macciocchi claims, to demolish bourgeois ideology from within. In accordance with the importance that both Gramsci and Mao attribute to the role of ideology in the class struggle, *Tel Quel* keeps emphasizing its role as an active instrument for the transformation of ideology. Because of the important role of ideological struggle in the preparatory phase of the socialist revolution, *Tel Quel* can now afford to take a certain distance from the party and the masses. This is certainly not what Gramsci and Mao are advocating, but attacking the PCF for its dogmatism, bourgeois revisionism, and Stalinism (not that *Tel Quel*'s critique is not on target) allows *Tel Quel* to sever a

---

Casanova, Claude Chabrol, Cixous, Henri-Georges Clouzot, Julio Cortazar, Pierre Daix, Marc Devade, Serge Doubrovsky, all the professors of the Department of Letters at Vincennes, Genet, Glissant, Jean-Joseph Goux, Henric, Denis Hollier, Anne-Marie and Jean-Louis Houdebine, Luce Irigaray, Joseph Kessel, Pierre Klossowski, Kristeva, Le Clézio, Violette Leduc, Joyce Mansour, Albert Memmi, Henri Meschonnic, François Mitterand, Ariane Mnouchkine, Jacques Monod, Pier Paolo Pasolini, Jacques Prévert, Claude Prévost, *Promesse*, *La Quinzaine Littéraire*, Alain Resnais, Jean-François Revel, Ricardou, Denis Roche, Sanguineti, Scarpetta, *Tel Quel*, Todorov, *Union des Ecrivains*, Jean Vilar). These petitions appeared in *Le Monde* on 8–9 and 11 November 1970. Texts by Pierre Guyotat appeared in *Tel Quel* 36 (an extract from *Eden, Eden, Eden)*; 43 (an interview with Thérèse Réveillé refused by *Le Monde* and *La Quinzaine Littéraire*); 45 (an analysis of the censoring of *Eden, Eden, Eden*); and 63. See also Guyotat's *Littérature interdite* (Paris: Gallimard, 1972).

62. Macciocchi, *Pour Gramsci* (Paris: Seuil, 1974), 18.

problematic alliance that has led it to assume counterrevolutionary positions, despite the theoretical and political gains they acknowledge having
made. *Tel Quel* finally concedes that their silence over the 1968 Soviet
invasion of Czechoslovakia was an error. It also confesses to having misread
the Chinese Revolution because it adhered to the petit bourgeois and
ouvriériste slant of a party that was also dogmatist. They had failed to realize
that dogmatism and revisionism are not necessarily contradictory. Together,
they lead to the same goal: the depoliticization of the masses, ideological
sclerosis, and the restoration of capitalism.[63] The June 1971 movement
contends that, from 1966 to 1970, too much was sacrificed to a right-wing,
opportunistic line of the consolidation of revisionism. In light of Macciocchi's
positions, *Tel Quel* opposes the Chinese Cultural Revolution to the revisionism and economism of European Communist parties as they attempt to gain
power through a politics of alliance, be it the "historic compromise" of the
PCI or the "common program" of the PCF. In criticizing the economist line
of the PCF, *Tel Quel* appears to share the same reservations that Breton had
in *Légitime défense*. And it is easy to understand why. The revisionist slant
of the PCF obviously places *Tel Quel* in a less than advantageous position.
To those critics who claim that *Tel Quel* overestimates the ideological
dimension of the revolution, the movement replies that their critique is based
on the separation between the infrastructure and superstructure on which
the dogmatism-revisionism of the PCF depends. By accusing the PCF of
economism, dogmatism, and revisionism, *Tel Quel* does indeed appear
revolutionary, for it is abandoning an alliance that is not only Stalinist, but
even bourgeois! Although the movement claims that it will continue with
alliances so long as its positions are not censored, it does state emphatically
that it will deal with its alliances without any intermediary taking its place
("Positions du mouvement de Juin 71" 140).

If *Tel Quel* is still able to assume revolutionary posturings in its break with
the party, what about its already ambiguous relationship with the masses?
The June 1971 movement specifies a struggle between two lines: that is,
"between a petit bourgeois line (in the service of the bourgeoisie and
revisionism) and a revolutionary line (in the immediate service, although in
the long term, of the proletariat)" (136). *Tel Quel* is evidently focusing more
on the preparatory phase leading to the takeover of power by the proletariat,
and thus on the important role it thinks it can play in attacking bourgeois
ideology from within. This is obviously a limited reading of both Mao and

---

63. "Positions du mouvement de Juin 71," 136–37.

Gramsci, but a convenient one for the group. The movement contests the pretension of dogmatic revisionist intellectuals claiming to represent the proletariat (141). It even pities those intellectuals, who, in good faith, think that they are supporting the masses, all the while condoning revisionism and thus supporting the bourgeoisie (138). It finally asks revolutionary intellectuals to combat this mystification by assuming responsibility for their specific work (141). *Tel Quel* is already beginning to look for a way out of the intellectual-masses dichotomy inherent both in engagement and the avant-gardes.

In choosing the Chinese Cultural Revolution over PCF "revisionism" in June 1971, *Tel Quel* was actually recognizing the legacy of May as a cultural one. Although they claimed to be breaking with the PCF for theoretico-political reasons, in effect, Mao's brand of Marxism was more appealing in that it was more "cultural." Mao accorded tremendous importance to the "cultural" revolution, which *Tel Quel* equated with its own "textual" revolution, its work in the signifier. The Chinese Cultural Revolution recognized the importance of theoretical work. Furthermore, unlike Althusser's "process without a subject," Mao's theory of contradiction seemed to make room for a (Freudian) theory of the subject, for that subjectivity which May 1968 had brought to the forefront of social change. Mao appeared to emphasize ideology over politics, thereby giving Telquelians the impression that, in China, writers and artists had a leading role to play.

In "Pourquoi j'ai été chinois" [Why I was Chinese], published in *Tel Quel* in 1981 (no. 88), Sollers reveals how China represented *Tel Quel*'s break with the PCF in the wake of May. May was a cultural alternative to politics, which ultimately led *Tel Quel* back to literature as a personal experience after the deviation resulting from theory. "Our Maoism was an anti-organizational, anti-partisan antidote, a utopia in pure form, which had nothing to do with the sects of the Left (which were weary of us and rightly so)," wrote Kristeva in 1983.[64] In the spring of 1974, several Telquelians—François Wahl, Kristeva, Pleynet, Sollers, and Barthes (Lacan was also supposed to accompany them, but at the last moment, declined)—traveled to China.[65] Kristeva retrospectively noted that

---

64. Kristeva, "My Memory's Hyperbole," 273.

65. See the special issue "En Chine" *Tel Quel* 59 (Autumn 1974). See also Kristeva's *Des chinoises* (Paris: Editions des Femmes, 1974), Pleynet's *Le Voyage en Chine* (Paris: Hachette, 1980), and Barthes's "Alors, la Chine," in *Le Monde*, 24 May 1974, 1, 14.

it was impossible for me to make French intellectuals and my friends from Eastern Europe recognize that the China of the Cultural Revolution represented hope for national and libertarian socialism. For some of us, this gesture of friendship and adherence to the Chinese revolution was a way of associating with a left-wing political movement devoid of the Communist Party legacy. For others, such as myself, who were not interested in political discourse, it was a means of finding another set of social and historical roots for "internal experience."[66]

Clearly, both motivations reveal a break from Marxism, the latter more pronounced than the former. For the "Paris-Peking-Paris" travelers, "this arduous journey, one that from the onset was more cultural than political, definitively inaugurated a return to the only continent that we had never left: internal experience" (Kristeva, "My Memory's Hyperbole" 275). Sollers even conceded that it was literature (or personal experience) and not politics (or collective experience) that first aroused his interest in China. *Drame* (1965) was a "Chinese novel." A certain experience of writing brought Sollers to Chinese philosophy and poetry, to an interest in the disposition of the Chinese body with respect to language and writing, to Taoism.[67] Kristeva also admitted, "What we were looking for in the spasms of Chinese anti-bureaucratism at a moment when the party machinery had exploded and women, after the young, were suddenly pushed to the front line, was Taoist culture, Chinese writing, and poetry, like jade, bland but subtle.[68] Both Sollers and Kristeva were influenced by Joseph Needham's *Science and Civilization in China*. Needham convinced Kristeva that "Mao, poet and writer, was the most faithful modern version of ancestral Taoism." In short, "it was classical China, dressed in the worker's blue suit of socialism, that we had gone to find."[69]

Nevertheless, "the romantic vision of an insurrectional China, which invents an entirely different model for society, had to revert fatally to something that would become, in essence, a mere coloration of Soviet

66. Kristeva, "My Memory's Hyperbole," 274.
67. Sollers, "Pourquoi j'ai été chinois," *Tel Quel* 88 (Summer 1981): 11.
68. Kristeva, "My Memory's Hyperbole," 274.
69. Ibid., 275. The two special issues of *Tel Quel* on China (nos. 48–49 and 50) published in 1972 contained excerpts from Needham's "Time and Eastern Man." The first number juxtaposes essays on Chinese language and writing to the polemic surrounding Macciocchi's book and *Tel Quel*'s break with the PCF. The second number contains articles on contemporary China (politics, psychiatry, acupuncture, and so forth).

experience, which Chinese history itself confirmed."[70] And yet, by focusing on the cultural side of China, *Tel Quel* actually saved itself from another delusion when the political myth of China crumbled. Was the Chinese Revolution, in fact, a cultural one? If, at one point, *Tel Quel* promoted China, it was with the hope that China was indeed a cultural and not a political phenomenon. Was it possible to integrate a revolution of language into an active and militant revolution? China temporarily fostered this illusion for *Tel Quel*. But the revelation that this was impossible and that the avant-garde dream was illusory came not only from the realization that China was perhaps as oppressive as the Soviet Union but, perhaps more important, from *Tel Quel*'s inability to come to terms with May.[71]

May 1968 marked a turning point for *Tel Quel*. It made *Tel Quel* aware of "the lack of coincidence between culture, language, and action." As a result, it challenged the very basis of the avant-garde wager: transforming language and transforming society. In 1981, Sollers admitted:

> I had this utopian idea, that I no longer have, that revolution in language and revolution in action are two things that must necessarily go hand in hand. This idea came from the Surrealists and the Futurists. It represents the illusion of the twentieth-century avant-gardes, which must be completely abandoned, because it is an error to want everything to go at the same speed.[72]

During May 1968, *Tel Quel* was lured by the possibility of defending the specificity of its work while assuming politically correct positions. The seduction was fostered by the break between theory and practice, resulting from *Tel Quel*'s reading of Althusser, Gramsci, and China. It was the distinction between theory and practice that allowed *Tel Quel* to assume pro-PCF political positions during May. It was also the distinction between theory and politics that permitted *Tel Quel* to abandon the PCF for the Chinese Cultural Revolution and, finally, Marxism and politics altogether. In hindsight, *Tel Quel*'s political positions had little in common with its literary convictions. In effect, its theoretical work was closer to the practice of May than to the PCF.

---

70. Sollers, "Pourquoi j'ai été chinois," 13.
71. For a "belated" look at May, see Sollers's February 1970 preface, "Printemps rouge" to Thibaudeau's *Mai 1968 en France* published in Collection Tel Quel (Paris: Seuil, 1970).
72. Sollers, "Pourquoi j'ai été chinois," 13.

CHAPTER FIVE

THE ALIBI
OF DISSIDENCE

Dissidence, what a magnificent alibi!
We are all "dissidents."

—David Cooper

While French politicians and public officials were busy commemorating the bicentennial of the French Revolution in 1989, a heated controversy that had begun in the late 1970s with the crisis of the French Left—over whether the "Revolution was finished"—erupted again among historians, philosophers, and writers. As Wajda's *Danton* had all too clearly demonstrated in 1983, the French Revolution is anything but anachronistic: its historical impact is central to contemporary political battles. In his film, Wajda telescopes two distant historical periods, thereby managing to eliminate the one hundred fifty years that separate the French Revolution from Bolshevism, the trials of March 1794 from the Stalinist purges, the Jacobin committees from the Communist parties. Wajda's ideological juxtaposition generates the premise that the Revolution is finally understood once it is viewed through the interpretive lens of the twentieth-century events it supposedly produced.[1]

A number of French intellectuals—Régis Debray among them—continued to adhere to the belief that to defend the Revolution is to defend the essence of

1. See Furet, "Camarade Danton," *Le Nouvel Observateur* (14–20 January 1983): 56–57.

the Republic. In *Que Vive la République*, Debray lashed out provocatively against those who proclaimed that the Revolution was finished. For Debray, they were one and the same as those who had supported Pétain and the Occupation. Even more controversial were the statements of contenders of the opposite tendency—those who not only viewed the Terror as the necessary outcome of revolutionary ideology but also saw a logical historical evolution from the Terror to the concentration camps and the gulags of this century. In *Le Monde* of 6 January 1989, Jean-Marie Benoist (who had with fellow "nouveaux philosophes" André Glucksmann, Bernard-Henri Lévy, and Maurice Clavel made the cover page of *Time* magazine on 5 September 1977, under the title "Is Marx dead?") contended that "to want to kill all the members of a category without exception, here the aristocrats, later the Jews in the Third Reich, is the recurrent form of genocide."[2] Consequently, those willing to celebrate the Revolution were, in effect, defending a political logic leading to totalitarianism and death camps.

Clearly both groups were reading and interpreting the Revolution in relation to the crisis of the French Left in the 1970s and from a reexamination of eighteenth- and nineteenth-century notions such as progress, revolution, and the avant-garde. Both sets of interpretations were therefore subject to biases that situated the interpreters politically. Communists and Socialists adhered to the Jacobin ideal; former (dissident) Communists and neoliberals claimed that the origins of contemporary terrorism and totalitarianism were to be found in the Revolution. It thus came as no surprise to hear Sollers equate cultural repression and political terrorism with the Terror. At a colloquium entitled "Revolutions, 1889–1989" held at Columbia University in the spring of 1989, Sollers, the keynote speaker, dedicated his talk, entitled "Art and Revolutions—The Great Misunderstanding," to Salman Rushdie and freedom of expression. In a tone reminiscent of the dissident intellectual and human rights advocate that he was during the mid- and late 1970s, Sollers went on to trace the origins of modern terrorism—as exemplified by Khomeini and Iran's actions against Rushdie and the Western world—in the Terror of the French Revolution. Through the juxtaposition of a carefully orchestrated slide presentation (which went from Fragonard and David to Picasso) and a reading of revolutionary texts (posthumous texts by Saint-Just and entries from the diary of a noted guillotine executioner), which focused on the suppression of individual rights and associated sexual repression with political violence, there was no mistaking Sollers's

---

2. Jean-Marie Benoist, "Au nom des Lumières . . . ," *Le Monde*, 5 September 1977, 2.

intent: modern terrorism (and totalitarianism) has its undeniable roots in the French Revolution. As Laurent Dispot had demonstrated all too well a decade earlier in *La Machine à terreur* (1978)—a book for which Sollers himself had written the preface—"terror" (*la terreur*) is a distinctively French term, a neologism of the French Revolution.[3]

Sollers contended that in debating on the meaning of the French Revolution, political thinkers and historians lost sight of the real issue: the Terror. What perspective could writers and artists bring to an issue that had been systematically bypassed by politicians? Speaking from the gap that often separated artists and writers from social and historical movements, Sollers argued for judging revolutions (and counterrevolutions) from the perspective of art, the collective from the individual, the rule from the exception. Since the opposite had always been prescribed, why not reverse the perspective and make it cultural rather than political? Sollers's premise was that the notion of revolution-counterrevolution is opposed to the extreme freedom or individualization of human bodies and denies sexual *jouissance* (expressed by the art of Fragonard, but denied in the work of David, the official painter of the Revolution, who represents the enslavement of the artist). The art of David reveals how Jacobinism gave birth to statism and the repressive state.[4]

---

3. Laurent Dispot contends that "terreur" does not derive from the Latin "terror," which belongs to a vocabulary of emotions and not to a political vocabulary. See *La Machine à terreur* (Paris: Grasset, 1978; Le Livre de Poche, 1984), 18.

4. Sollers, "L'Art et les Révolutions: le grand malentendu," Sixth International Colloquium on Twentieth Century French Studies ("Revolutions, 1889–1989"), Columbia University, New York, 30 March 1989.

Sollers's talk at Columbia was actually the answer that he had not been able to give to an American socialite, the wife of a prominent banker, who at a "tout Paris" dinner had ventured to ask him whether he too was actively involved in the preparations for the bicentennial of the French Revolution. With typical Sollersian flourish he had replied, "But, Madam, I am not commemorating the Revolution, I am making it." Surprised, she merely answered, "Again?" Was Sollers making the revolution or further contributing to its demise? An American woman in the Columbia audience, asked "What was so revolutionary about showing women's asses?" Would she have been less disturbed to see the numerous figurines of the revolutionary greats on sale with the usual T-shirts of Paris in front of the Galeries Lafayette? After the presentation, French graduate students lamented the image of France that Sollers had projected and the departmental funds that had been lavished on such a speaker. (I remembered how those of us who were graduate students in the mid-1970s had made identical remarks about Lacan's visit to Columbia.) Whether Sollers was still making the revolution or merely personifying an aging conservative at the site of another failed revolution (Columbia), one thing was certain. He could still perturb and offend public opinion, as he had done in the late 1960s and early 1970s.

JE PARLE POUR DANS DIX SIECLES et je prends date
on peut me mettre en cabane

Tel Quel's ethical preoccupations of the mid-1970s coincide with what François Furet has called the end of the ideological era. According to Furet, "the Revolution is over." Sollers argues that Furet's *Penser la Révolution française* (1978) signals the end of the Left-Right era.[5] In this pivotal work, Furet establishes a line from the French Revolution to Bolshevism, from the Terror to twentieth-century Nazi and Stalinist camps. For Furet, the Revolution is over: the political worldview it generated and the camps of partisans and opponents it produced have disappeared.[6] (Did Furet foresee the end of the cold-war period, marked by the demolition of the Berlin Wall and the dissolution of Soviet hegemony in Eastern Europe?) A long revolutionary cycle has come to an end. Furet believes that ideological politics are finished, that is, "a specific set of ideas about human beings and the state and the notion that all that is needed in order to implement these ideas in reality is sufficient political will and the right political organization" (Berger, "The French Revolution" 56). What is implied is the sacrifice of the individual for the sake of the common good. For Furet, apocalyptic scenarios are no longer possible in today's society. The death of ideology in our postmodern age stems from the realization of what it leads to: the Terror, Auschwitz, and the gulag. Ideologies "entail and legitimize the coercion of human beings in aspects of their lives that have to be beyond the reach of political authority if freedom is to be preserved" (Berger, "The French Revolution" 58).

The ethical function of art is diametrically opposed to the ideological function of politics and society: "The conception of the ethical function of art separates us, in a radical way, from one that would commit art to serving as the representation of a so-called progressive ideology or an avant-garde socio-historical philosophy."[7] Similarly, dissidence does not represent an alternative, but rather a form of resistance to politics. Unlike the avant-garde, dissidence does not propose a social project or program. It is a negative ethics.[8] The demise of the avant-gardes in the 1970s is bound up with the crisis of Marxism and the revolutionary project. At the heart of the

---

on peut me rire au nez ça dépend de quel rire
JE PROVOQUE A L'AMOUR ET A LA
REVOLUTION
YES! I AM UN IMMENSE PROVOCATEUR
                    (Léo Ferré, "Le Chien")

5. Sollers, "Gauche, droite . . . ," 339.
6. Suzanne Berger, "The French Revolution in Contemporary French Politics," *French Politics and Society* 8, no. 2 (Spring 1990): 56.
7. Kristeva, *Revolution in Poetic Language*, 233.
8. Scarpetta, *Eloge du cosmopolitisme*, 197.

avant-garde project was the belief that society would evolve and follow suit. This belief was founded on the notion of progress and on the evolutionary myth contested by both the dissidents and the new philosophers.

Tel Quel's depoliticization (intended from Marxism) in the mid-1970s, represents, in effect, the successful coming together of its aesthetics and ethics. To a notion of literature conceived from a political perspective, which in the instances of postwar engagement and socialist realism equates with the subordination of literature to a political ideology, *Tel Quel* opposed an ethics stemming from the literary experience itself. Such an ethics is based on the premise that questions of political oppression and ideological totalitarianism are initially implanted "in the relation that each subject holds with his language and his culture, and with that which goes beyond them."[9] Ethics is therefore not to be intended as a prescriptive or coercive practice that relies on the notion of language as "common measure" and has the assurance of community cohesion as its major objective. Rather, it is an aesthetic experience associated with the explosion of limits, the transgression of identities, and the crossing of boundaries. What is implied by *Tel Quel*'s notions of "poetic language" and writing as an "experience of limits" is "that language, and thus sociability, are defined by boundaries admitting of upheaval, dissolution, and transformation."[10] To situate a critical discourse or practice of writing near these boundaries is to inevitably endow them with an ethical impact (Kristeva, "The Ethics of Linguistics" 25).

Necessarily cosmopolitan, the dissident writer or intellectual must transcend all boundaries, whether linguistic, ideological, national, or political. In defending ethical values that are no longer specific to a political regime or ideology, a social group or nation, in using the unique language of the individual as an arm against the annihilating Word that purports the Good of the Nation, the Welfare of Society, the dissident movement of the 1970s coincides with literary modernity. Together, they represent a new conjunction of ethics and aesthetics "having the power to set an obstacle in the path of the steamroller of ideology, of the totalitarian machine."[11]

The explosion of *Tel Quel* between 1968 and 1975 is the explosion of the Marxist reference.[12] Whether we situate the beginning of *Tel Quel*'s last phase in 1968 with the events of May, in 1971 with *Tel Quel*'s shift from the

---

9. Ibid., 290.
10. Kristeva, "The Ethics of Linguistics," 25.
11. Scarpetta, "Dissidence et littérature," *Tel Quel* 76 (Summer 1978): 48.
12. Sollers, "Pourquoi j'ai été chinois," 16.

PCF to China, or in 1974 with *Tel Quel*'s break with China, all three events designate the turn from a political to a cultural perspective. In this final turn, *Tel Quel* relinquishes the avant-garde dream of revolutionizing society along with literature. It abandons a totalizing aesthetico-political program (*théorie d'ensemble*) and with it any interest in a progressive, collective movement. In fact, it disposes once and for all of the guilt-ridden dichotomy of the intellectual and the masses bequeathed by nineteenth-century Marxism and socialism. Curiously enough, it does so through the political phenomenon of dissidence, which it interprets from a cultural optic.

Tel Quel refused to limit its interpretation of dissidence to a political reading. As writers, Telquelians were able to understand the rupture of community and the cosmopolitanism exceeding the framework of national traditions espoused by the dissidents. If politicians had difficulties under-standing the dissident message during the 1970s, it was because the vocabulary of dissidence differed markedly from the vocabulary of politics. Politics is a question of the state, nations, alliances, diplomacy, treatises, communities, consensus, and the collective; whereas dissidence concerns individuals, revolt, singularities, human rights, ethics, religion, exile, departure, universality.[13] How symptomatic, remarks Scarpetta, that writers and philosophers supported the dissidents, whereas politicians did not. The dissident message is not merely anti-Communist but anticommunity (*Eloge du cosmopolitisme* 197–98). It is bound up with the impossible community theorized by Freud and Bataille. In a lecture entitled "What Is a Dissident Intellectual?" delivered at the Pompidou Cultural Center (Beaubourg) on 23 May 1977 and subsequently published in *Tel Quel* (no. 74), Kristeva maintained that the role of the writer was no longer to deal out "globalizing doctrines," but instead to express "the impossibility of cohesion." For "social consensus— even when it advocates the well-being of the majority—represents in its *massiveness* a germ of *totality*, and ultimately a promise of *totalitarianism*."[14] *Tel Quel*'s crisis with Marxism in the mid-1970s stems precisely from a fear of the "massification" of culture and society and the subordination of the individual to the collective. This explains *Tel Quel*'s total abandonment of Marxism in favor of human rights during its last phase.

The mid-1970s mark the spectacular disappearance of Marxism as an obligatory reference in French intellectual thought, cultural practice, and

13. Scarpetta, "Eloge du cosmopolitisme, 197.
14. Kristeva cited in Jean-Louis Chiss, "Julia Kristeva et le rôle des intellectuels," *La Nouvelle Critique* 107 (October 1977): 63.

political life. In the thirty years following World War II, Marxism so dominated the French intellectual scene that it succeeded in subsuming modes of thought as ideologically alien to it as existentialism and structuralism. With no hegemonic doctrine to follow suit, French intellectuals found themselves without familiar landmarks in the vast militant space that had opened up. Many, including the *Tel Quel* group, relinquished their Marxist vulgate in favor of an antitotalitarian discourse in the name of human rights.

The crisis of Marxism also brought an end to the traditional status of the French intellectual, both as a universal conscience speaking out for others in the name of justice and truth, and as the representative of the cultural and political concerns of subordinate groups. In an interview with Deleuze in March 1972, Foucault stated:

> The intellectual's role is no longer to place himself "somewhat ahead and to the side" in order to express the stifled truth of the collectivity; rather, it is to struggle against the forms of power that transform him into its object and instrument in the sphere of "knowledge," "truth," "consciousness," and "discourse."[15]

During the 1970s, the totalizing notions of "universal," "engagé," and even "organic" that qualified the contemporary intellectual were abandoned, to a large degree, in favor of such counterhegemonic notions as "specific" and "dissident." Whereas the engaged intellectual took his place alongside the masses to defend globalizing doctrines, the dissident intellectual, on the other hand, advocates the impossible community.

In the opening editorial entitled "Un nouveau type d'intellectuel: Le dissident" [A new type of intellectual: The dissident] that appeared in the Winter 1977 issue of *Tel Quel* devoted to "Feminine Research,"[16] Kristeva states that our representation of the intellectual, both as engagé and organic, is bound up with an insurmountable opposition between the masses and the individual, which, governed by the Hegelian master-slave dialectic, generates

15. Foucault, "Intellectuals and Power," in *Language, Counter-Memory, Practice,* 207–8.
16. Kristeva's text on the dissident intellectual figures in an issue devoted to "feminine research." A introductory note indicates that such research will now form an integral part of *Tel Quel.* Much has already been written on Kristeva's relationship to feminism, which I shall not enter into here. Suffice it to note, however, that *Tel Quel*'s dissident turn and its ethical emphasis on the individual finally also accounts for sexual difference. This is a belated interest for *Tel Quel.* In her piece on the dissident intellectual, Kristeva sees sexual difference as a form of dissidence.

pity and guilt. Insofar as there has not been, according to Kristeva, any fundamental questioning of the relationship between the individual and the masses and, even more important between the intellectual and the social group, the intellectual has all too often seen his role as limited to patching up social groups. As a result, intellectuals "have used their superior historical perspective inherited from the nineteenth century to devote themselves to a cause whose ideal of social and economic equality is evident but which serves both to swallow up the particular characteristics of intellectual work and to perpetuate the myth of a successful society whose messianism, when not Utopian, has turned out to border on totalitarianism."[17] In their preoccupation with social causes, intellectuals have maintained, in too many instances, a division between their political militancy and their own work, say, as writers, linguists, philosophers, or teachers. They have thus failed to recognize that "each individual's specific activity [can] serve as the basis for politicisation."[18] Political militancy often became a diversion from the urgent need to reflect on the specificity of one's own work, and on the moral and political implications that logically ensue.

Nevertheless, between 1968 and 1972, *Tel Quel* had attempted to articulate its theory and practice of writing in terms of the class struggle. Position statements such as the following were thus common:

> We affirm that in producing a new practice (a new relationship of the subject to meaning and to ideological norms) and a new understanding of this practice, the specific struggle of the avant-garde on the ideological and political front objectively serves the struggle of the masses. In this sense, our struggle joins theirs.[19]

Tel Quel's position vis-à-vis the masses was ambiguous: Just exactly *where* was the *Tel Quel* group with the masses? *How* was it for them? If "for whom?" remains a valid question, it is clear that, given the elitist nature of the journal (price, choice of material, highly esoteric language), *Tel Quel* was hardly destined to be read by the masses, let alone many intellectuals. In an interview, Kristeva conceded that *Tel Quel* was for the intellectual petite

17. Kristeva, "A New Type of Intellectual: The Dissident," in *The Kristeva Reader*, trans. Seán Hand, 293. Originally published as "Un nouveau type d'intellectuel: Le dissident," *Tel Quel* 74 (Winter 1977).

18. Foucault, "Truth and Power," 127.

19. "Le dogmatisme à la rescousse du révisionnisme," 189.

THE ALIBI OF DISSIDENCE

bourgeoisie that was expanding as an audience thanks to the university.[20] How ironic that a review that always positioned itself against the university should depend on a university-trained public for its readership and be subsidized—as Pleynet noted in an interview—largely by library subscriptions.[21] If the so-called masses were not even reading *Tel Quel*, how exactly was the group supporting them in their class struggle? Obviously the only epidermal contact that Sollers, Kristeva, and other Telquelians had with "the masses" in the late 1960s and early 1970s were a few guest appearances at Communist-run "Maisons de la Culture" or the annual "Fête de l'Humanité." A *Tel Quel* sympathizer nonetheless assured me that Sollers had read portions of his novel *H*(composed of one sentence) in factories and that the workers had not objected to the lack of punctuation!

Historians like Perry Anderson have pointed out, all too well, that Western Marxism has generally been characterized—and this was particularly true in the 1960s and 1970s—by a dichotomy between theory and practice. Marxist theory, relegated as it is to the university (or to elitist cultural experiments), has no direct bearing on mass movements.[22] Carrying out a signifying practice and an ideological struggle that aim to undermine the foundations of Western idealist thought and cultural practice does not necessarily imply a socialist or proletarian stance. Walter Benjamin, for example, affirmed that the "proletarianization of the intellectual hardly ever makes him a proletarian." This is because the dominant social class, the bourgeoisie, has endowed the intellectual with a means of production, in the form of culture, that, because of the social privilege it implies, creates a reciprocal bond of solidarity between the intellectual and the dominant social class.[23]

In 1970, Sartre reiterated such a position by stating that "no *political denunciation* can compensate for the fact that in his social being [the intellectual] remains objectively an enemy of the people."[24] Sartre argued that the intellectual could not remain at the stage of a "guilty conscience" (characterized by idealism and inefficacy); he had to negate his *intellectual moment* in order to achieve a new *popular* status (227). Although Telquelians were only too eager to rid themselves of any latent "guilty conscience,"

20. Kristeva, personal interview, Paris, 15 February 1978.
21. Pleynet, personal interview, Paris, 15 June 1987.
22. Perry Anderson, *Reflections on Western Marxism* (London: New Left, 1976).
23. Walter Benjamin, "The Author as Producer," 102.
24. Sartre, *Between Existentialism and Marxism*, trans. John Mathews (New York: Pantheon, 1974), 257.

they were not about to relinquish the intellectual moment. How would *Tel Quel* resolve this contradiction, without resorting to a certain form of idealism that they had so contested in Breton, or to a blind adherence to political dogma (as in the case of Aragon)? How could they once again affirm their unflinching allegiance to literature, as they had for more than fifteen years, without appearing reactionary in the new historical circumstances? The solution, oddly enough, lay in recasting the relationship between the intellectual and the masses: "Whether Euro-communist or not, the future of Western society will greatly depend on a re-evaluation of the relationship of the masses to the individual or intellectual, and on our ability to break out of the dialectical trap between these oppositions and to recast the whole relationship."[25] The implicit analogy between the intellectual and the individual is central to this recasting. In effect, it is in the notion of the individual subject as an irreducible singularity that Kristeva sees the possibility of an ethics of resistance to the potentially totalitarian notions of the "Greatest Number" and "Everyone's Idea of Good."

For Kristeva, the recasting of the relationship of the individual to the community has been central to the languages of modernity, which are more and more directed against an "equalizing Word" of a secular and militant nature. Political machinery, including that on the Left, has been caught up in a large history that excludes the specific histories of discourses, dreams, and *jouissance* ("A New Type of Intellectual: The Dissident" 294). Diametrically opposed to Althusser's "process without a subject" (Marxism liberated from Hegel) is Kristeva's "subject in process/on trial" (Hegelianism liberated by Bataille). Insofar as it has become an all-embracing rationality, Marxism has ended up filling in the gaps and stemming all escape, thereby becoming a "magic password that closes the door and reinforces the belief in a society shaped by constraint, thus justifying the obsessional dialectic of the slave." In opposition to politics, Kristeva posits a new conjunction of aesthetics and ethics: "Communal but singular, addressed to all but specifically realized by each one of us, such is the culture of our age, when it is not an echo-chamber of the past. From this point on, another society, another community, another body start to emerge" (294).

When I asked Kristeva who read *Tel Quel* and whether the elitist nature of the journal was not incompatible with the "organic" intellectual stance that *Tel Quel* had adopted in the late 1960s, she responded, "But who reads

25. Kristeva, "A New Type of Intellectual: The Dissident," 293.

Mallarmé?"[26] Such a reply is actually a loaded question. According to Kristeva, *Tel Quel* "does not address people as individuals determined by their places in production. It addresses people as determined by their dreams, their sleep, their sex; in that instance, their social status is not essential." Although most of us would concur that our identity is a function of our socioeconomic status, it is nevertheless necessary to take Kristeva's statement beyond its apparently idealistic face value. Through her statement, Kristeva is contesting the economic reductionism that has characterized Marxist cultural analysis, whereby literature is merely a reflection of the social relations and productive forces of a particular class, and the individual is determined solely by his national and social dimensions. In stating that art and literature "are the phenomenal forms and consequences of the development of the material forces of production and the class struggle,"[27] Lukács is practically implying that each epoch necessarily produces a homogeneous art. Obviously, this statement is far from accurate, as it denies that art and literature have anything to do with individual expression. Arguing for the radical heterogeneity separating the world of the artist from the one of the politician, Camus wrote, "The work of art, by the mere fact that it exists, negates the conquests of ideology."[28]

Is the notion of art as the expression of individual difference the privileged posture of an elite in a society where the majority are denied this possibility? Is artistic creativity a solitary act imposed by the conditions of capitalism? Perhaps the intolerance displayed toward individualistic cultural expression in former socialist regimes provides some clarification. If a certain form of art was problematic for Marxist regimes, was it solely because it reflected a bourgeois order based on class exploitation, or because it also undermined the totalitarian nature of the new order? "The real force of art is that it appears threatening to those against whom it is directed."[29] According to Winfred Gaul, "Hitler as well as Stalin, the Fascist dictatorship as well as the Communist one knew and feared this: art is often the only oasis of individual thought, sentiment, or will in a totally regimented world" (20). Fascism and Stalinism share a "hatred both for the diversity of languages and for what such a diversity opens up, that is, a transgressive and critical position with

26. Kristeva, personal interview, Paris, 15 February 1978.

27. Lukács cited in Verdès-Leroux, *Le Réveil des Somnambules*, 315.

28. Albert Camus, "Le Témoin de la liberté," *Actuelles I* in *Essais*, ed. Roger Quilliot and Louis Faucon (Paris: Bibliothèque de la Pléiade, 1965), 404.

29. C. Linfert cited in Winfred Gaul, "Opinioni eretiche di un produttore d'arte," *Settanta* (April 1972): 20.

respect to normative codes."[30] Economic reductionism goes hand in hand with the subordination of art to political ends. To recognize the irreducible quality of art implies endangering the Marxist edifice as well as, in the short term, the right of politicians to intervene in art.[31] The economic determinism and cultural interventionism that sustained the notion of socialist realism revealed that what was at stake was less a question of aesthetics than of a power struggle between intellectuals and politicians leading to the subservience and destruction of culture as the expression of individual difference.

The question still remains whether the freedom of individual expression and the solitary moment of creativity are, in fact, inherent in an elitist culture or are more generally necessary conditions for the production of knowledge and artistic creation. Sollers maintains that it is not possible to make the moment of scientific discovery or artistic creativity, which is necessarily elitist, coincide with its democratic reception by all.[32] Cultural time and social time do not necessarily coincide. Not only is the notion of a simultaneous whole erroneous, it is also totalitarian: "If you think that the speaking species can be contemporaneous with itself in a whole, the rest ensues. We shall quickly reach a 'biologism,' a 'massification' such that we shall not need Mr. Y, Z, Artaud, who hinder the development of socialism" (Sollers, interview). Kristeva does not believe in mass culture: "There is no mass culture. Mass culture is a fantasy for a homogeneous society that has never existed" (interview).

While I concur with Kristeva and Sollers that the notion of a homogeneous society or culture is neither realistic nor desirable, I do not believe, however, that they actually address the question of the democratization of culture implied by their prior "organic" positions. Kristeva finds fault with the concept of a popular or democratic culture, which is perhaps accessible to all but not of much value. She concedes that "the masses have the 'maisons de la culture,' where one can see a play by Beaumarchais or Molière, which is not bad in itself, but as far as intellectuals are concerned, it is essential that [they] continue [their] work in language" (interview). Kristeva and Sollers clearly do not want their cultural research to be stifled by either the "masses" or the political parties representing them. To a large degree, they adhere to Elio Vittorini's idea of the "dual articulation of culture." On the one hand, there is culture as research, that is, avant-garde culture, which is

30. Pleynet, *Transculture* (Paris: Union Générale d'Editions, 1979), 232.
31. Verdès-Leroux, *Le Réveil des Somnambules*, 315.
32. Sollers, personal interview, Paris, 5 July 1979.

beyond the reach of the masses; on the other hand, there is culture as action, that is, culture that does not lose contact with the masses.[33] In refusing to let the "real" culture (culture as research) be arrested by the level of the masses and in advocating the autonomy and freedom of cultural activity, Sollers and Kristeva nevertheless continue to situate their cultural politics within an idealist framework, thereby conferring a socially (class) privileged status on culture and the intellectual. Once again, culture is seen as separate from material social life, which has been the dominant tendency in idealist cultural thought.[34]

Between 1967 and 1971, *Tel Quel* endeavored to articulate the singular experience of writing with "the needs of the whole ideological community" (Gramsci) only to conclude that the collective ends up being defined in relation to ideology and not to practice.[35] Inspired by Bataille, Sollers maintained that practice is necessarily singular, whereas a collectivity is always established in relation to ideological consensus. Whether theological or political in nature, the latter can never be a collectivity of singularities. There is no collective unconscious, only singular or particular cases. This is why *Tel Quel* always upheld the concept of heterogeneity or singularity (Sollers, "Pourquoi j'ai été chinois" 17). It is also why it refused the notion of a mass culture accessible to all. Kristeva contended that it is not possible to give something positive to all ("donner du bien à tous") because all are diverse ("tous sont très différents"). Those who try to reach "all" ultimately eliminate what "exceeds." What disturbs Kristeva about the democratization of culture is that it implies a process of homogenization that always begins from the base. It always eliminates what exceeds: a Dostoevsky or a Kandinski (interview). It was, in fact, Dostoevsky who claimed that "There is something incommensurable in mankind."[36] There is a fundamental absence of common measure among the elements or dimensions that con-

---

33. As a dissident Communist at odds with his party in 1947, Vittorini felt compelled to make this distinction in a heated polemic with Palmiro Togliatti, the head of the PCI. In so doing, he sought to preserve his cultural review, *Il Politecnico* (1945–47), from the two extremes of his time: "insufficient politicization" ("a culture of consolation") and "political saturation" (culture subordinate to politics, i.e., Zhdanovism). Unlike *Tel Quel*, however, *Il Politecnico* was a cultural review destined to be read by the masses. See Elio Vittorini, "Politica e cultura: Lettera a Togliatti," *Il Politecnico* 35 (January–March 1947). See also my "Culture and Politics: The *Politecnico* Experience," *The Minnesota Review* 26 (Spring 1986): 83–98.

34. Raymond Williams, *Marxism and Literature* (Oxford: Oxford University Press, 1977), 19.

35. See Sollers, "Pourquoi j'ai été chinois," 17.

36. Dostoevsky cited in Houdebine, *Excès de langages*, 102.

stitute what we consider to be "mankind" (Houdebine, *Excès de langages* 102).

Tel Quel advocated that the history of humanity be viewed from the perspective of exceptions. In 1980, Sollers declared, "We wish to illuminate history from the exception, and not from the rule or the community."[37] If this appeared to be an elitist posture, it was—claimed *Tel Quel*—because art was considered from a political perspective where the individual continued to be a right-wing notion and the masses a left-wing one. Such a perspective was also adopted by the political Left when it criticized dissidence for being an elite movement that had only touched a narrow stratum of intellectuals associated with scientific and cultural production.[38] *Tel Quel* rejected this political perspective of dissidence and art that once again sets the intellectual or artist in opposition to the masses. Sollers claimed that political society, whether left-wing or right-wing, tends automatically to reduce creativity to a totalitarian model. There must be a correspondence between opinions and art.[39] Within such a paradigm, the artist or writer who dares to affirm the specificity of his or her work is always seen as standing out with respect to the rest of society. If artists and writers are indeed privileged, then why, asks Camus, have they traditionally been the first victims of modern tyrannies, be they left- or right-wing?[40] Why was a death warrant issued against an apparently harmless, quasi-unknown novelist by a powerful political and religious leader with a following of millions? Further intensifying Sartre's famous slogan, Sollers notes that God—or the Community—is not an artist, even if artists have made use of this horizon in privileged historical moments.[41] Could a subjective reverie threaten the massive following of Khomeini? Could a work of fiction challenge religious dogma? For Sollers, Khomeini's death wish is ultimately against language as the expression of the most intense individualism. What Big Brother abhors, above all, is the individual as an unstable, varied, incalculable, and irreducible entity—like literature.[42]

It is symptomatic that one of the last political events responsible for freeing many French intellectuals of any lingering illusions with respect to

---

37. Sollers, "On n'a encore rien vu," 24.
38. Dominique Lecourt, *Dissidence ou révolution?* (Paris: Maspero, 1978), 8.
39. Sollers, "Gauche, droite . . . ," 330.
40. Camus, "Conférence du 14 décembre 1957," *Essais*, 1094.
41. Sollers, "L'Art et les Révolutions: le grand malentendu."
42. See Sollers, "Lettre sur l'individualité littéraire," *Magazine Littéraire* 264 (April 1989): 34–35.

Marxism would be interpreted as a cultural phenomenon by the *Tel Quel* group: "It is time to realize that dissidence is not a 'political party,' but above all, a cultural movement."[43] With this statement, Scarpetta does not seek to reduce dissidence to a mere question of literature and art, but rather to raise art and literature to an ethical dimension where the notion of the individual is foremost. What, in fact, is intended by the notion of dissidence (related to the Russian *inakomysliatchi,* that is, "those who think differently") is the birth of an individual relationship to existence: "Moral resistance to violence and injustice has no relation to politics. It is the most simple demonstration of individualism."[44] Insofar as dissidence affirms "the right to singularity and the specificity of speech" as a political value (Kristeva), "the appearance of difference as a political occurrence" (Sollers), it can be considered a synonym for art.[45] It brings into play notions such as the following: the necessity of speaking one's own language (not necessarily equated with one's native tongue) in its irreducible singularity (Scarpetta); the crossing of all linguistic and national boundaries (Kristeva); the free circulation of ideas, discourses, and individuals; the rejection of any utopian vision of an ideal society, or of any political reduction of reality; the refusal of the mutilation of the subjective by the collective (Scarpetta). In this respect, dissidence is less a set of social and political values than a cultural ethics.[46]

As a phenomenon associated with human rights, dissidence challenges the traditional dichotomy that has served "to make people keep in step in reference exclusively to the last two centuries."[47] *Tel Quel* claimed that by refusing to listen to the message of dissidents, many European intellectuals were merely acknowledging their inability to question the fundamental relationship of the intellectual to society and to social change. Furthermore, by devoting their energies to deciding whether supporting the dissidents was actually a right-wing move against the rise to power of the Left in France, or rather a new manifestation of critical Marxism, pitted against the oppressive tactics of Soviet Communism as well as Eurocommunism, these intellectuals continued to pose the question of dissidence in global political terms. In so doing, they lost sight of the singular nature of the dissident appeal for the respect of individual rights in the face of ideological totalitarianism and

---

43. Scarpetta, *Eloge du cosmopolitisme*, 198.
44. Tatiana Khodororovitch, "Dissident?" *Le Monde* (17 November 1977): 21.
45. "La dissidence n'est finalement que le synonyme de l'art." Andrei Siniavsky, "L'art est supérieur à la réalité," *Tel Quel* 76 (Summer 1978): 57.
46. Scarpetta, "Eloge du cosmopolitisme, 198.
47. Sollers, "Gauche, droite . . . ," 333.

political oppression, whether left-wing or right-wing. Perhaps one of the most acute statements came from the Soviet dissident Vladimir Bukovsky: "I am neither in the camp of the Right nor the camp of the Left; I am in the concentration camp."[48]

Did the concentration camp belong to the Left or the Right? Did it really matter? The dissidents merely confirmed what was becoming the realization of many French intellectuals in the 1970s: that the Left-Right dichotomy had become an anachronism in both the cultural and political spheres. In 1976, Sollers contended that France was in a period of regression. As the Left attempted to come to power—supposedly as an oppositional force—French society should have been seeing both a political program of transformation and an ideological, cultural one.[49] If it was time to abandon politics in the name of culture, it was perhaps because culture held an invaluable lesson for politics, that is, about "the right in the left" (Lévy): "We have finally come to the conclusion that, culturally, the Left, which was all evolution, progress, generosity, humanism, had with respect to questions of art and literature, the most regressive, most reactionary, most conservative opinions, thereby making it converge with the political right."[50] The distinction between progress and reaction seemed to have disappeared in the 1970s, and, with it, the political division between the Left and the Right. In maintaining the Left-Right dichotomy, intellectuals and politicians were refusing to come to terms with the totalitarian phenomenon, which, in effect, brought an end to the possibility of dividing roles between something that resists and conserves, and something that seeks progress and evolution.[51] Back in 1947, the "dissident" Vittorini had chided Togliatti and the Italian Communist Party for applying purely political criteria to cultural phenomena in order to determine whether they were innovative or retrograde: "The line that divides progress from reaction, in the cultural sphere, does not coincide exactly with the dividing line in the political domain."[52]

Could the dividing line in culture be the revealing one? Perhaps it was from the site of culture that one could learn the truth about politics. If moving over to a domain that had apparently nothing to do with the political distinctions of left and right did not imply abandoning politics, it

48. Vladimir Bukovsky cited in Sollers, "Gauche, droite . . . ," 329.

49. Sollers, "Nous vivons une période de régression," *Les Nouvelles Littéraires*, 28 October 1976, 19. See also "Gauche, droite . . ."

50. Sollers, "Gauche, droite . . . ," 329.

51. Ibid., 328.

52. Elio Vittorini, "Politica e cultura: lettera a Togliatti," 105.

was because of the wager that a politician could be judged more by his literary tastes, his conception of modern art, or his definition of culture, than by his views on unemployment or the construction of socialism.[53] Politics could be illuminated by the cultural choices that stand in its shadows or margins, or on the other side of its mirror, as its most assured foundation or its inevitable sanction (281). This had been the *Tel Quel* wager for twenty-two years. Perhaps *Tel Quel* had something to tell us about Fascism and its alter ego, Stalinism. For *Tel Quel*, the 1970s meant coming to terms with a Fascism "aux couleurs de la France" (a "French-tinged Fascism"). To those who criticized *Tel Quel* for supporting Giscard over the Common Program, Sollers responded: "Of course a liberal [in the French sense of the term] like Giscard is more left-wing than the PC, it seems obvious to me, but it disturbs, it disturbs, it is not accepted."[54] Who was right-wing, Giscard or Hitler? Hitler or Stalin? How did one account for the socialist roots of Hitler and Mussolini? Was Fascism, as Sollers contends, merely left-wing discourse pushed to the limit? After all, Fascism was a phenomenon that had not only arisen on the Left, but in France as well. To the vast majority who criticized *Tel Quel*'s turn toward the United States in 1977 as a right-wing action, Sollers replied that, unlike Europe, the United States had not experienced Fascism. Was Fascism merely the logical development of capitalism? Then why hadn't the United States known it? From 1940 to 1942, France had its Fascist configuration. Was it a mere foreign occupation? Or one rooted in French nationalism, in the Jacobin ideal? With questions like these raised by Sollers, Scarpetta, Pleynet, Houdebine, and Henric during the 1970s, it was not surprising that they found a soulmate in the author of *L'Idéologie française*: the "new philosopher" Bernard-Henri Lévy.

Lévy was appealing to Telquelians in that he advocated ethics over politics, the individual over the community, the artist or moralist over the ideologue. Lévy's anti-Marxism became "the contemporary form of the fight against politics."[55] In making ethics the foremost concern of philosophical thought, he also attributed a key historical position to the artist or writer. In an interview published in *Tel Quel* in 1978, Lévy maintained that artists and

53. Bernard-Henri Lévy, "La gauche, telle quelle," in *Questions de principe* (Paris: Denoël, 1983), 279. Angelo Rinaldi, the literary critic of *L'Express* dubbed François Mitterrand's style a "lyrisme d'orphéon": "Imagine a lyrical notary and you get the picture more or less," comments Guy Hocquenghem in an interesting analysis of French culture under the early Mitterand regime, "The New French Culture," *October* 19 (Winter 1981): 106.
54. Sollers, "Gauche, droite . . . ," 337.
55. Lévy, *Barbarism With a Human Face*, 189–90.

poets have always accounted for the "monsters of the historical unconscious." According to Lévy, the greatest classical theory of power was not
written by Machiavelli, but by Shakespeare (*King Lear, Richard III*). The
origins of World War I are best illustrated by Musil's *A Man Without
Qualities*; the horrors of the Spanish civil war are best depicted by Picasso's
Guernica. As for the gulag, one need only read Solzhenitsyn.[56] It was, in fact,
the publication of Solzhenitsyn's *The Gulag Archipelago* in 1973, coupled
with a profound disillusionment with the unfulfilled aspirations of May
1968, that prompted the "nouveaux philosophes" to attack Marxism and
socialism relentlessly.

The "nouveaux philosophes" were an eclectic group of young philosophers who took the media by storm in the late spring and summer of 1977.
André Glucksmann's *Les Maîtres penseurs* and Lévy's *La Barbarie à visage
humain* became overnight best-sellers.[57] Within a few months, the "new
philosophers," who had been launched by *Les Nouvelles Littéraires* in June
1976, became media celebrities in Europe and America; as cited earlier, *Time*
devoted a cover story to them on 5 September 1977 entitled "Is Marx
Dead?" In addition to Lévy and Glucksmann, the group included Jean-
Marie Benoist, Guy Lardreau, Christian Jambet, Jean-Paul Dollé, Michel
Guérin, Philippe Nemo, and Maurice Clavel. Critics accused these "disc
jockeys of ideas" of "philosophical marketing"; Deleuze denounced the
whole phenomenon as "a media racket mounted by the Right."[58] Coming
from divergent political backgrounds, they nevertheless shared a common
hostility toward Marxism and the notions of progress, revolution, and the
state. Even though the new philosophers claimed to be opposed to all
political ideologies, in effect, their main target of attack was Marxism. The

56. Lévy, "La preuve du pudding," *Tel Quel* 77 (Autumn 1978): 31.

57. Thirty-seven thousand copies of Lévy's book were sold in two weeks; 30,000 of
Glucksmann's in less than a month! When they appeared on "Apostrophes" on 27 May 1977,
their viewing audience was calculated at six to seven million! See Valerio Riva, "Tutto finisce in
Gulag," *L'Espresso*, 19 June 1977, 68.

58. In an interview of 5 June 1977, Deleuze criticized the new philosophers for their shoddy
philosophical reasoning— "they use broad concepts, as big as cavities"—and for subordinating
thought to media demands. See "A propos des nouveaux philosophes et d'un problème plus
général" in *Recherches* 30 (November 1977): 179. According to the Italian journalist, Valerio
Riva, this interview was published as a pamphlet, at Deleuze's own expense, and distributed free
in bookstores, like antismoking propaganda. See "Tutto finisce in Gulag," 69. Deleuze's
interview was subsequently reprinted in a special issue of *Recherches* entitled "Les Untorelli"
[The plague carriers] devoted to the Italian uprisings and Bologna Conference Against Repression of 1977. Portions of the interview were also published as "Nuovi filosofi, siete zero," in *La
Repubblica*, 25 June 1977, 10–11.

success of the "nouveaux philosophes" is to be attributed less to the ideas they put forward, which date back to the 1950s (Camus is usually seen as their prototype), than to their timing. They appeared on the French political scene just prior to the legislative elections of March 1978, when a victory of the Left seemed imminent. For anyone opposed to a Communist-Socialist takeover in France, these "pub-philosophers" who benefited from what Debray calls the media cycle (1968–) were just the solution. In fact, their intense media exposure greatly determined their success. The underlying premise of François Aubral and Xavier Delcourt's *Contre la Nouvelle philosophie* was that behind the success of the new philosophers was nothing but a mass-media exploitation.[59]

Philosophical marketing certainly gave the "nouveaux philosophes" a visibility they could never have achieved from their ideas alone, many of which, incidentally, were well founded even if they were often posed in simplistic terms and pretentious rhetoric. This media hype explains perhaps why *Tel Quel* formed an alliance with the "nouveaux philosophes" in spite of its long-standing aversion to mass culture. I suspect that *Tel Quel* was only too pleased to have many of the ideas it shared with the new philosophers broadcast in such a direct and hyperbolic manner. Perhaps it even detected the end of the publishing hegemony and thus ultimately its own demise. In fact, a few years down the road, Sollers (who in January 1983 with *Femmes* became the best-selling novelist of realist fiction)[60] would be only too happy to make regular appearances on French television, even to the point of appearing on a show like "De quoi j'ai l'air?" [What do I seem like?] (France 2) along with Lova Moor and Jean-Paul Gaultier on 3 August 1993.

If public attention turned to the "nouveaux philosophes," this was due not only to the success of the media but also to the times: the new philosophers' hyperbolic condemnation of Marxism in the mid-1970s coincided with the rise of Eurocommunism and terrorism. Cornelius Castoriadis and Claude Lefort's *Socialisme ou Barbarie* certainly had not been accorded the same attention and publicity in the early 1950s when it attacked the Soviet myth. The same holds true for East European and Soviet dissidents who were not taken very seriously in France at the time. At odds with the

59. See François Aubral and Xavier Delcourt, *Contre la nouvelle philosophie* (Paris: Gallimard, 1977).

60. "Le retour du 'je': de la littérature d'avant-garde à la conquête des magazines féminins," note Anne Simonin and Hélène Clastres in *Le Débat: Les Idées en France, 1945–1988*, 394.

"revisionist" politics of the PCF in 1971, *Tel Quel* appeared even more troubled by the looming possibility of a Communist-Socialist takeover of the French superstructure in 1978. It thus allied itself with the new philosophers, the dissidents from Eastern Europe and the Soviet Union, the Metropolitan Indians and Untorelli (plague carriers) in Italy, and the intellectuals of CIEL (The Committee of Intellectuals for a Europe of Liberties). All of these currents had Marxism and Communism as their prime target.

Tel Quel published both essays by and interviews with the new philosophers: Glucksmann's "Réponses" (no. 64), Nemo's "Job et le mal radical" [Job and radical evil] (no. 70), Lévy's "La preuve du pudding" [The proof of the pudding] (no. 77), "C'est la guerre," [It's war], and "Discours au mémorial" (no. 82), and Benoist's "La normalisation" (no. 84) and "Une nouvelle critique de la raison pratique" [A new critique of practical reason] (no. 85). In May 1977, Kristeva joined Lévy and Benoist at the Beaubourg conference devoted to the theme "A quoi servent les intellectuels?" [What purpose do intellectuals serve?]. Her presentation was part of a series that included such speakers as Jean Daniel, Jean-Toussaint Desanti, Clavel, and Glucksmann. Toward the middle of her presentation on the intellectual as a dissident, Kristeva was continually interrupted as she tried to defend her positions. Members of the audience wanted to know on what grounds she could possibly compare herself to a Soviet or Chilean dissident. What was the point of talking about dissident intellectuals in France where, after all, there was freedom of expression and where the Left was just coming to power? It was necessary, responded Kristeva, considering that, culturally, the Common Program of the Left was full of clichés dating back some thirty to fifty years. When someone in the audience decided to get a more political response out of Kristeva by asking her for whom she was planning to vote in the upcoming March 1978 legislative elections, Kristeva was at a loss, but Glucksmann immediately got up and pointed an arm at the audience while screaming, "We've finally gotten there! Control of party cards, of loyalty to the party. Here's why we already need to be dissenting in France . . . the Gulag has already begun."[61] The hyperbolic nature of Glucksmann's remark reflects the confusion established by both the new philosophers and Telquelians over the cultural and the political. And this confusion owes much to the

---

61. See Riva, "Tutto finisce in Gulag," 69, 71. Needless to say when "barbarism" came to power in May 1981, neither the new philosophers nor Telquelians fared that badly! Kristeva even accompanied President Mitterand on a trip to Bulgaria in 1989. See "An Interview with Julia Kristeva: Cultural Strangeness and the Subject in Crisis," *Discourse* 13, no. 1 (Fall–Winter 1990–91): 149–80.

concerted efforts of *Tel Quel* and other Althusser-influenced currents in the late 1960s to separate the theoretical from the political, to the point of privileging the former as a means of political militancy.

In *The French New Left*, Arthur Hirsh perceptively notes that the new philosophers clearly revealed their debt to their mentor Althusser in that their brand of anti-Marxism was merely another form of theoreticism.[62] One of the trademarks of the "new philosophy" was the claim that the evils of twentieth-century socialism and communism were inherent in nineteenth-century Marxist theory. Hirsh claims that the Soviet experience was

> conditioned by a host of historical, social, economic, and cultural factors as well as the impact of marxism. To consider a theory as the sole cause of social reality implies that reality is a construction of our minds in the way that fantasy is. In fact this is consistent with the previous political and theoretical efforts of the new philosophers: i.e., maoism and Althusserianism. What we see then is a progression from one fantasy type of thinking to another. (200)

In her Beaubourg presentation on the dissident intellectual (subsequently published in *Tel Quel*), Kristeva conglomerates the various categories of dissidents—"the rebel who attacks political power," "the psychoanalyst who transforms the dialectic of law-and-desire into a contest between death and discourse," "the writer who experiments with the limits of identity," and finally "sexual difference, women: isn't that another form of dissidence?"[63]—in order to stress the theoretical aspects of the phenomenon: "For true dissidence today is perhaps what it has always been: *thought*" (299). In so doing, she practically implies that writers, psychoanalysts, and women, are de facto dissidents of the same order as political rebels. She thus fails to distinguish between the very real political situation that distinguishes French intellectuals from dissidents in Chile or the Soviet Union. And if true dissidence is thought, what about the very different political repercussions for thought in France versus the Soviet Union? When Kristeva claims that "exile is already in itself a form of *dissidence*, since it involves uprooting oneself from a family, a country, or a language" (298), is she acknowledging that exile is perhaps the only form of "dissidence" that she actually experi-

---

62. Arthur Hirsh, *The French New Left: An Intellectual History from Sartre to Gorz* (Boston: South End, 1981), 200.

63. Kristeva, "A New Type of Intellectual: The Dissident," 295–96.

enced? In order to defend her legitimacy as a dissident intellectual in France, Kristeva alludes to the retrograde cultural ideas of the PCF and PSF (French Socialist Party). Such a remark, however, does not account for the fact that as a "dissident" intellectual in France, she is politically better off than Chileans under Pinochet or Soviets under Brezhnev. And yet, when she is once again put on the spot regarding her concrete politics—that is, when she is asked for whom she will cast her vote—Glucksmann feels compelled to intercede on her behalf by having recourse to the "gulag." Obviously a question posed to a French intellectual concerning her vote does not constitute the gulag as Soviet dissidents experienced it.

Scarpetta would probably take issue with the objections I am raising here. He maintains that there is a danger in inferring that there is no relation between the dissidents from Eastern Europe and intellectuals in the West because of the contention that the latter have not experienced the repression of the former. He claims that a division of this sort ends up, on the one hand, isolating the testimony of the dissidents, and, on the other, devalorizing the thought of Western intellectuals who try to draw lessons from the dissidents and consequently articulate these lessons with their own specific practice against the cultural and political conformism of the West, and the totalitarian risks it contains.[64] While I concur that the former danger was a real one, I believe, however, that the latter was perhaps the real center of concern for Western-style "dissidents." In *Past Imperfect*, Tony Judt goes to great lengths to show how French intellectuals ignored the message of East European dissidents when it was not useful to them as "Western" Europeans. According to Judt, French intellectuals enjoyed a special status in the postwar years. For Parisian writers, it meant having the right to speak out in the name of humanity even when local politics were the real issue. Judt argues that French intellectuals not only risked few consequences for their actions, they also revealed a lack of historical gravity.[65] Judt acerbically remarks that "[t]he community of the universal intellectual was redefined [after 1945] to exclude those who were victims of Stalinism" (279). In the 1940s and 1950s, the dissident and exiled intelligentsia of Eastern Europe had been confined to the margins and ostentatiously ignored by dominant circles of the time (277). This obviously was not the case in the mid-1970s

---

64. Scarpetta, "Dissidence de l'inconscient et pouvoirs," *Art Press International* 17 (April 1978): 24.

65. Tony Judt, *Past Imperfect: French Intellectuals, 1945–1956* (Berkeley and Los Angeles: University of California Press, 1992), 275–76.

with the dissident appeal echoing in France at a time when the return to power of the Left seemed imminent and many intellectuals—including Telquelians and the new philosophers—sought a political justification to bury their former entanglements with Marxism once and for all. Now it was not only chic to listen to the dissidents, but even more chic to consider oneself a dissident.

In "L'art est supérieur à la réalité" published in *Tel Quel* (Summer 1978), Siniavsky notes that "the artistic situation of an era is not defined solely by what is created at that time, but also by what, arising from the past, enters our perception with a particular intensity, abolishing the distance of time and space."[66] Thus, in 1978 *Tel Quel* publishes Joseph Brodsky, Andrei Siniavsky, and Georges Konrad. But does it succeed in masking the distance of time and space by emphasizing the artistic or cultural dimension of dissidence? It is not for artistic reasons that these writers were completely ignored by *Tel Quel* during the 1960s. While I commend *Tel Quel* for making the dissident texts presented at the Biennale of Venice during the autumn of 1977 available to the French reading public, I cannot dismiss what I consider to be a self-serving strategy. After all, what was *Tel Quel* publishing when Siniavsky and Daniel were sent to the gulag in 1966 or when the Solzhenitsyn bombshell exploded in 1968? How nice that *L'Infini* devoted so much attention to Kundera in the early 1980s or that Scarpetta emphasized the importance of Eastern and Central European writers in *L'Impureté* (1985)—a book, incidentally, opposed to the notion of the avant-garde.

By emphasizing the cultural over the political in its appropriation of dissidence in the 1970s, *Tel Quel* was advocating once again the disengagement of literature, a position with which it was exceedingly well acquainted. But if in 1960 it had defended literature from the reigning ideologies of the cold-war years merely by speaking from the site of its own literary practice, in 1977–78, *Tel Quel* had to resort to a foreign event that was—no matter how hard *Tel Quel* tried to reduce (or raise) it to its cultural dimensions— not a literary movement, after all, but rather the direct consequence of a concrete, political reality. Was *Tel Quel* once more "constru[ing] the foreign culture as a critical instrument applied to local contradictions?"[67] It had already used China to move away from PCF revisionism in 1971 and to justify its "cultural" turn.

Furthermore, *Tel Quel* also turned to the United States in the summer of 1977 to defend its cultural—or, perhaps, political—positions. For many

---

66. Siniavsky, "L'art est supérieur à la réalité," 57.
67. Annette Michelson, "The Agony of the French Left," *October* 6 (Fall 1978): 22.

critics of *Tel Quel*, the special triple issue on the United States (nos. 71–73) merely confirmed the group's abdication of Marxism in favor of monopoly-capitalism and imperialism, which they claimed was also supported by *Tel Quel's* alliance with the new philosophers and dissidents. This triple issue of *Tel Quel* was deemed important enough to receive a detailed review entitled "L'Internationale transatlantique ou un gauchisme de croisière" [The trans-atlantic international or a cruise-like leftism] on page 2 of *Le Monde* (5 November 1977). The author of the piece was Jérome Bindé, a "Normalien" and "agrégé" professor of literature at that political stronghold known as L'Ecole Polytechnique. *Le Monde* added its own subtitle—"Sur les nou-veaux philosophes" [On the new philosophers]—to the essay, thereby linking *Tel Quel* to the movement that had been mesmerizing French intellectual circles for months. In this time of crisis for the West, notes Bindé, "we are turning to intellectuals, looking for prophecies, as we did in the '30s." As part of the new "chic liberal pessimism," Bindé considers two "symptoms" in the French intelligentsia as worthy of notice: the "nouveaux philosophes" and *Tel Quel's* change of line from a militant Sinophilia to an Atlantism. Although Bindé acknowledges in passing the theoretical originality of these two "microcosms of European intelligence"—note his use of "European" rather than "Parisian" or "French"—he is more interested in situating these two currents within the orbit of two international movements of broader scope: a generalized attack on Marxism's hold on the petit bourgeois of the West—social democracy included—and a resurgent human rights movement.

"After China, the United States," writes Bindé. He contends that it would have been impossible to see texts by William Burroughs, John Ashbery, or Bob Wilson fifteen months earlier. While this remark is partially correct—texts on and by American writers and artists were symptomatically absent from *Tel Quel* during its Marxist phase (1967–76)—Ashbery and Bur-roughs were present in *Tel Quel* from 1964 (no. 18) and 1966 (no. 27), respectively. Bindé is wrong to accuse *Tel Quel*—as he does—of an anti-Americanism, unless we consider the ethnocentric bias of *Tel Quel's* views on the States as a form of anti-Americanism (which he really does not address as such). Despite an anti-Americanism that prevailed among French intellectuals, *Tel Quel* supported American culture—thanks particularly to the efforts of Pleynet and his pioneering critical work on the plastic and performing arts. Denis Roche was also the French translator of Pound.[68] *Tel*

68. Texts by Pound, trans. Denis Roche, were already published by *Tel Quel* in nos. 6 (Summer 1961) and 11 (Autumn 1962). E.E. cummings was introduced in *Tel Quel* (no. 11) by

Quel's interest in American culture was not surprising to anyone truly familiar with the journal.

However one may have felt about the choice of texts published in the special issue (which, as some critics have claimed, seem to be more written *in* than *on* the United States),[69] what really unleashed a fury of commentary were the remarks on the United States contained in the opening editorial entitled "Pourquoi les Etats-Unis?" [Why the United States?], which consisted of a conversation among Kristeva, Pleynet, and Sollers. In opening the conversation on the United States, Pleynet immediately deferred to Kristeva because she was the only one to already have written and published something about one of her visits to the States (a piece entitled "D'Ithaca à New York" published in *Tel Quel*'s satellite journal *Promesse* in 1974 and subsequently reprinted in *Polylogue*). By deferring to her in this manner, Pleynet gave Kristeva a certain authority. To explain the interest of the three in the American plastic and performing arts, Kristeva noted that American culture excelled in its "non-verbal" dimension, adding that "there is no great American literature today, apart from a few exceptions, which are in any case of English origins, and nostalgically oriented towards a Kafkaesque Jewish humour."[70] Commenting on the American audience of her lectures and classes in the mid-1970s, she noted:

Roche. Pleynet wrote on Mark Rothko, Charles Olson (no. 12), Robert Rauschenberg—he compared his painting to Roche's poetry—(13, 18), John Ashbery (18, 20, 27), John Cage (18), Merce Cunningham (18), Cy Trombly (67), Pound (70). See also Pleynet's essays on American art in *Transculture* and *Art et Littérature* published in Collection Tel Quel in 1977. Poetry by Ashbery and Robert Creeley (translated by Roche) appeared in no. 20, prose by William Burroughs in nos. 27 and 66, a text by Richard Foreman in no. 68.

69. The opening conversation among Kristeva, Pleynet, and Sollers was immediately followed by an interview with Sollers conducted by David Hayman in 1975, followed by an excerpt from *Paradis*. Next comes Kristeva's text "Actualité de Céline" (a lecture she gave at Columbia and Yale), followed by Pleynet's poem "La Gloire du ciel." Then we finally get some "American" texts: interviews with Gregory Corso, Stanley Hoffmann, Merce Cunningham, Robert Wilson, Viola Farber, Michael Snow (a reprint of a 1968 interview), a poem by John Ashbery taken from *The Double Dream of Spring*, and texts by Philip Roth, Norman Birnbaum, Domna Stanton, Tom Bishop, and Harry Blake on literature, foreign policy, and women's studies. These are complemented by texts by American academics like Leon Roudiez and Jan Kott on Malraux and Shakespeare, and Telquelians (Pleynet on Robert Motherwell, Scarpetta on American experimental theater). There is also a poem by Marc Hanrez entitled "Wisconsin." The issue closes with other texts by Daniel Sibony, Philippe Nemo, Dominique Desanti, and Gilles Susong.

70. Kristeva, "Why the United States?" in *The Kristeva Reader*, 276. Originally published as "Pourquoi les Etats-Unis?" in *Tel Quel* 71–73 (Autumn 1977).

despite their naïvety, the American audience gives the European intellectual the impression that there is something he can do on the other side of the Atlantic, namely that he can speak in a place where it [ça] doesn't speak. This entails, of course, speaking like a psycho-analytic patient: into a void which returns little more than a dim presence and the punctuation of sounds, colours and gestures. It is very stimulating, I think, for any intellectual work; in any case, it was for mine. (275–76)

Elsewhere, in an article entitled "Des campus pleins d'étoiles" [Campuses full of stars] that appeared in *Le Nouvel Observateur* of 1 January 1978, Kristeva reaffirmed her position, stating that "American civilization . . . is not a civilization of discourse: it's a civilization of sounds, gestures, colors, numbers" and saying, "I feel then that our refinements in the human sciences here, on the old continent, concerning language, literature, religion, or history correspond to something *lived* intensely over there, but on which they have no '*discours*'" (58). Little wonder that many were scandalized by this "condescending description of the non-verbalized American void, which [was] supposedly crying out to be filled with the discourse of European (French?) intellectuals."[71] *Tel Quel*'s interest in American culture was thus considered just another ethnocentric gesture, like its previous fascination with China.

Kristeva claimed that it was necessary to change continents—as she had done for China a few years earlier (273). In her retrospective look at the *Tel Quel* years, "Mémoire" [published subsequently as "My Memory's Hyper-bole"], Kristeva nonetheless admitted that her journey to China had been more cultural than political and had constituted "a return to the only continent that [they] had never left: internal experience [*l'expérience intérieure*]."[72] Kristeva was once again grafting her internal experience—and consequently also her own cultural preoccupations and intellectual prejudices—onto a new continent, but doing so allowed her and fellow Telquelians to construe a political justification for breaking away from the Marxist idols to which they had paid at least theoretical homage a few years earlier. "One only discovers the America that one dreams about at home," wrote Kristeva for *Le Nouvel Observateur*. Thus, the United States represent "a polyvalent, polylogical, cultural space. A chance for freedom with respect

71. Toril Moi, introductory note to "Why the United States?" 272.
72. Kristeva, "My Memory's Hyperbole," 275.

to the ever bi-polar European tradition? A dream, a utopia." If Kristeva's interest in China represented "an anarchist outbreak with Marxism,"[73] where exactly in relationship to Marxism was this "utopian" turn to the States to be situated? Kristeva states: "I feel that American capitalism . . . is a system of permanent recuperation, of patching-up of crisis. Here I don't mean to be pejorative, but rather want to convey a sense of the most livable possibility of survival" (274). Bindé ironically notes that "[o]ne would have been stoned for less than that, only five years ago, in the halls of Vincennes or Nanterre, or even in the seminars of the Rue d'Ulm." No matter how hard Kristeva tries to valorize a so-called American "polyvalent" cultural space and to dismiss the oppressive dimensions of "ghettoization," she never addresses head-on the "divide and rule" strategy that is unmistakenly American and unfortunately successful as an oppressive strategy. Furthermore, in emphasizing the polyvalent cultural subversion of the States, she completely fails to mention the literature—the words, in addition to the colors and gestures that have arisen out of our ethnic enclaves: the great American literature of American minorities. To mention a few authors in passing: Alice Walker, Leslie Marmon Silko, Toni Morrison, Maxine Hong Kingston—who incidentally do not have English origins! But perhaps this cultural nearsightedness coincides with the hexagonal view of literature espoused by *Tel Quel* over the years, which—and this will probably come as no surprise—never published any francophone literature from Africa or the Americas.

Is Kristeva's remark about the lack of a great American literature in the 1970s (in her earlier text "D'Ithaca à New York" she is more specific when she remarks that there is "no contemporary American literature in the sense of 'an experience of limits' "[74]), merely a continental displacement meant to conceal that there is perhaps no great French literature during this period and that the real writing of limits is situated in the outskirts of the French ethnocentric empire—in Africa and the Americas? Furthermore, in stating that she felt "that even though [she] was using a specialized language, [she] was speaking to people [her American audience] who knew what it was about, even if they found it difficult. It corresponded to a lived experience, whether pictorial, gestural or sexual," Kristeva symptomatically omits the adjective "writerly," in the same way she fails to account for an American— and I use this word in its broad denotation to include the rich cultural tradition and practices of all the countries constituting the Americas—

---

73. Kristeva, "Why the United States?" 273.
74. Kristeva, "D'Ithaca à New York," in *Polylogue*, 500.

writing of the experience of limits that has arisen out of the very polyvalent cultural space from which she constructs her theoretical discourse. Perhaps Americans had not needed to theorize about an experience of limits that, as *lived*—rather than *constructed*—experience, has produced a rich, literary expression. In her essay entitled "The Agony of the French Left," which accompanied the American translation of the *Tel Quel* editorial on the States in the Fall 1978 issue of *October*, Annette Michelson concludes, "It is, however, the hypertrophy of the theoretical function in a once artistically productive culture and the operations of a dominantly theorizing elite within its economy which constitute a central problem to be explored by that elite in Giscardian France."[75]

What is important for *Tel Quel* is perhaps not so much the naive image of American culture and society that it projects—it is symptomatic that the adjective "naive" crops up again and again in "Pourquoi les Etats-Unis?" to qualify the people and culture of the States—as what this projection says about the Telquelians' own practice as writers and intellectuals. That is really the crux of the question: "The question is perhaps precisely the kind of vision we offer of America," remarks Pleynet (282). Over and over in their conversation, Kristeva, Sollers, and Pleynet (who maintains a more modest position throughout; most of the remarks in the editorial are, in fact, by Kristeva and Sollers) ask themselves what they are looking for in the States, thereby acknowledging their own intellectual biases:

> We ought to find out what it is we are looking for in them. It's not so much "why do they do this and not that?" as "why do they interest us?" Isn't it because they make an appeal to us by their gap in verbalization [*ce trou de verbalisation*]? And when facing this void we feel we are being called, perhaps not exactly chosen [*élus*], but at least called. (Kristeva 281)

Just how different is Kristeva's language here from that of the European missionaries who came to "civilize" the Americas a few centuries ago? No wonder Michaël West Oborne, an American intellectual living and working in Paris, remarks that this second discovery of the New World has not been less interesting than the first for certain Parisian intellectual circles.[76] He writes:

75. Annette Michelson, "The Agony of the French Left," 23.
76. Michaël West Oborne, "Les Etats-Unis: Pays de Mission?" unpublished paper of 1978.

If, on the other side of the Atlantic, it [ça] doesn't speak, on this side of the ocean, it surprisingly speaks the language of cultural imperialism. In other times, inspired missionaries, informed tradesmen, and slave traders from everywhere felt compelled to answer the call of God or Civilization, thereby discovering the void that justified their business transactions. And, of course, it was not in the name of their business that they claimed to speak, but in the name of a cause that went beyond borders.

Tel Quel, too, is speaking in the name of a cause that goes beyond borders: cosmopolitanism, dissidence. Their vision is neither French nor American, claims Pleynet, because it is not a national one (282). It is, however, distinctly European. Thus, the few exceptions of great American literature are of English origins; Artaud and surrealism seem to be continually present in American culture; and at the source of what they call American art is the grafting of the European avant-garde onto the United States (276, 279, 280). Sollers notes:

> Now, what happened in the twentieth century with the First and Second World Wars? Strangely, we witnessed a completely spectacular grafting of the different subjective liberations which had erupted in Europe as dissidence or marginality. Naturally, I see the main graft at the time of the Second World War as being the draining of marginalized European personalities into an American exile. Let's call it the grafting of the European avant-garde on to the United States. (280)

Pleynet states that he is "very much interested in the fact that the exile of artists and intellectuals to the United States is not only that of the Surrealists; I mean it's not only the exile of the French, it's the exile of all of Europe" (282). While it is true that many exiles from Europe sought political refuge in the States from Fascism and Nazism and this produced a form of transnational art, American art cannot simply be reduced to European dissident and marginal sources, even if this is the form of art valorized by *Tel Quel*. Considering that these intellectuals purport to be cosmopolitan or transnational, it is ironic that they continually insist on theorizing American

---

Kristeva, in effect, states, "there is a passionate search, and a feeling of discovery, even if it sometimes involves discovering the bicycle a century late." In "Why the United States?" 275.

culture from the perspective of its European graft—for which the word *roots* (which they obviously do not care for) could just as easily be substituted. One is left with the feeling that not only are they unable to see anything but the European dimension in American culture, but also that they are trying to reappropriate—if only through the role they assign to themselves of a theoretical "stand-in" (*bouche-trou*; Oborne, in "Les Etats-Unis: Pays de Mission?")—that modernity which European Fascism took away from them. In reducing American culture to its distinctly European dimension, all they see is Europe, that is, themselves. There is nothing very transnational or cosmopolitan (at least from the subversive perspective they attribute to these words) about their discourse on the so-called American arts. Kristeva is more on target (and less ethnocentric) when she concedes: "They took Artaud and Duchamp but produced Pollock, which couldn't have happened in either France or Moscow. So there's something specific and interesting in America" (281). Unfortunately, they are unable to appreciate this specificity, preoccupied, as they are, by themselves. Who is really speaking in this issue on the United States? asks Oborne. What machine has produced this "enormously exhibitionistic discourse" (Sollers 291)?[77]

What business transaction does the American void justify? Are the three Telquelians "talking around the problem of having to redefine a place, (if indeed it is a question of place) for the artist and intellectual that would be neither what one might want to establish in France nor what one can see in the United States?" (Pleynet 287). In wielding the United States as a cultural arm, what exactly is *Tel Quel* trying to combat? Kristeva's desire to change continents—she also admits having gone to the States with "almost the same desire for discovery and change that took [her] from Bulgaria to Paris ten years [earlier]" (273)—was prompted by the realization that "what was happening in France—due to the various developments of a Gaullism in its death-throes on the one hand and the growing power of the so-called masses or petit-bourgeois masses on the other—was making the history of the European continent predictable, so that if one were interested in the breaks within history, culture and time, one had to change continents" (273). Was Kristeva concerned about the so-called demise of Gaullism (which, after all, had not been unkind to her)?

---

77. Oborne uses the term "machine" in response to Kristeva. "It is an immense machine turning Western discourse into refuse," remarks Kristeva about the way Americans "may be getting bogged down today [as] they take anything and everything from Parisian intellectual cuisine" ("Les Etats-Unis: Pays de Mission?" 281).

I came to France because of General de Gaulle. He had a megaloma-
niac idea which consisted of connecting Europe from the Atlantic to
the Urals and he gave fellowships to young nationals from the East
whom the authorities would not send. They were afraid that the
nationals would stay in the West, and they were right.[78]

And what about the growing power of the masses or, more precisely, the
petit-bourgeois masses (who were, according to Kristeva, *Tel Quel*'s constituency)? Let us recall Bindé's assessment of *Tel Quel*'s transatlantic cruise,
for whom the change of continent must be viewed in conjunction with a
generalized attack on Marxism's hold on the petit bourgeois of the West—
social democracy included. Had Kristeva lost faith in *Tel Quel*'s petit-
bourgeois constituency that was on its way to accepting social democracy in
France? Or did the growing power of the masses (petit-bourgeois or other)
represent a threat for the cultural practice of *Tel Quel*? This appeared to be
Barthes's contention when he stated: "In fact, if France becomes a petit-
bourgeois country, intellectuals will lose their identity more and more."[79]
And Michelson wrote: "*Tel Quel*, fearful of Left domination of the superstructure, prefers the cultural permissiveness of a regime whose policy of
economic austerity will, in any case, continue to be paid for by the working
class."[80]

A direction for *Tel Quel*'s cultural practice was certainly not to be found
in the United States, where intellectuals did not appear to have an important
role. Kristeva recognizes that the States do not "accord the status to the
intellectual that exists in Europe . . . where it essentially comes from the
French Revolution's idea of the intellectual as a mediator between the
different political parties and thought."[81] In *Pour Gramsci*, Macciocchi
notes that "France is the country in which the 'conservation' of the intellectual is the object of the most scrupulous attention."[82] For Gramsci, the
consecration of French intellectuals coincides with the important role they
play "as the dominant group's assistants in the exercise of the subaltern
functions of hegemony." As a pivot between the infrastructure and super-

78. Kristeva, "Cultural Strangeness and the Subject in Crisis," *Discourse*, 172.

79. Barthes, "The Crisis of Desire," in *The Grain of the Voice*, trans. Linda Coverdale (New
York: Hill and Wang, 1985), 361. Originally published in *Le Nouvel Observateur* (20 April
1980) and subsequently in *Le Grain de la voix* (Paris: Seuil, 1981).

80. Michelson, "The Agony of the French Left," 19.

81. Kristeva, "Why the United States?" 277.

82. Macciocchi, *Pour Gramsci*, 256.

structure, intellectuals play an irreplaceable role in the bourgeois hegemony of a "cultivated" country (*Pour Gramsci* 254). Macciocchi notes that the "self-conservation" or "self-exaltation" reflected in the superiority complex of Parisian and French intellectuals with respect to foreign cultures merely reinforces bourgeois hegemony and its cosmopolitan rage. Cosmopolitanism—as opposed to internationalism[83]—is, for Gramsci, the diffusion of the dominant bourgeois culture and consequently an elitist phenomenon (*Pour Gramsci* 257). Macciocchi includes engaged intellectuals in this cosmopolitan category:

> One could even say that precisely insofar as it is projected on an international level, the *engagement* of the French intellectual confirms, in its modern configurations, the cosmopolitan role France has played since the Enlightenment through its universal cultural mission, and that intellectuals continue to be the best cultural "ambassadors" of the French nation. (*Pour Gramsci* 262–63)

Judt comes to almost the same conclusions even though he reaches them from a very different political orientation (liberal rather than Marxist). In *Past Imperfect*, he criticizes French intellectuals of the postwar years for taking on international causes, that ended up being, for the most part, self-serving rather than altruistic or humanitarian. The universal dimension of the engaged intellectual and the transnational realities it supported (Soviet, Third World) merely reinforced the status of the French bourgeois, cosmopolitan intellectual. Such an identity could not be lost in engagement.[84]

Judt writes again and again of the lost opportunities for French intellectuals represented by the years 1956–74:

> Starting from a shared premise—that November 1956 marked the end of an era in which communism had dominated the radical imagination—they moved not closer to their eastern European audience but further away, to the point of losing all contact with a large part of their internal constituency. In 1956, French intellectuals thus parted company from much of the rest of the European intellectual

---

83. Scarpetta prefers the bourgeois or elitist term "cosmopolitanism" to "internationalism." In *Eloge du cosmopolitisme*, he writes "Internationalism—or rather: cosmopolitanism" and "As though internationalism, that old term soiled in the congresses of senile bureaucrats and the petrified language of politburos, were once again becoming a new idea in Europe," 12.

84. Judt, *Past Imperfect*, 203.

community at just the moment when they could still have reasserted their leadership, in East and West alike. (281–82)

Judt notes that East and West diverged to the point that the "Prague Spring" of 1968 met uncomprehending and even hostile reactions from certain members of the French Left (281). The Prague reformers were considered petit-bourgeois not only by members of the Parti Socialiste Unifié, as Judt notes, but also by *Tel Quel*, which was supposedly adhering to the PCF party line in not opposing the Soviet invasion of Czechoslovakia. In an interview, Scarpetta admitted that *Tel Quel* had viewed the Prague explosion as a social democratic phenomenon, adding that *Tel Quel*'s enemies, at that time, were social democrats: "*Tel Quel* read Prague through the eyes of Paris—the Latin Quarter and Vincennes clouded their perspective."[85] Let us note, in passing, that Faye, unlike *Tel Quel*, supported the Prague Spring. Therefore, Judt's premise that "only after 1974, and then for reasons of their own that had little to do with the course of events in the Soviet bloc, did the Parisian intellectual community once again begin to look eastward, this time with a modicum of sympathy if not understanding" (281) is also valid for the *Tel Quel* group.

For one last time, during the 1970s and 1980s, French intellectuals "engage polemically with the fellow-travelers of the forties and fifties, calling back across the decades to remind them of their ill-judged commitments and marshaling in evidence the continuing repression of dissidence and opposition within the Soviet bloc."[86] If *Tel Quel* now feels compelled to join this chorus line, it is not because of what changed but because of what remained the same after 1956 (Henric, for example, joined the PCF in 1955; Houdebine, in 1956). Had there been a thorough evaluation of Stalinism in France during the mid-1950s, *Tel Quel* would not have been able, to a large degree, to reenact the drama of left-wing writers in the 1920s and 1950s. The Left's failure to deal with Stalinism initially helped *Tel Quel* in its combat for intellectual hegemony in the aftermath of 1956. *Tel Quel* received the enthusiastic support of a broad spectrum of writers with different ideological leanings, who nevertheless seemed to share a passion for literature and even, in several instances, a nostalgia for those times when writers had not had to dirty their hands in politics. Was the turn to literature another way of overlooking the Stalinist truth after 1956? If this had not

85. Interview with Scarpetta, Paris, 23 June 1987.
86. Judt, *Past Imperfect*, 294.

been the case, *Tel Quel* could not have drawn attention away from the polarizing role played by the Algerian War in the Left's attempts to come or not come to terms with de-Stalinization. But the failure to deal with Stalinism in the 1950s caught up with French writers and intellectuals— including *Tel Quel*—during the late 1960s and 1970s.

Tel Quel was continually criticized for its anachronistic and opportunistic politics: "Strange avant-garde, which politically is always one train behind."[87] I recall a piece—I believe published in *Libération*—that compared *Tel Quel* to a caboose: by not being at the front of the train (where it would have to guide) or in the middle, it could easily remove itself when the right occasion came along and quickly hook up with some other train. But the analogy of the train was also used to criticize Sartre. At the colloquium "Camus and Politics" held in June 1985 at the University of Paris X at Nanterre, Ilios Yannakakis argued that "Sartre [had] always missed the trains of history. When an express left, he hopped onto a bumpy slow train ("omnibus") or onto a train that was staying behind at the station."[88] It was perhaps because his generation missed the express that *Tel Quel*'s would be one train behind. Yannakakis, a former Greek Communist who had sought exile first in Czechoslovakia and then in France after the Soviet invasion of 1968, recalls how already in 1963 Prague was a cultural bridge—albeit a fragile one—between the East and the West: "1968 began in 1963."[89] A certain de-Stalinization had already begun, affecting even the cultural realm where a writer like Kafka had been "rehabilitated." It was with great anticipation that Yannakakis and his Czechoslovakian university students awaited Sartre and Beauvoir's officially sponsored visit to Prague in 1963, only to be violently disappointed to hear Sartre praise socialist realism as the "future of literature" and advocate the "engagé" intellectual: "Your Sartre dropped his pants in front of the authorities," lamented Yannakakis's students (39). Was Sollers then so wrong to claim in 1967 that he "did not think that Sartre, in pursuing such an irresponsible discourse on the literature of the past and that of his time, demonstrated a real understanding of *Marxism?*"[90] Judt also faults Sartre for not being truly "engagé": he had

87. Roger-Pol Droit, "Sollers, philosophe et traducteur de Mao," *Le Monde*, 1 February 1974, 18.

88. Ilios Yannakakis, "Discussion," in *Camus et la politique*, ed. Jeanyves Guérin (Paris: L'Harmattan, 1986), 94.

89. Yannakakis, "Concilier Sartre et la dissidence," *Libération*, special issue on Sartre (1980): 39.

90. Sollers, "Un fantasme de Sartre," *Tel Quel* 28 (Winter 1967): 85.

criticized Flaubert and Goncourt for their failure to speak out against the repression of the Communards, yet he himself never spoke out against Soviet anti-Semitism or in defense of the victims of the show trials.[91]

Judt contends that "the intransigent self-confidence of the postwar intelligentsia survived largely unscathed the experience of the Stalinist years. Were this not the case, the wilder shores of *tiers-mondisme* and Althusserian Marxism of the mid-sixties could never have been reached" (286). Although *Tel Quel* never expressed an interest in the Algerian War, it did turn to Althusserian Marxism as it took on the avant-garde wager in the mid-1960s. Annexing Althusserian Marxism to its theoretical chain seemed innocent enough, and certainly not very compromising. *Tel Quel* could now join the class struggle without abandoning the specificity of writing as Aragon, Sartre, and others had done. The theory-practice articulation seemed painless. Besides, in his 1967 preface to the English translation of *For Marx*, Althusser had even conceded that he had failed to discuss the problem of the "union of theory and practice":

> No doubt I did speak of the union of theory and practice within "theoretical practice," but I did not enter into the question of the union of theory and practice within *political practice*. Let us be precise; I did not examine the general form of historical existence of this union: the "fusion" of Marxist theory and the *worker's movement*. I did not examine the *concrete forms of existence* of this fusion.[92]

Tel Quel was thus spared any danger of being exposed on the political front. Thanks to this "theoreticist deviation," they could keep on doing what they had always done—defending the specificity of the practice and theory of writing as revolutionary in itself—and further consolidate their prestige as revolutionary writers by situating it in the aura of the class struggle. *Tel Quel* continued to defend the absolute necessity of the theory-practice articulation right through the tumultuous events of May 1968, despite the risk of appearing—and perhaps even being—Stalinist in their support of the PCF, even as it failed to recognize the importance of the Chinese Cultural Revolution and to denounce the Soviet invasion of Czechoslovakia. Following Althusser, *Tel Quel* advocated the necessity of theory for revolutionary

91. Judt, *Past Imperfect*, 306.
92. Althusser, "To My English Readers," in *For Marx*, trans. Ben Brewster (New York: Vintage, 1970), 15.

practice and denounced all forms of empiricism. The emphasis on theory allowed *Tel Quel* to put down a movement that not only seemed eclectic and empirical, but that also did not adhere to their schematization of the revolution. And it allowed them to validate the only thing they had: theoretical, not political, practice. Besides, they were not about to take to the streets like their perennial foe, Sartre, with his ever-present guilt complex regarding the role of the intellectual. Nor were they about to join a movement that threatened their social prerogative as writers. The imaginary in the streets and shared by all? Never! Eluard had already made it clear in 1946 that "there would no longer be poets where everyone could be a poet."[93]

With Althusser, Telquelians thought they were safe from any real encounters with Stalinism. But by May 1968, *Tel Quel* was entangled in politics and not just as Marx-spouting theoreticians at an institutionalized gathering at Cluny. This was apparent in *Tel Quel*'s language, which from 1968 to 1971 became more and more hard-line (even Stalinist, as Faye and many other critics claimed). No wonder Faye, acknowledged by several Telquelians, including Sollers and Thibaudeau, as having brought a left-wing political slant to a journal that had initially been apolitical,[94] abandoned the group in 1967, followed by Ricardou and Thibaudeau in 1971. The avant-gardism with Maoist overtones had become unbearably oppressive for them. Scarpetta claimed that *Tel Quel* pushed the avant-garde logic to the point of exasperation. It could go no further.[95] Both in supporting and breaking with PCF revisionism and dogmatism, *Tel Quel* adopted the most hard-line, terroristic—that is, avant-garde—language. Its language is politically overcharged not only in its attempts to legitimate the "fusion" of theory and practice in its avant-garde enterprise, but also in its realization—after 1968—that politics are no longer just theoretical, but real. In its June 1971 manifesto, *Tel Quel* adopts the most excessive language to justify a break that marks, after all, the privileging of theory over politics, and ultimately the break from politics. *Tel Quel*'s language has indeed become "revolutionary," in the true sense of the term.

Tel Quel also ended up dancing a seductive but menacing *paso doble* with the Communist party, just as Sartre, and before him the surrealists, had done. Had *Tel Quel* been unfaithful to literature and ended up sacrificing its

93. Paul Eluard, "La poesia non è sacra," *Il Politecnico* 29 (May 1946): 38.
94. Interviews with Sollers (5 July 1979) and Thibaudeau (19 May 1979).
95. Interview with Scarpetta (23 June 1987).

mission of re-creating a new *NRF* in the wake of *Les Temps Modernes*? Had it duplicated Sartre's or Aragon's dance steps? Not according to former PCF militants Henric and Scarpetta. As Henric so eloquently put it: "Contrary to the avant-garde writers who preceded us, it seems that we caught ourselves in time. Whatever may have been our mild or not so mild ideological deliriums, we never sacrificed our literary and artistic convictions to the political slaughterhouse. Literature is what saved us."[96] Scarpetta also seconded Henric's assertion that their literary and artistic choices never varied: "Let those who talk about our 'changing colors' reflect on this little detail, not the least trivial."[97] What is implied by this assertion that literature saved them from politics? Or, in the midst of accusations about their incessant political oscillations, why this continual recourse to their literary stability? Is it to draw attention away from their politics? To reinforce their strong points? Why are two former PCF militants who abandoned the French Communist Party for *Tel Quel* making this statement? Does this statement assume even more importance given its spokespersons? Are they merely trying to justify abandoning politics for literature? And what about Barthes, who stated that he'd rather be wrong in politics and right in literature?[98] Is he merely assuming the traditional bourgeois idealist stance of "art for art's sake"?

Would Sartre have preferred to be right in politics rather than in litera-ture? In hindsight, critics today acknowledge that he was wrong in literature. Sartre was criticized by *Tel Quel* and other groups for having subordinated literature to a politics that turned out to be the counterpart of the Fascism that had prompted the need for engaged writing: Stalinism. Was he also wrong in politics? After all, while engaging the writer-intellectual in the service of Communism, Sartre also ended up defending the horrors of Stalinism, to the point of losing a number of friends, including David Rousset, Merleau-Ponty, and Camus, and taking some rather outrageous positions. Rousset, for example, failed to understand how in 1950 Sartre could acknowledge the concentration-camp nature of the Soviet regime and yet write that this reality did not have any social and political significance for him.[99] Did Sartre's work as a writer ultimately endorse this totalitarian reality? Although he was considered the loser to Sartre in the famous

96. Henric, "Quand une avant-garde . . ."
97. Interview with Scarpetta (23 June 1987).
98. Barthes cited in Combes, *La Littérature et le mouvement de mai 68*, 236.
99. David Rousset is referring to Sartre's editorial "Les jours de notre vie" published in *Les Temps Modernes* in 1950. See Rousset, "Le drame de l'affrontement politique," in *Le Matin*,

polemic of '52, Camus seems to have survived the vissitudes of history better. But the Telquelians had neither the political determination of Sartre nor the moral vision of Camus. They were, in effect, closer in their practice to the surrealists, and not just (as they hoped) to the dissident Bataille, but also (and perhaps more so) to the idealist Breton.

As it "call[s] back across the decades" to Sartre and Aragon, *Tel Quel* aims to show that, despite their ideological deliriums and political entanglements of the 1960s, they did not end up sacrificing literature for politics. For this reason, in the mid- and late 1970s, *Tel Quel* feels compelled to refer continually to the cultural—and not the political—dimension of dissidence. They are only too happy to see in the dissident movement of the 1970s an ethics that seems to validate their modernist aesthetics. If the dissidents are victims of Marxist and socialist regimes, all the better for *Tel Quel*, eager as it is to show that art and literature can be a liberation from politics. And they are only too eager to advocate a vague humanitarian appeal for human rights that goes beyond all national boundaries and political ideologies, and emphasizes the individual (and, of course, the writer or artist) as a lone ranger.

Marxism ceased to intimidate French intellectuals in the 1970s. Although they claimed to be preoccupied with the advent of Eurocommunism and disturbed by the political reality from which the dissidents had fled, they no longer felt obliged to wave a French-tinged Marxist flag in front of their artistic or intellectual production, as they had done in the past. If political distinctions had formerly divided writers into two camps, the new emphasis on "culture above all" ("la culture avant tout") led to new alliances. In January 1978, a number of Telquelians (Sollers, Kristeva, Pleynet, Devade, Henric, Scarpetta, and Houdebine) joined—along with other intellectuals and artists such as Raymond Aron, Eugène Ionesco, Fernando Arrabal, Emmanuel Levinas, Claude Simon, Emmanuel Le Roy Ladurie, Edgar Morin, Jean-François Revel, Jean-Marie Benoist, and Gérard Depardieu— CIEL (The Committee of Intellectuals for a Europe of Liberties), whose manifesto "La culture contre le totalitarisme. La liberté ne se négocie pas" [Culture against totalitarianism. Freedom is not to be negotiated] occupied a full page of *Le Monde* on 27 January 1978. The manifesto appeared two months before the legislative elections that the Left was supposed to win. The CIEL coalition once again prompted critics of *Tel Quel* to claim that

---

special issue on Sartre (May 1980): 32, and "L'histoire d'une rupture," *Libération*, special Sartre issue (1980): 39.

they had become reactionary since they were now associating with right-wing writers. How could a former Maoist like Sollers possibly sign manifestos with someone like Ionesco, who had supported political regimes like South Korea?[100] Without hesitation, Sollers replied that "above all, he and Ionesco were writers. The time had come to realize that an understanding among writers of supposedly different ideological backgrounds could be possible by the mere fact that they were writers."[101] Not everything could be determined by political criteria, even if this continued to be the hegemonic vision (Sollers, "Eco perché vado d'accordo con Ionesco" 14).

CIEL was thus able to bring together liberal intellectuals of the postwar years like Aron, politically conservative writers like Ionesco, East European dissidents, new philosophers, and Telquelians "to defend the synonymy of these three words: Europe, culture, freedom."[102] A Marxist like Debray was anything but pleased that intellectuals associated with CIEL were taking a "cultural" turn just before the March elections. For him, the engagement implied by CIEL was really one of disengagement, where no negotiation between culture and politics seemed possible.[103] The CIEL manifesto read: "Let it be understood that 'politics first' and 'politics above all' must yield to 'culture first and foremost.'"[104] For Sirinelli, CIEL was part of a neo-liberal revival in the mid- and late 1970s that Judt believes brought a welcome end to the notion of the engagé or universal intellectual.[105] The intellectual no longer accepts the Jacobin model of acting as a mediator between political parties and thought (Kristeva, "Why the United States?" 277) but also does not accept the role of specialist in the American sense given to the term by *Tel Quel*: "I feel that when the political class in the United States calls upon intellectuals—which it does constantly—it calls upon them as specialists."[106] In France, however, notes Pleynet, "intellectuals are called upon to argue about ideas; they can't produce real, objective knowledge and take concrete action" ("Why the United States?" 278). In comparing the propo-

---

100. An interview with Ionesco, "L'homme en question," conducted with Pierre-André Boutang and Sollers for FR3 (the television channel France Région 3) in July 1978, appeared in *Tel Quel* 78 (Winter 1978).
101. Sollers, "Eco perché vado d'accordo con Ionesco," *La Repubblica* (22 June 1978): 14.
102. "Manifeste du comité des intellectuels pour l'Europe des libertés," in Jean-François Sirinelli, *Intellectuels et passions françaises: Manifestes et pétitions au XXe siècle* (Paris: Fayard, 1990), 278. Originally published in *Le Monde*, 27 January 1978.
103. Régis Debray, *Le Scribe* (Paris: Grasset, 1980), 231.
104. "Manifeste du comité des intellectuels pour l'Europe des libertés," 277.
105. Sirinelli, *Intellectuels et passions françaises*, 280. See also Judt, *Past Imperfect*.
106. Pleynet, "Why the United States?" 278.

nents of CIEL with the dissenters of the 1930s, Jean-Marie Domenach—
who incidentally also adhered to CIEL—observes that the latter did not
separate criticism from proposition, and did not defer to politicians the
concern for the institution and monopoly of power.[107] Were intellectuals
once more rendering to Caesar what was Caesar's, thereby also allowing
Caesar to control the "spirit"—culture?[108]

The intellectuals who rallied around CIEL were attempting, on a collective
level—which nevertheless reflected their individual work as writers—to
define a practice that moved beyond the Sartrean notion of engagement and
ideological straitjackets. Although they continued to sign petitions as intellectuals had done in the past, these petitions were more cultural than
political in nature. Since the demise of humanism in the 1930s, writers and
intellectuals had been categorized more by the political positions they had
assumed than by their creative works. Sollers contended that with the
explosion of the Marxist paradigm in the mid-1970s, writers and artists
were less willing to subordinate themselves to a political vision of the world.

Founded in January 1978 by former Marxist-Leninist Alain Ravennes,
CIEL had as its essential mission the refusal to reduce the world and thought
to politics. By reaffirming the primacy of culture over politics, the individual
over the collective, CIEL strove to emphasize that national borders could
never become cultural limits. CIEL sought to defend a liberal, European,
cultural space against chauvinism and xenophobia. Although CIEL focused
essentially on the European community, its objective was the reunification of
Eastern and Central Europe with Western Europe. In this respect, it acknowledged its debt to the dissidents for having eliminated the dichotomy
between East and West, Left and Right. CIEL's founder Ravennes contended
that "Marxism certainly was not its only enemy, but [that] the major danger
today was obviously a certain Marxism" bound up with Eurocommunism
and terrorist Italy.[109]

For CIEL, human rights had no ideological determinations. In the texts
denouncing the intellectual silence surrounding the death of Aldo Moro,
written for CIEL and subsequently published in *Tel Quel* (no. 78, Winter
1978), Leonardo Sciascia, Macciocchi, and Sollers lamented that for the past
fifty years intellectuals had been thinking and acting according to two

107. Jean-Marie Domenach, *Enquête sur les idées contemporaines* (Paris: Seuil, 1981), 60.

108. Vittorini used this metaphor in the opening editorial "Una nuova cultura" of *Il
Politecnico* 1 (29 September 1945): 1.

109. Alain Ravennes cited in Bernardo Valli, "Tutti uniti in nome del Ciel," *La Repubblica*
(22 June 1978): 14.

systems of weights and measures. Left-wing intellectuals were continually obsessed with a possible recuperation by the Right. Sollers condemns the "less heavy weight" of the Italian cadaver of Moro. He remarks that not one petition was made in France asking for public opinion to intercede on behalf of Moro's life. In Italy, discussions became deadlocked in the political dimension. To take a position on behalf of Moro was to be immediately for or against terrorism. Sollers maintains that in refusing to judge violence and death with equal measures, intellectuals lost sight of the Fascist and Stalinist horizon of this century.[110]

If Italy held particular interest for *Tel Quel* in 1977–78, it was because the "historic compromise" foreshadowed what might take place in France if the Communists and Socialists came to power. Thus the Italian backdrop of the Biennale "Cultural Dissidence in the East" held in Venice in December 1977 was pivotal for *Tel Quel*.[111] As the Italian Communist Party went from opposition to power through the notorious "historic compromise," or politics of coexistence with conservative forces, it bore substantial blame for socioeconomic crisis and political repression in Italy. During the spring 1977 student uprisings in the Communist-run cities of Bologna and Rome, the party was inculpated for supporting police intervention and brutality and for attempting to set the working class against the youth movement. These and similar events led to the "French Appeal Against Repression in Italy," launched by such intellectuals as Sartre, Deleuze, Guattari, and Macciocchi, that culminated in the Bologna mass rally of September 1977. The Biennale on dissidence that took place two months later in Venice was boycotted by Italian intellectuals: only Alberto Moravia participated.[112]

Tel Quel's interest in the dissident movement of the 1970s derived not only from the political site from which it stemmed (the Soviet Union and Eastern European countries adhering to the Soviet model), but also to which it emigrated (Western Europe), and from which it actually spoke (exile). *Tel Quel*'s support of the dissidents coincides, on a theoretical level, with its desire to redefine a working definition of the intellectual outside Marxist (and political) parameters and, on a political level, with the rise of Eurocom-

---

110. Sollers, "Nous sommes tous des intellectuels italiens," *Tel Quel* 78 (Winter 1978): 94–96.

111. A number of the proceedings of the Biennale were published in *Tel Quel* 76 (Summer 1978).

112. In "L'Art est supérieur à la réalité," Siniavsky acknowledges Moravia as being not only the sole Italian writer to join the dissidents in Venice, but also among the first Italian writers to speak out on behalf of Daniel and himself during the 1966 trial (56).

munism and, more precisely, with the possibility of a Communist-Socialist government takeover in France. *Tel Quel* refused to draw a distinction not only between Soviet-style Marxism in the East and Eurocommunism in the West, but also between Communist oppression and ultra-left-wing terrorism. Writing on the painful silence surrounding Moro's death, Macciocchi argued that intellectuals had been anesthetized into tolerating crime as a function of ideology. It was time for political crimes to stop benefiting from ideological impunity and mythological justification.[113]

For *Tel Quel*, Moro's death was of the same "weight" as that of Pier Paolo Pasolini. An unrelenting critic of the Christian Democrat Party, Pasolini nevertheless characterized Moro as "he who seems the least implicated in all the horrid acts organized since 1969, whose objective, achieved up to today, is to conserve power."[114] These words were uttered the same year Pasolini himself was assassinated. Macciocchi views these two crimes as sacrificial: "The cadaver of Pasolini, the greatest Italian intellectual, and the cadaver of Moro, the most honest statesman of the Christian Democrat Party, suddenly appear almost simultaneously at the heart of Rome and its outskirts" ("Le crime italien" 100). As celebrities, Pasolini and Moro were antagonists: one was a heretic, the other a moderate. Why did terrorist violence choose the exception (the Communist-Catholic homosexual writer and artist) and the average (a moderate politician and family man) as sacrificial scapegoats (100)? Macciocchi ventures that the "obscure law that kills tolerates neither the singular exception, nor the reserved, 'private' man" (101).

In advocating a dissident politics or singular ethics in the mid- and late 1970s, *Tel Quel* opposed a sacrificial ideology embedded in a political vision of the world. Although such a stance coincided with a new historical crisis that ultimately led to the demise of Marxism-Communism and the avant-garde project, it was not new or original. In many respects, it coincided with the definition of the writer that *Tel Quel* had defended from the onset, even though it had subsequently taken on more pronounced ethical dimensions. Bound up with literary modernity, writing for *Tel Quel* continued to be an "experience of limits," an "inner experience," whose prototypes were Dante, Sade, Kafka, Joyce, Céline, Artaud, Bataille, and Pasolini. In many respects, dissidence merely highlighted the conjunction between literature and ethics that *Tel Quel* had advocated all along. The times had changed, however. If the notion of disengagement had been viewed with extreme

---

113. Macciocchi, "Le crime italien," *Tel Quel* 78 (Winter 1978): 97.
114. Pier Paolo Pasolini cited in Macciocchi, "Le crime italien," 100.

suspicion from the 1940s to the 1970s, by the time *Tel Quel* came to a close in 1982, it had come to stand for a liberation from the mania of political ideologies that had terrorized literature and philosophy for more than thirty years. Disengagement was now perceived as a manner of affirming individual rights over ideological totalitarianism.

In 1980, Sollers declared that *Tel Quel* had put an end to the avant-garde experience. Was *Tel Quel* thus able to prophesy its own end? The death of the avant-garde was bound up with the fall of Marxism, which *Tel Quel* had proclaimed in the mid- and late 1970s. In defending the dissident movement in an era dominated by the rise of Eurocommunism, *Tel Quel* revealed a certain visionary spirit that placed it ahead of its time. It had already foreseen the end of the cold-war or postwar era. Although more than a decade has passed, the recent collapse of Marxism-Communism is certainly a testament to *Tel Quel*'s prophetic vision. The demise of Communism sanctified the death of a review that had lost its very raison d'être. *Tel Quel*'s foremost premise was that literature is invincible. Its long-standing and tenacious opposition to engagement was aimed at asserting this premise. Hence, the downfall of Communism, and with it the Marxist tenets that immobilized the intellectual in the knots of engagement, would have left *Tel Quel* with an immense void. We may venture to say that *Tel Quel* foresaw this void before it could permeate its existence. It was therefore inevitable that *Tel Quel* would cease to be. But *Tel Quel*'s formidable odyssey was not in vain. Despite what many judged to be its palinodes, disengaging literature was its principal mission from the beginning to the end. With the demise of engagement, literature is, in a sense, at peace again. It hardly needs to be defended. *Tel Quel* would say: "Mission accomplie." That *Tel Quel* became *L'Infini* symbolizes, in many respects, the end of a particular historical climate. With *L'Infini*, literature thrives, for the time being, in the equanimity that the *NRF* fostered and savored—if only fleetingly.

CONCLUSION

In 1980, Sollers claimed that *Tel Quel* was on the verge of an extraordinary explosion: it was just getting started after a preparatory phase of twenty-odd years. Two years later, *Tel Quel* had become *L'Infini*. There had been an explosion all right. The path had been cleared once again, and this time it had taken more than the disposal of a few Telquelians. It was now time to change publishers, and so *Tel Quel* was no more. Twenty-odd years. The duration of a journal and the age of its founders in 1960. They were now in their forties. Had they reached midlife crises? After the Revolution, Restoration? In *Carnet de nuit*, Sollers notes, " '68–'78: incredible freedom on the whole. Before is before, and after, after. Enough to write fifty novels."[1] Sollers had time to write his novels now that literature no longer appeared to be under siege. And he was writing them at the rate of almost one a year.[2]

Although *Tel Quel* ceased publication in 1982, its odyssey is, in a sense,

---

1. Sollers, *Carnet de nuit* (Paris: Plon, 1989), 88.
2. *Femmes* (1983), *Portrait du joueur* (1984), *Paradis II* (1986), *Le Coeur absolu* (1987), *Les Folies françaises* (1988) and *Le Lys d'or* (1989), *La Fête à Venise* (1991), *Le Secret* (1992).

not over. Unable to carry over its name after its founder Sollers abandoned the Editions du Seuil for the more prestigious publishing house Gallimard in January 1983, *Tel Quel* relinquished its original name for *L'Infini*. The opening editorial of *L'Infini* suggests that *Tel Quel* was merely a threshold (*seuil*) that had been crossed by now. In crossing this threshold, did Sollers realize the *NRF* dream? After all, he acquired a broad audience with the publication of his first literary best-seller, *Femmes* (1983), by the most powerful publishing house in France. Sollers had had his eye on the *NRF* and Gallimard since the late 1950s. In 1957, despite the intercessions of Ponge and Paulhan on his behalf, Sollers's "Introduction aux lieux d'aisance" was rejected by Marcel Arland, who found it too scatological for the *NRF*.[3] In the summer of 1960, Sollers had also tried to leave Seuil for Gallimard.[4] Furthermore, in an interview in 1987, one Telquelian confidentially confided to me that Sollers had been most disappointed when he had not been entrusted with the editorship of the *NRF* in 1987.[5]

Does Gallimard's patronage of *Tel Quel*'s successor indicate that it finally attained the status of the *NRF*? Certainly not. The *NRF* and its writers enjoyed a consecration in the temporal sphere—the *NRF* not only founded its *own* publishing house, already a remarkable achievement, but the *most* prestigious one in France—that gave the writer an authority and influence he would never again have. Sollers and his cohorts have not achieved the literary status of Proust, Gide, or Malraux. In making these comparisons, I am not just establishing an aesthetic distinction but an economic one as well. As a writer today, Sollers cannot enjoy the kind of prestige that Proust or Gide did. The *NRF* represented a merger among the three realms of production, distribution, and legitimation, which today are split up. Or to "put it another way, the merger then operated at the level of the producers and according to their norms, whereas it now operates at the level of the distributors and according to theirs."[6] The *NRF* succeeded in creating an autonomous literary milieu, independent of the university, which, according to Debray, had established its hegemony from 1880 until 1930. The apogee of the publishing cycle, which subsumed and prolonged the one of the university, marked the golden age of French thought—florescence, equilib-

---

3. It was published anonymously in the second issue of *Tel Quel* (Summer 1960) and subsequently reprinted in *L'Intermédiaire*. On the vicissitudes of the text, see Paulhan and Ponge, *Correspondance II (1946–1968)*, 208–12.

4. See Paulhan and Ponge, *Correspondance II*, 303.

5. Jacques Réda replaced Georges Lambrichs in September 1987.

6. Régis Debray, *Teachers, Writers, Celebrities*, 67.

rium, and maturity (*Teachers, Writers, Celebrities* 65–66). As much as he seeks to resuscitate this golden age, it is not one that Sollers will enjoy. Perhaps the demise of the *NRF* during the Occupation and the rise of Sartrean engagement are less to blame than the media's supplanting of the publishing hegemony: "The hegemony of the publisher, symbolized by the Gallimard imprint, lasted until the 1960s, when the publishing world began to lose the economic and intellectual initiative. As it ceased to polarize the magnetic field of the literary intelligentsia, it began itself to be polarized by a very different system of gravitation" (Debray, *Teachers, Writers, Celebrities* 62).

In attempting to resuscitate the *NRF* as *Tel Quel* in the 1960s and then being taken on by Gallimard in the 1980s, Sollers does not establish the infrastructure for his symbolic mission the way the *NRF* did. It is a major shortcoming, considering how much Sollers advocated an extrainstitutional status for *Tel Quel* over the years. The review may have succeeded in preserving its independence from the university milieu (and then only superficially, considering its university-trained readership)—in a period ("les trente glorieuses") when the explosion of the university posed a new threat to the publishing hegemony—but it did not, like the *NRF*, set in place an oppositional infrastructure to legitimate its symbolic conquest. The best that Sollers could do was to join Seuil—in the shadow of Gallimard—and subsequently Gallimard, in the shadow of the *NRF*. *Tel Quel* could only take its place at the end of a cycle that it unsuccessfully tried to duplicate. It may have continually fought off the university, thereby deluding itself into thinking that it preserved a sort of extrainstitutional status (even though it was always at the mercy of Seuil); but in failing to create a new form of cultural action, that is, its own infrastructure, it merely marked the end of an era.

Grandiose as its new title may seem, *L'Infini* is not *Tel Quel*. Indeed, the media and intellectual interest sparked by *Tel Quel* has dissipated. In "Goodbye to All That," the concluding chapter to *Past Imperfect*, Judt writes: "The 'little' journals of the intelligentsia continue to come and go; but no one now waits with bated breath for the latest number of *Temps modernes* or *Tel Quel*."[7] Debray would probably equate this loss of public interest in the review-form with the end of the publishing era, which nevertheless also coincides with the collapse of Marxism-Communism and the expiration of the avant-gardes. The revolutions in Eastern Europe and

---

7. Judt, *Past Imperfect*, 295.

the collapse of the Soviet Union appear to have eliminated whatever was left of one of the major political and ideological pillars of postwar European life.[8] Who, asks Judt, now takes seriously the promises of Marxism, the assurances of even modest utopian futures (*Past Imperfect* 294)? An era guided by the belief that a revolutionary cultural practice must go hand in hand with the struggle for socialism appears to have come to an end. In a 1980 interview provocatively entitled "On n'a encore rien vu" [You haven't seen anything yet], Sollers contended that *Tel Quel* had put an end to the century-old contradiction between art and political commitment. They were now ready to begin something else.[9] Whether *Tel Quel* put an end to the avant-garde adventure or was merely part of an era that dismissed the feasibility and desirability of such an enterprise, the group had at least come to the realization, as Sollers claimed in 1978, that the "avant-garde" is an expression paradoxically applied to the arts when the evolutionary myth is already a regression in the real (Fascism, Nazism, Stalinism).[10]

Telquelians may have relived the adventure of the twentieth-century avant-gardes, but if they never entirely gave in to politics, it is largely because they were more interested in theoretical rather than political practice. It is in the name of a revolutionary theoretical practice that they initially stood by the PCF during the events of May 1968 and subsequently broke with the party for Mao's more liberating brand of Marxism, and finally separated themselves from Marxism altogether in the mid-1970s. Maoism was definitely better for *Tel Quel* in that it was more theoretical—a distant mirage to ward off the looming reality of social democracy in France. As *Tel Quel* continued to look for a brand of Marxism that increasingly emphasized the superstructure to the exclusion of the infrastructure, it finally made the total break between politics and culture. The "cultural" turn to China thus became, in Kristeva's own words, a return to the only continent they had never left (or abandoned, as Henric claimed): inner experience or literature. "In any case, what never changed was the preoccupation of rigorously preserving the independence of the experience of writing, of literature."[11] Telquelians could thus claim that they had never abandoned literature for politics, despite some rather opportunistic measures taken in the process to assert and preserve themselves in the intellectual field.

8. Ibid., 294.
9. Sollers, "On n'a encore rien vu," 25.
10. Sollers, "Crise de l'avant-garde?" *Art Press International* 16 (March 1978): 6.
11. Sollers, "On n'a encore rien vu," 25.

In one important sense, they did not give in to politics. Unlike Sartre, they never once experienced guilt about being writers. Debray estimated that a day of freedom for Sollers (or himself) devoted to the profession of scribe costs, at the very *least*, ten children's lives.[12] Sartre had known this all along: "*Nausea* doesn't really measure up against a child dying of hunger." And yet he also stated that "literature must be universal. The writer must thus place himself on the side of the greatest number, of the two billion who are starving, if he wants to address all and be read by all."[13] If one of his literary masterpieces cannot measure up to the reality of a dying child, just what exactly is the writer doing on the side of the starving? Will the starving populace read his work? There is an implicit arrogance in a writer claiming to be a universal conscience speaking out for others. Especially if that writer is a European speaking for the "Third World" or a bourgeois speaking for the "masses." It is a privilege that, according to Judt, changes nothing with respect to the bourgeois identity of the European writer.

Bernard Pingaud, Sartre's associate for eight years at *Les Temps Modernes*, contends that Sartre did not really abandon or renounce the mission of writing: he simply accomplished it while denouncing it.[14] The power of literature led to a certain humility, compensated, however, by what many consider to be a presumptuousness in the intellectual or political realm. Pingaud nonetheless argues that Sartre always wrote against the writer that he fundamentally was. This detour was the price to be paid for sacrificing what never ceased to fascinate him—art, and even style:

> *Les Mots* were supposed to be "*an adieu to literature.*" But I do not think that it is a coincidence if the work concludes, or rather interrupts itself, with the monumental *Flaubert*. Whatever Sartre may have said in this "*true novel*" where he presents a writer who is detested and admired, both a foil and a model, it is he with whom we meet up, he and literature which are one, his only true passion. ("Sartre: La Littérature et les Autres" 29)

Sartre's *Flaubert* was perhaps his ultimate masterpiece—not the *Critique*—like Aragon's *Aurélien*. Had engagement thus been in vain? Merely "politics by proxy" (Merleau-Ponty)?

12. Debray, *Le Scribe*, 242.
13. Sartre cited in Ricardou, "Une question nommée littérature," in *Problèmes du nouveau roman* published in Collection Tel Quel (Paris: Seuil, 1967), 16.
14. Bernard Pingaud, "Sartre: La Littérature et les Autres," *Le Matin*, special issue on Sartre (1980): 29.

Telquelians, including Macciocchi, never stopped admonishing Sartre for his schizophrenic relationship with writing, which they argued stemmed from engagement. Sartre may have been at Billancourt or with the barricaders of May, but that did not prevent him from progressing with his Flaubert project, volume after volume: "I'll finish my Flaubert." That is, he continued to do what *Tel Quel* had done all along, without feeling guilty or obliged to divert attention elsewhere. For Macciocchi, "engagement" implied "disengagement"; it just served to create an alibi in the absence of an "organic link" with the proletariat (whereas a structural link exists with the bourgeoisie). Engagement, claims Macciocchi, allows us to understand why intellectuals in France, thanks to their support of a noble cause or their "revolt," are always said to be on the Left—theoretically ["en principe"]. Furthermore, membership in the party merely gives them the illusion of being in the circuit of the masses.[15] This is not to say, of course, that *Tel Quel*'s relationship with the masses was any more organic than Sartre's had been, no matter how much they sought to delude themselves and others with their reading of Gramscian, Maoist, and Althusserian theory.

There was one marked difference, however, between Sartre and the Telquelians. It had to do with guilt: that notion that historians and sociologists coming from such diverse ideological backgrounds as Macciocchi, Judt, and Gilbert Joseph[16] claim is the basis of engagement. Remorse for being a writer was a sentiment never shared by the *Tel Quel* group. Sartre continually confessed that the intellectual, in his being (that is, as a bourgeois), was always an enemy of the people. Yet Sartre never abandoned the intellectual role despite what appeared to *Tel Quel* and others to be schizophrenic or even self-serving behavior. Sartre himself admitted that even though he felt powerless as a writer, he would go on writing. Telquelians, on the other hand, were just as consistent in their polar opposite stance. They not only refused to feel guilty as writers (and elitist ones at that) but even claimed that they had nothing to feel guilty about because their practice was a safeguard from a guilt complex that had prevented writers from satisfactorily accomplishing what they had set out to do—write—and also led them to let their practice be swallowed up by totalitarian causes that ended up making them the servants of one gulag or another. Were they merely manifesting the "art for art's sake" syndrome? In many respects, their views converged with the

15. Macciocchi, *Pour Gramsci*, 263.
16. See Gilbert Joseph's *Une si douce Occupation: Simone de Beauvoir et Jean-Paul Sartre (1940–1944)* (Paris: Albin Michel, 1991).

nineteenth-century Romantics' emphasis on the self as the only certitude in a time of change and on the "superior reality" of Art in a era when a bourgeois market-oriented society had replaced the aristocratic patronage of the arts. In 1986, Sollers claimed that he was living in a nihilistic period where he could only recommend the greatest possible disengagement.[17] Were writers and intellectuals suffering from what Judt, paraphrasing Kundera, called the "unbearable lightness" of their being (306)? Had we reached a phase of intellectual burnout? Between Sartre's guilt complex and *Tel Quel*'s smugness, where do we draw the line?

The line is perhaps a historical one, and a fragile one at that. Today, the French writer and intellectual no longer feels the need to be "engaged" so as not to appear a musty reactionary and residual collaborator. Today, so it seems, it is the engaged writer or intellectual who is obsolete. "The intellectual-as-hero is a dying genre," concludes Judt (*Past Imperfect* 294). No wonder Larry Kritzman entitles his review of Anna Boschetti and Howard Davies's critical texts on *Les Temps Modernes* "Those Oldies but Goodies," and begins with "the painful consciousness of the passing of that now prehistoric creature known as the politically committed French intellectual."[18] Kritzman concludes that reading again about *Les Temps Modernes* allows "us to reflect on a time when politics, ethics, and the demands of history come together to create the enabling myth of the committed French intellectual" (102). Kritzman is entitled to be nostalgic about a time when intellectuals could associate their writing with great revolutionary causes. But would Judt call Kritzman a "latter-day nostal-gic" for taking such a position? Judt claims that the years 1944–56

> were not a golden age of intellectual responsibility but quite the reverse; never were French intellectuals so *irresponsible*, saying and writing whatever they desired, pronouncing angrily on a subject one month, neglecting it thereafter for years to come, at no cost either to their reputations or their skins. Their engagements and affiliations smack less of a sense of collective moral responsibility or a desire to influence public sentiment than of the need to give themselves a clean social and political conscience. (307)

17. Sollers, "Voir ce qui est, et en jouir," *Art Press International* 102 (April 1986): 44.
18. Larry Kritzman, "Those Oldies but Goodies: *Les Temps Modernes* Revisited," *L'Esprit Créateur* 29, no. 4 (Winter 1989): 97.

I do not entirely agree with Judt, however, that the postwar years were special only because intellectual confidence and self-promotion were carried to unusual heights (307). It is true, as Judt notes, that the intellectual privilege associated with that era was not unique and belonged to a century-old tradition. That the moral underpinnings and political repercussions of such a tradition need to be critically examined on a regular basis goes without saying. Even Barthes acknowledged this when he defended Sollers's oscillations as a healthy deconstruction of the intellectual mission. In the aftermath of the Dreyfus affair, when the intellectual emerged as a social entity, he became "a kind of prosecuting attorney on the side of angels."[19] Barthes does not question the intellectual's need to act, but is interested by the possibility that Sollers offers "of disturbing the splendidly robed figure of an impeccably clear conscience"; as a consequence, "the superego of the intellectual as an emblem of Fidelity, of the moral Good," is called into question (*Writer Sollers* 98).

The need for a clean social and political conscience went hand in hand with the search for a new culture during the war and postwar years. Writers had to come to terms with an intellectual stance of "nonparticipation": "the writer was marked, compromised up to his furthest retreat."[20] The Occupation had convinced Sartre's generation that they were responsible. Michel-Antoine Burnier notes: "Their inactivity during the prewar period [had] not [been] a retreat from an absolutely indifferent world, but resignation—permissiveness toward History and those who were leading it toward catastrophe."[21] For Sartre, Beauvoir, Merleau-Ponty, and the other founders of *Les Temps Modernes*, it was time to put an end to the idealist illusion. This meant taking an intellectual stance that no longer favored the realm of abstract thought over direct action, the comfortable intellectual distance of the ivory tower over the malaise of being "situated" in one's sociopolitical reality. If postwar writers became overzealous in their search for a new culture based on a different set of values than the ones bequeathed by an idealist "culture of consolation" (Vittorini, "Una nuova cultura" 1) to the point of advocating a less than utopian alternative worldview and reality, it is because of the history they witnessed, lived, or tried to hide from the 1930s to the 1950s. But it is true that despite the economic difficulties of postwar Europe, engaged writers and intellectuals benefited from a context that had

19. Roland Barthes, *Writer Sollers*, 98.
20. Sartre, "Présentation," *Les Temps Modernes* 1 (October 1945): 3.
21. Burnier, *Choice of Action*, 8.

left prewar culture—and the terrain heretofore cultivated by the *NRF*—razed to the ground. Sartre knew that the Liberation had been the intellectuals' "perfect moment": "with the traditional powers in collapse or disarray, the mandarinate had enjoyed an unexampled public emminence; its very word seemed laden with portentous meaning."[22] Drawing from Michel Crozier, H. Stuart Hughes notes, however, that if intellectuals never quite succeeded in defining a content for their doctrine of universal responsibility, it is because they oscillated erratically "between the total liberty of the individual revolutionary and the total constraint of Stalinism" (*Obstructed Path* 263).

Today, French intellectuals have certainly lost the power that they wielded in the postwar era. But then the sociopolitical reality is a very different one. France, fortunately, is not in the aftermath of war and the Occupation. This is not to say that *Tel Quel* did not reap the benefits of a historical context characterized—especially after 1956—by a profound disillusionment with, if not antipathy for, political ideologies that had led to marriages of convenience and had not necessarily eliminated the causes of intellectual guilt. We can therefore understand why a generation born at the eve or the morning after the demise of the Third Republic, for whom the backdrop of childhood was the Occupation and adolescence the Algerian War, could have, like Huguenin, despised the generation of its elders and deemed their engagement a belated justification for their between-the-wars happiness. We can also see why they did not believe that they had to share that generation's guilt: they thought that they had already sufficiently paid for their elders' debts, "their miserable between-the-wars happiness" (Huguenin, "Aimer la vie" 56). Besides, what was so bad about advocating that literature be free of political ideologies? What good had politics done if instead of so-called bourgeois (disengaged) literature they now had bourgeois literature wrapped in socialist cellophane? *Tel Quel* went back to "literature" with a clear conscience. Nevertheless, according to Camus, "Man is not entirely guilty, for he did not begin history, nor is he entirely innocent, since he continues it."[23] Vladimir Jankélévitch maintained that no moral conscience could exist without a certain sentiment of guilt.[24] While it may take years to form a moral conscience, centuries to build a more just society, it takes very little time to destroy all our

22. H. Stuart Hughes, *The Obstructed Path*, 262–63.
23. Camus cited in a special dossier entitled "Relire Camus" in *Le Point* 1091 (14 August 1993): 59.
24. Vladimir Jankélévitch cited in Elisabeth Badinter, "Le grand silence des déserteurs," *Le Nouvel Observateur*, 29 July 1983, 29.

efforts (Badinter, "Le grand silence des déserteurs"). Where peace is cultivated, also takes root the time of dangers.[25]

A few weeks before his death in January 1960, Camus was asked whether he was driven by the preoccupation of being a "guide" for his generation. Camus replied that he found such a notion amusing. He claimed that he did not speak for anyone; he had enough trouble finding his own language: "I don't guide anyone: I don't know, or I barely know, where I'm going. I don't live on a tripod: I walk at the same pace as everyone else in the streets of time."[26] Today, Camus's words seem less blasé than realistic. Do writers understand society or know themselves better than anyone else in the world? What is so special about writing that it automatically confers a certain social aura on an individual? Wasn't one of Sartre's and *Tel Quel*'s objectives to be done with the valorizing and sacralizing notions of author and work? As Barthes repeatedly stated, writers merely had a certain relationship to language, but that did not imply that they were missionaries or prophets, roles that, unfortunately, even certain Telquelians and new philosophers have perpetuated. For even in liberating literature from political engagement, Telquelians attributed to literature—and themselves—a rather privileged status in a world where most still have more urgent matters to tend to than reading, let alone reading the "greats." And we should not ignore that one of their main reasons for seeking to free literature from politics was so that they could once again have the power that the *NRF* group had wielded in the years between the wars. These writers were not just defending literature for literature's (art for art's) sake, but for themselves.

This is not to say that literature—if there can be a consensus around this term that is not guided solely by power relations—and writers have no importance in this world. Perhaps Sartre, anguishing over political commitment and his realization that he was indeed a writer and that he enjoyed being one, too quickly dismissed the sword in the pen in his autobiographical work, *Les Mots*. There is something far from inconsequential about literature when we consider the fates of Salman Rushdie, Rachid Mimouni, and Taslima Nasreen who have been forced into exile and hiding, or Tahar Djaout who was assassinated. Victims of a new form of ethnic totalitarianism stemming from the most recent resurgence of nationalisms and funda-

25. Bernard Henri-Lévy quotes a verse from Hölderlin that Camus particularly liked: "Là où croît le danger, croît aussi ce qui sauve," remarking that, today, Camus would probably say "Là où vient la paix, croît aussi le temps des dangers." See "Si Camus était vivant," *Le Point*, 14 August 1993, 51–52.

26. Camus, "Dernière Interview d'Albert Camus (20 December 1959)," in *Essais*, 1925.

mentalisms, they have been sentenced to death because they write. Words are still to be feared even in today's world of sophisticated technological power. A certain form of writing that advocates the rights of individuals over and above oppressive ideologies is still alive and well, even as its proponents risk being killed. *Tel Quel* can be commended for defending the rights of writers for whom, as Camus repeatedly noted, there are no privileged executioners. But it is not enough to pay lip service to a cause. It is not enough to say, as does *L'Infini*, that writers are necessarily in the opposition. Telquelians spoke too quickly and irresponsibly on behalf of the revolution, thereby also allowing themselves to be lured by the specters of Stalin. The connivances were perhaps less consequential the second time around if only because the stakes were purely theoretical. Advocating that the work of intellectuals no longer be guided by "universal" but rather by "specific" concerns, Foucault was not entirely convinced that intellectuals were a desirable social category. What he was certain about, however, was that intellectuals should exercise more care in taking on revolutionary causes: "I dream of the intellectual . . . who asks whether revolution is worth the trouble and which one (I mean which revolution and which trouble), it being understood that only those who risk their lives to make the revolution are entitled to answer this question."[27] I am afraid that the Telquelians are not among those Foucault had in mind. Clearly, very few writers—"engaged," "dissident," or "other"—are entitled to answer this question that continues to haunt us today. Writers like Giame Pintor, Pier Paolo Pasolini, Primo Levi, Mouloud Feraoun, Anna Gréki, Rachid Mimouni, Jean Sénac, and Tahar Djaout paid the ultimate price for defending the "irreducible alterity" of individuals. Whether writing against Fascism or Communism, colonialism or nationalism, anti-Semitism or homophobia, religious or political terrorism, they paid more than lip (pen) service to revolutionary ideals and dissident beliefs.

---

27. Foucault, "The End of the Monarchy of Sex," in *Foucault Live*, 155. I have used my own translation from the original French version, "Non au sexe roi," *Le Nouvel Observateur*, 12 March 1977.

SELECT BIBLIOGRAPHY

Abraham, Pierre, and Roland Desne, ed. *Manuel d'histoire littéraire de la France.* Vol. 6. Paris: Editions Sociales, 1982.

Althusser, Louis. *Reading Capital.* Translated by Ben Brewster. New York: Pantheon, 1970.

———. *For Marx.* Translated by Ben Brewster. New York: Vintage, 1969, 1970.

Anderson, Perry. *Reflections on Western Marxism.* London: New Left, 1976.

Aragon, Louis. *J'abats mon jeu.* Paris: Réunis, 1959.

Artaud, Antonin. "Chiote à l'esprit." *Tel Quel* 3 (Autumn 1960): 3–8.

Aubral, François, and Xavier Delcourt. *Contre la nouvelle philosophie.* Paris: Gallimard, 1977.

Badinter, Elisabeth. "Le grand silence des déserteurs." *Le Nouvel Observateur,* 29 July–4 August 1983, 29.

Bann, Stephen. "The Career of *Tel Quel: Tel Quel* becomes *L'Infini.*" *Comparative Criticism* 6 (1984): 327–39.

Barthes, Roland. "L'aventure sémiologique." *Le Monde,* 7 June 1974, 28.

———. *Critical Essays.* Translated by Richard Howard. Evanston: Northwestern University Press, 1972.

———. *Criticism and Truth.* Translated by Katrine Pilcher Keuneman. Minneapolis: University of Minnesota Press, 1987.

———. *The Grain of the Voice.* Translated by Linda Coverdale. New York: Hill and Wang, 1985.

———. *The Rustle of Language.* Translated by Richard Howard. New York: Hill and Wang, 1986.

———. *Sur Racine.* Paris: Editions du Seuil, 1963, 1966.

———. "To Write: An Intransitive Verb?" In *The Language of Criticism and the Sciences of Man,* edited by Richard Macksey and Eugenio Donato. Baltimore: Johns Hopkins University Press, 1970.

———. *Writer Sollers.* Translated by Philip Thody. Minneapolis: University of Minnesota Press, 1987.

Bataille, Georges. *Death and Sensuality.* New York: Walker, 1962.

———. *Inner Experience.* Translated by Leslie Anne Boldt. Albany: State University of New York Press, 1988.

————. "La 'vieille taupe' et le préfixe *sur* dans les mots *surhomme* et *surréaliste*." *Tel Quel* 34 (Summer 1968): 5–17.

Baudry, Jean-Louis. "Linguistique et production textuelle." Paper presented at the colloquium "Linguistique et Littérature" (Colloque de Cluny, 16–17 April 1968). Published in *La Nouvelle Critique*, special issue (1968): 48–54.

————. "La Tragédie racinienne: Une oeuvre ouverte." *Tel Quel* 15 (Autumn 1963): 65–67.

Benjamin, Walter. *Understanding Brecht*. Translated by Anna Bostock. London: New Left, 1973.

Benoist, Jean-Marie. "Au nom des Lumières . . ." *Le Monde*, 5 September 1977, 2.

Benveniste, Emile. *Problems in General Linguistics*. Translated by Mary Elizabeth Meek. Coral Gables: University of Miami Press, 1971.

Berger, Suzanne. "The French Revolution in Contemporary French Politics." *French Politics and Society* 8, no. 2 (Spring 1990): 261–67.

Bertherat, Yves. "Essais." *Esprit* 33, no. 334 (January 1965): 284–86.

————. "La pensée folle." *Esprit* 35, no. 360 (May 1967): 862–81.

Bindé, Jérome. "L'Internationale transatlantique ou un gauchisme de croisière." *Le Monde*, 5 November 1977, 2.

Blanchot, Maurice. *L'Espace littéraire*. Paris: Gallimard, 1955, 1968.

————. *Michel Foucault as I Imagine Him*. In *Foucault/Blanchot*, translated by Jeffrey Mehlman and Brian Massumi. New York: Zone Books, 1987.

Boisrouvray. "Du surréalisme, quand même." *Tel Quel* 10 (Summer 1962): 69–70.

Boschetti, Anna. *The Intellectual Enterprise: Sartre and "Les Temps Modernes."* Translated by Richard McCleary. Evanston: Northwestern University Press, 1988.

Breton, André. *Oeuvres complètes*. Vol. 2. Paris: Gallimard, 1992.

————. *Situation du surréalisme entre les deux guerres*. Paris: Editions de la Revue Fontaine, 1945.

Brochier, Jean-Jacques. "Tel quel, du nouveau roman à la révolution culturelle." *Magazine Littéraire* 65 (June 1972): 9–10.

Buin, Yves, ed. *Que peut la littérature?* Paris: Union Générale d'Editions, 1965.

Burnier, Michel-Antoine. *Choice of Action*. Translated by Bernard Murchland. New York: Random House, 1968.

Camus, Albert. *Essais*. Edited by Roger Quilliot and Louis Faucon. Paris: Bibliothèque de la Pléiade, 1965.

————. "Ce qu'il disait." *Le Point* 1091 (14–20 August 1993): 59.

Césaire, Aimé. *Discourse on Colonialism*. Translated by Joan Pinkham. London: Monthly Review Press, 1972.

————. *Letter to Maurice Thorez*. Paris: Editions Présence Africaine, 1957.

Charvet, Monique, and Ermanno Krumm. *Tel Quel: Un'avanguardia per il materialismo*. Bari: Dedalo, 1970.

Châtelet, François. "Récit." *L'Arc* 70 (1977): 3–15.

Chiss, Jean-Louis. "Julia Kristeva et le rôle des intellectuels." *La Nouvelle Critique* 107 (October 1977): 63–64.

Clément, Catherine. "A l'écoute de Derrida." *L'Arc* 54 (1973): 16–19.

Cohen, Francis. "Le sens d'un colloque." Paper presented at the colloquium "Littérature et idéologies," (Cluny II, 2–4 April 1970). Published in *La Nouvelle Critique*, special issue 39a (1970): 6–8.

Combes, Patrick. *La Littérature et le mouvement de Mai 68*. Paris: Seghers, 1984.

Cooper, David. *Qui sont les dissidents*. Paris: Editions Galilée, 1977.

Culler, Jonathan. "Jacques Derrida." In *Structuralism and Since*, edited by John Sturrock. New York: Oxford University Press, 1981.

Daix, Pierre. "Et si nous étions passés à côté de la littérature soviétique?" *Les Lettres Françaises*, 7–13 July 1966, 11–12.

Debray, Régis. *Que vive la République*. Paris: O. Jacob, 1989.

———. *Le Scribe*. Paris: Grasset, 1980.

———. *Teachers, Writers, Celebrities: The Intellectuals of Modern France*. Translated by David Macey. London: NLB and Verso, 1981.

Deleuze, Gilles. "A propos des nouveaux philosophes et d'un problème plus général." *Recherches* 30 (November 1977): 179–84.

———. "Nuovi filosofi, siete zero." *La Repubblica*, 25 June 1977, 10–11.

Della Volpe, Galvano. "Settling Accounts with the Russian Formalists." *New Left Review* 113–14 (January–April 1979): 133–45.

Derrida, Jacques. *Of Grammatology*. Translated by Gayatri Chakravorty Spivak. Baltimore: Johns Hopkins University Press, 1974, 1976.

———. "La parole soufflée." *Tel Quel* 20 (Winter 1965): 41–67.

———. *Positions*. Translated by Alan Bass. Chicago: University of Chicago Press, 1981.

———. *Writing and Difference*. Translated by Alan Bass. Chicago: University of Chicago Press, 1978.

Descombes, Vincent. *Modern French Philosophy*. Translated by L. Scott-Fox and J. M. Harding. New York: Cambridge University Press, 1980.

Dispot, Laurent. *La Machine à terreur*. Paris: Grasset, 1978, 1984.

Domenach, Jean-Marie. *Enquête sur les idées contemporaines*. Paris: Seuil, 1981.

Droit, Roger-Pol. "Sollers, philosophe et traducteur de Mao." *Le Monde*, 1 February 1974, 18.

Eluard, Paul. "La poesia non è sacra." *Il Politecnico* 29 (May 1946): 38.

Erlich, Victor. *Russian Formalism*. The Hague: Mouton, 1955, 1980.

Faye, Jean-Pierre. "Le camarade 'Mallarmé.'" *L'Humanité*, 12 September 1960, 5.

———. *Commencement d'une figure en mouvement*. Paris: Editions Stock, 1980.

———. "Interphone." *Tel Quel* 30 (Summer 1967): 93–94.

———. "Mise au point." *L'Humanité*, 10 October 1969, 9.

———. Personal interviews. Paris, 23 and 30 May 1979.

———. *Le Récit hunique*. Paris: Seuil, 1967.

Felman, Shoshana. *Writing and Madness*. Ithaca: Cornell University Press, 1985.

Foucault, Michel. *The Birth of the Clinic: An Archaeology of Medical Perception*. Translated by A. M. Sheridan Smith. New York: Pantheon, 1973.

———. *Death and the Labyrinth: The World of Raymond Roussel*. Translated by Charles Ruas. Garden City, N.Y.: Doubleday, 1986.

———. "The Discourse on Language." In *The Archaeology of Knowledge*, translated by A. M. Sheridan Smith. New York: Harper and Row, 1972.

———. "Distance, Aspect, Origine." In *Théorie d'ensemble*. Collection Tel Quel. Paris: Seuil, 1968.

———. *Foucault Live*. Edited by Sylvère Lotringer. New York: Semiotext(e) Foreign Agents Series, 1989.

———. *Language, Counter-Memory, Practice*. Translated by Donald Bouchard and Sherry Simon. Ithaca: Cornell University Press, 1977.

———. *Maurice Blanchot: The Thought from Outside*. In *Foucault/Blanchot*, translated by Jeffrey Mehlman and Brian Massumi. New York: Zone Books, 1987.

———. "Nietzsche, Freud, Marx." In *Cahiers de Royaumont 6: Nietzsche*. Paris: Seuil, 1967, 183–92.

———. *The Order of Things*. New York: Vintage, Random House, 1973.

———. *L'Ordre du discours*. Paris: Gallimard, 1971.

———. *Power/Knowledge: Selected Interviews and Other Writings (1972–1977)*. Edited by Colin Gordon. Translated by Colin Gordon, Leo Marshall, John Mepham, and Kate Soper. New York: Pantheon, 1980.

———. *The Thought From Outside*. Translated by Brian Massumi. New York: Zone Books, 1987.

Fourny, Jean-François. "La Deuxième Vague: *Tel Quel* et le Surréalisme." *French Forum* 12, no. 2 (May 1987): 229–38.

———. "A Propos de la Querelle Breton-Bataille." *Revue d'Histoire Littéraire de la France* 84, no. 3 (May–June 1984): 432–38.

Furet, François. "Camarade Danton." *Le Nouvel Observateur*, 14–20 January 1983, 56–57.

———. "Les intellectuels français et le structuralisme." *Preuves* 192 (February 1967): 3–12.

———. *Penser la Révolution française*. Paris: Gallimard, 1978.

Gaul, Winfred. "Opinioni eretiche di un produttore d'arte," *Settanta* 3, no. 23 (April 1972): 20–22.

Genette, Gérard. *Figures I*. Paris: Seuil, 1966.

———. "Le Travail de Flaubert." *Tel Quel* 14 (Summer 1963): 51–57.

Goux, Jean-Joseph. "Marx et l'inscription du travail." In *Théorie d'ensemble*. Collection Tel Quel. Paris: Seuil, 1968.

Grisoni, Dominique. "Années soixante: La Critique des philosophes." *Magazine Littéraire* 192 (February 1983): 43–44.

Guérin, Jeanyves, ed. *Camus et la politique*. Paris: L'Harmattan, 1986.

Guyotat, Pierre. *Littérature interdite*. Paris: Gallimard, 1972.

Hallier, Jean-Edern. *La Cause des peuples*. Paris: Seuil, 1972.

Hamon, Philippe. "La lente percée des formalistes-structuralistes." *Magazine Littéraire* 192 (February 1983): 38–40.

Heath, Stephen. *The Nouveau Roman: A Study in the Practice of Writing*. Philadelphia: Temple University Press, 1972.

Hefner, Robert. "The *Tel Quel* Ideology: Material Practice upon Material Practice." *Sub-Stance* 8 (Winter 1974): 127–38.

Henric, Jacques. Personal interview. Paris, 24 June 1987.

————. "Pour une avant-garde révolutionnaire." *Tel Quel* 40 (Winter 1970): 58–66.

————. "Quand une avant-garde (littéraire) rencontre une autre avant-garde (politique) . . ." Unpublished paper (December 1986), 15 pp.

Hirsh, Arthur. *The French New Left: An Intellectual History from Sartre to Gorz.* Boston: South End, 1981.

Hocquenghem, Guy. "The New French Culture." *October* 19 (Winter 1981): 105–17.

Hollier, Denis. *The Politics of Prose.* Translated by Jeffrey Mehlman. Minneapolis: University of Minnesota Press, 1986.

————. "Le savoir formel." *Tel Quel* 34 (Summer 1968): 18–20.

Houdebine, Jean-Louis. "André Breton et la double ascendance du signe." *La Nouvelle Critique* 31 (February 1970): 43–51.

————. "Le 'Concept' d'écriture automatique: Sa signification et sa fonction dans le discours idéologique d'André Breton." Paper presented at the colloquium "Littérature et idéologies" (Cluny II, 2–4 April 1970). Published in *La Nouvelle Critique*, special issue 39a (1970): 178–85.

————. *Excès de langages.* Paris: Denoël, 1984.

————. Personal interview. Paris, 23 June 1987.

————. "Première approche de la notion de texte." In *Théorie d'Ensemble.* Collection Tel Quel. Paris: Seuil, 1968.

Hughes, H. Stuart. *The Obstructed Path: French Social Thought in the Years of Desperation, 1930–1960.* New York: Harper and Row, 1966, 1968.

Huguenin, Jean-René. "Aimer la vie, vivre l'amour!" *Réalités* 184 (May 1961): 56–64.

————. *Le Feu à sa vie.* Paris: Seuil, 1987.

————. *Journal.* Paris: Seuil, 1964.

Jakobson, Roman. "Du réalisme artistique." In *Théorie de la Littérature*, edited and translated by Tzvetan Todorov. Paris: Editions du Seuil, 1965.

————. "Glossolalie," *Tel Quel* 26 (Summer 1966): 3–9.

————. *Language in Literature*, edited by Krystyna Pomorska and Stephen Rudy. Cambridge: Harvard University Press, 1987.

Jean, Raymond. "Linguistique et Littérature." *Le Monde des Livres*, 27 April 1968, II.

————. "Trajet politique et romanesque." *Magazine Littéraire* 166 (November 1980): 12–14.

Johnson, Barbara. Translator's Introduction to *Dissemination*, by Jacques Derrida. Chicago: University of Chicago Press, 1981.

Judt, Tony. *Past Imperfect: French Intellectuals, 1945–1956.* Berkeley and Los Angeles: University of California Press, 1992.

Juin, Hubert. "L'étonnante aventure de la revue *Tel Quel.*" *Le Monde*, 30 January 1981, 19.

————. "Pourquoi une nouvelle revue?" *Les Lettres Françaises*, 18 February 1960, 4.

Julliard, Jacques. "La réussite gaullienne." In *Le Débat: Les Idées en France (1945–1988).* Paris: Gallimard, 1989.

Khodororovitch, Tatiana. "Dissident?" *Le Monde,* 17 November 1977, 21.

Knapp, Bettina. *French Novelists Speak Out.* Troy, N.Y.: Whitston, 1976.

Kramer, Jane. "A Reporter in Europe." *New Yorker,* 30 June 1980, 42ff.

Kristeva, Julia. "Des campus pleins d'étoiles." *Le Nouvel Observateur,* 1–8 January 1978, 58.

———. *Desire in Language.* Edited by Leon Roudiez. Translated by Thomas Gora, Alice Jardine, and Leon Roudiez. New York: Columbia University Press, 1980.

———. "The Ethics of Linguistics." In *Desire in Language,* edited by Leon Roudiez; trans. Thomas Gora, Alice Jardine, and Leon Roudiez. New York: Columbia University Press, 1980.

———. "An Interview with Julia Kristeva: Cultural Strangeness and the Subject in Crisis." *Discourse* 13, no. 1 (Fall–Winter 1990–91): 149–80.

———. "Julia Kristeva: Pouvoirs de l'horreur." *Tel Quel* 86 (Winter 1980): 50–53.

———. *The Kristeva Reader.* Edited by Toril Moi. New York: Columbia University Press, 1986.

———. *Language: The Unknown.* Translated by Anne Menke. New York: Columbia University Press, 1989.

———. "Linguistique et sémiologie aujourd'hui en U.R.S.S.," *Tel Quel* 35 (Autumn 1968): 3–8.

———. "Littérature, sémiotique, marxisme." *La Nouvelle Critique* 38 (November 1970): 28–35.

———. "My Memory's Hyperbole." In *The Female Autograph,* edited by Domna Stanton and Jeanine Parisier Plottel. New York: New York Literary Forum, 1984.

———. "The Pain of Sorrow in the Modern World: The Works of Marguerite Duras." *PMLA* 102, no. 2 (March 1987): 138–52.

———. Personal interview. Paris, 15 February 1978.

———. *Polylogue.* Paris: Seuil, 1977.

———. *The Powers of Horror.* Translated by Leon Roudiez. New York: Columbia University Press, 1982.

———. "Problèmes de la structuration du texte." Paper presented at the colloquium "Linguistique et Littérature" (Colloque de Cluny, 16–17 April 1968). Published in *La Nouvelle Critique,* special issue (1968): 55–64.

———. *Revolution in Poetic Language.* Translated by Margaret Waller. New York: Columbia University Press, 1984.

———. "The Ruin of a Poetics." In *Russian Formalism,* edited by Stephen Bann and John E. Bowlt. New York: Harper and Row, 1973.

———. *Séméiotiké: Recherches pour une sémanalyse.* Paris: Seuil, 1969.

———. "Sujet dans le langage et pratique politique." *Tel Quel* 58 (Summer 1974): 22–27.

———. "Within the Microcosm of 'The Talking Cure.'" In *Interpreting Lacan,* edited by Joseph Smith and William Kerrigan. New Haven: Yale University Press, 1983.

Kritzman, Larry. "Those Oldies but Goodies: *Les Temps Modernes* Revisited." *L'Esprit Créateur* 29, no. 4 (Winter 1989): 97–103.

Lacan, Jacques. *Ecrits*. Paris: Seuil, 1966.

———. *Ecrits (A Selection)*. Translated by Alan Sheridan. New York: Norton, 1977.

———. *Le Séminaire*. In *Encore* 20. Edited by Jacques-Alain Miller. Paris: Seuil, 1975.

Lecourt, Dominique. *Dissidence ou révolution?* Paris: Maspero, 1978.

Leenhardt, Jacques. *Lecture politique du roman*. Paris: Minuit, 1973.

———. "Nouveau Roman et Société." In *Nouveau Roman: hier, aujourd'hui*, vol. 1, edited by Jean Ricardou and Françoise Van Rossum-Guyon. Paris: Union Générale d'Editions, 1972.

Lefebvre, Henri. *L'Idéologie structuraliste*. Paris: Seuil, 1971, 1975.

Lévy, Bernard-Henri. *Barbarism With a Human Face*. Translated by George Holoch. New York: Harper and Row, 1979.

———. *La Barbarie à visage humain*. Paris: Grasset/Livre de Poche, 1977, 1979.

———. "La preuve du pudding." *Tel Quel* 77 (Autumn 1978): 25–35.

———. *Questions de principe*. Paris: Denoël, 1983.

———. "Si Camus était vivant." *Le Point* 1091 (14–20 August 1993): 51–52.

Lyotard, Jean-François. "Foreword: A Success of Sartre's." In *The Poetics of Prose* by Denis Hollier. Translated by Jeffrey Mehlman. Minneapolis: University of Minnesota Press, 1986.

Macciocchi, Maria-Antonietta. *Après Marx, Avril*. Paris: Seuil, 1978.

———. "Le crime italien," *Tel Quel* 78 (Winter 1978): 96–101.

———. *Polemiche sulla Cina*. Milan: Feltinelli, 1972.

———. *Pour Gramsci*. Paris: Seuil, 1974, 1975.

———. "Réponse à 'La Nouvelle Critique': De la nouvelle critique ou des racines de la sinophobie occidentale." *Tel Quel* 48–49 (Spring 1972): 71–101.

Macherey, Pierre. *A quoi pense la littérature?* Paris: Presses Universitaires de France, 1990.

———. *Pour une théorie de la production littéraire*. Paris: Maspero, 1966, 1978.

Magny, Claude-Edmonde. *Histoire du roman français depuis 1918*. Paris: Editions du Seuil, 1950.

Marx, Karl. "Excerpt-Notes of 1844." In *Writings of the Young Marx on Philosophy and Society*, edited and translated by Lloyd Easton and Kurt Guddat. Garden City, N.Y.: Anchor Books, 1967.

Marx-Scouras, Danielle. "Culture and Politics: The *Politecnico* Experience." *The Minnesota Review* 26 (Spring 1986): 83–98.

Matignon, Renaud. "Flaubert et la sensibilité moderne." *Tel Quel* 1 (Spring 1960): 83–89.

Mauriac, François. *Bloc-Notes*. Paris: Flammarion, 1958.

———. "Une goutte de la vague." *L'Express* 338 (12 December 1957): 36.

Mehlman, Jeffrey, and Brian Massumi, trans. *Foucault/Blanchot*. New York: Zone Books, 1987. (Contains complete texts of Michel Foucault, *Maurice Blanchot: The Thought from Outside*; and Maurice Blanchot, *Michel Foucault as I Remember Him*.)

Merleau-Ponty, Maurice. "La guerre a eu lieu." *Les Temps Modernes* 1 (1 October 1945): 48–66.

———. *Signs*. Translated by Richard McCleary. Evanston: Northwestern University Press, 1964.

Meschonnic, Henric. *Pour la poétique*. Vol. 2. Paris: Gallimard, 1973.

Michelson, Annette. "The Agony of the French Left." *October* 6 (Fall 1978): 18–23.

Morin, Edgar. "Le symbole d'une errance." *Libération*, special issue (1980): 37.

Nadeau, Maurice. *Histoire du surréalisme*. Paris: Seuil, 1964, 1970.

La Nouvelle Critique. "Tel Quel nous répond." *La Nouvelle Critique* 8–9 (1967): 50–54.

Oborne, Michaël West. "Les Etats-Unis: Pays de Mission?" Unpublished paper (1978), 7 pp.

Paulhan, Jean, and Francis Ponge. *Correspondance II (1946–1968)*. Paris: Gallimard, 1986.

Peytard, Jean. "Rapports et interférences de la linguistique et de la littérature." Paper presented at the colloquium "Linguistique et Littérature" (Colloque de Cluny, 16–17 April 1968). Published in *La Nouvelle Critique*, special issue (1968): 29–34.

Picard, Raymond. "M. Barthes et la 'critique universitaire.'" *Le Monde*, 14 March 1964, 12.

———. *Nouvelle Critique ou nouvelle imposture?* Paris: Pauvert, 1965.

Pingaud, Bernard. "Où va 'Tel Quel?'" *La Quinzaine Littéraire* 42 (1–15 January 1968): 8–9.

———. "Sartre La Littérature et les Autres." *Le Matin*, special no. (1980): 29.

Pintor, Giaime. *Il sangue d'Europa*. Edited by Valentino Gerratana. Turin: Einaudi, 1966.

Pleynet, Marcelin. *Art et littérature*. Paris: Editions du Seuil, 1977.

———. "La pensée contraire." *Tel Quel* 17 (Spring 1964): 55–68.

———. Personal interview. Paris, 15 June 1987.

———. "La poésie doit avoir pour but . . ." In *Théorie d'ensemble*. Collection Tel Quel. Paris: Seuil, 1968.

———. *Transculture*. Paris: Union Générale d'Editions, 1979.

Pomorska, Krystyna. *Russian Theory and Its Poetic Ambiance*. The Hague: Mouton, 1968.

Ponge, Francis. *Entretiens de Francis Ponge avec Philippe Sollers*. Paris: Gallimard, 1967, 1970.

Prévost, Jean. "*L'Humanité*, 19-9-1969: sur 'le camarade Mallarmé.'" *Tel Quel* 39 (Autumn 1969): 101–2.

Quaranta, Guido. "Quell'eretica di Maria." *Panorama*, 16 August 1977, 38.

Revel, Judith. "Histoire d'une disparition." *Le Débat* 79 (March–April 1994): 82–90.

Ricardou, Jean. "Nouveau Roman: Un entretien de Jean Thibaudeau avec Jean Ricardou." *La Nouvelle Critique* 60 (January 1973): 62–70.

———. *Problèmes du nouveau roman*. Paris: Seuil, 1967.

Rieffel, Rémy. "L'empreinte de la guerre d'Algérie." In *La Guerre d'Algérie et les intellectuels français*, edited by Jean-Pierre Rioux and Jean-François Sirinelli. Paris: Editions Complexe, 1991.

Rioux, Jean-Pierre, and Jean-François Sirinelli. *La Guerre d'Algérie et les intellectuels français*. Paris: Editions Complexe, 1991.

Ristat, Jean. *Qui sont les contemporains*. Paris: Gallimard, 1975.

Riva, Valerio. "Tutto finisce in Gulag." *L'Espresso*, 19 June 1977, 68–74.

Robbe-Grillet, Alain. "Alain Robbe-Grillet: géomètre du temps." *Arts* 20–26 March 1953, 5.

———. *For a New Novel*. Translated by Richard Howard. New York: Grove, 1965.

———. *Ghosts in the Mirror*. Translated by Jo Levy. London: John Calder, 1988.

———. Interview. *Le Monde*, 13 May 1961, 9.

———. *Last Year at Marienbad*. Translated by Richard Howard. New York: Grove, 1962.

———. "La littérature, aujourd'hui—VI." *Tel Quel* 14 (Summer 1963): 39–45.

———. *Le Miroir qui revient*. Paris: Minuit, 1984.

Robitaille, Louis-Bertrand. "'Tel Quel,' ou comment peut-on être Chinois?" *La Presse*, 5 April 1975, D2.

Rossi, Aldo. "La ragione letteraria delle ultime leve francesi, 'Tel Quel.'" *Paragone* 132 (December 1960): 125–36.

Rotman, Patrick. "Une seule solution la révolution" (Rotman and Hervé Hamon interviewed by Chantal De Rudder). *Le Nouvel Observateur*, 6–12 March 1987, 44–47.

Rottenberg, Pierre. "Breton et le spiritualisme de Valéry." Paper presented at the colloquium "Littérature et idéologies" (Colloque de Cluny II, 2–4 April 1970). Published in *La Nouvelle Critique*, special issue 39a (1970): 256–59.

Roudiez, Leon. *French Fiction Today*. New Brunswick: Rutgers University Press, 1972.

———. Introduction to *Desire in Language*, by Julia Kristeva. Edited by Leon Roudiez. New York: Columbia University Press, 1980.

———. "With and Beyond Literary Structuralism." *Books Abroad* (Spring 1975): 204–12.

Roudinesco, Elisabeth. *Jacques Lacan & Co. (A History of Psychoanalysis in France, 1925–1985)*. Translated by Jeffrey Mehlman. Chicago: University of Chicago Press, 1990.

———. "A propos du 'concept' de l'écriture. Lecture de Jacques Derrida." Paper presented at the colloquium "Littérature et idéologies" (Colloque de Cluny II, 2–4 April 1970). Published in *La Nouvelle Critique*, special issue 39a (1970): 219–30.

Rousset, David. "Le drame de l'affrontement politique." *Le Matin*, special issue (1980): 32.

———. "L'Histoire d'une rupture." *Libération*, special issue (1980): 39.

Saporta, Sol. "The Application of Linguistics to the Study of Poetic Language." In *Style in Language*, edited by Thomas A. Sebeok. Cambridge: M.I.T. Press, 1960.

Sarraute, Natalie. *L'Ere du soupçon*. Paris: Gallimard, 1956, 1972.

Sartre, Jean-Paul. *Between Existentialism and Marxism*. Translated by John Mathews. New York: Pantheon, 1974.

———. Preface to *The Wretched of the Earth*, by Frantz Fanon. Translated by Constance Farrington. New York: Grove, 1963.

———. "Présentation." *Les Temps Modernes* 1 (October 1945): 2–21.

———. "Questions de méthode." In *Critique de la raison dialectique*. Vol. 1. Paris: Gallimard, 1960.

———. "Replies to Structuralism: An Interview with Jean-Paul Sartre." *Telos* 9 (Fall 1971): 110–15.

———. *Situations, V.* Paris: Gallimard, 1964.

———. *What is Literature?* Translated by Bernard Frechtman. New York: Philosophical Library, 1949.

———. *The Words.* Translated by Bernard Frechtman. New York: George Braziller, 1964.

Sartre, Jean-Paul, Bernard Pingaud, and Dionys Mascolo. *Du rôle de l'intellectuel dans le mouvement révolutionnaire.* Paris: Eric Losfeld, 1971.

Scalia, Gianni. "L'esempio del Politecnico." *Letterature moderne* 10, no. 5 (1960): 638–44.

Scarpetta, Guy. "Brecht et la Chine." Paper presented at the colloquium "Littérature et idéologies" (Cluny II, 2–4 April 1970). Published in *La Nouvelle Critique*, special issue 39a (1970): 231–36.

———. *Eloge du cosmopolitisme.* Paris: Grasset, 1981.

———. "Dissidence de l'inconscient et pouvoirs." *Art Press International* 17 (April 1978): 24.

———. "Dissidence et littérature." *Tel Quel* 76 (Summer 1978): 46–49.

———. *L'Impureté.* Paris: Grasset, 1985.

———. Personal interview. Paris, 23 June 1987.

Schalk, David. *The Spectrum of Political Engagement.* Princeton: Princeton University Press, 1979.

Sichère, Bernard. "L'Autre Histoire: A partir de Michel Foucault." *Tel Quel* 86 (Winter 1980): 71–95.

———. "Michel Foucault singulier." *L'Infini* 11 (Summer 1985): 111–27.

Simonin, Anne. "Les Editions de Minuit et les Editions du Seuil." In *La Guerre d'Algérie et les intellectuels français*, edited by Jean-Pierre Rioux and Jean-François Sirinelli. Paris: Editions Complexe, 1991.

Simonin, Anne, and Hélène Clastres. "Une chronologie." *Le Débat: Les Idées en France (1945–1988).* Paris: Gallimard, 1989.

Siniavsky, Andrei. "L'art est supérieur à la réalité." *Tel Quel* 76 (Summer 1978): 56–60.

Sirinelli, Jean-François. *Intellectuels et passions françaises: Manifestes et pétitions au XXe siècle.* Paris: Fayard, 1990.

———. "Les intellectuels français en guerre d'Algérie." In *La Guerre d'Algérie et les intellectuels français*, edited by Jean-Pierre Rioux and Jean-François Sirinelli. Paris: Editions Complexe, 1991.

Sollers, Philippe. "A. Robbe-Grillet: Pour un nouveau roman." *Tel Quel* 18 (Summer 1964): 93–94.

———. "L'Art et les Révolutions: le grand malentendu." Sixth International Colloquium on Twentieth Century French Studies ("Revolutions, 1889–1989"), Columbia University, New York, 30 March 1989.

———. *Carnet de nuit*. Paris: Plon, 1989.

———. "Crise de l'avant-garde?" *Art Press International* 16 (March 1978): 6.

———. "De *Tel Quel* à *L'Infini*." *Autrement* 69 (April 1985): 8.

———. "Ebranler le système." *Magazine Littéraire* 65 (June 1972): 10–17.

———. "Eco perché vado d'accordo con Ionesco." *La Repubblica*, 22 June 1978, 14.

———. "Editorial." *L'Infini* 1 (Winter 1983): 3–6.

———. *L'Ecriture et l'expérience des limites*. Paris: Seuil/Points, 1971.

———. "Ecriture et révolution" (interview with Jacques Henric). In *Théorie d'Ensemble*. Collection Tel Quel. Paris: Seuil, 1968.

———. "L'Ecriture fonction de transformation sociale." In *Théorie d'Ensemble*. Collection Tel Quel. Paris: Seuil, 1968.

———. "L'expérience 'Tel Quel.'" *Les Lettres Françaises* (23 January 1964): 5.

———. "Un fantasme de Sartre." *Tel Quel* 28 (Winter 1967): 84–86.

———. "Folie: Mère-Ecran." *Tel Quel* 69 (Spring 1977): 97–102.

———. *Francis Ponge*. Paris: Seghers, 1963.

———. "Gauche, droite . . ." In *La Droite aujourd'hui*, edited by Jean-Pierre Apparu. Paris: Albin Michel, 1979.

———. "La grande méthode." *Tel Quel* 34 (Summer 1968): 21–27.

———. "Le G.S.I." *Tel Quel* 86 (Winter 1980): 10–17.

———. "*L'Humanité*, 19-9-1969: 'camarade' et camarade." *Tel Quel* 39 (Autumn 1969): 100–101.

———. *L'Intermédiaire*. Paris: Seuil, 1963.

———. "Lettre sur l'individualité littéraire." *Magazine Littéraire* 264 (April 1989): 33–35.

———. "Littérature: Le Retour des précieux." *Le Nouvel Observateur* 525 (2–8 December 1974): 73.

———. "Logicus Solus." *Tel Quel* 14 (Summer 1963): 46–50.

———. *Logiques*. Paris: Seuil, 1968.

———. "La lutte idéologique dans l'écriture de l'avant-garde." Paper presented at the colloquium "Littérature et idéologies" (Colloque de Cluny II, 2–4 April 1970). Published in *La Nouvelle Critique* special issue 39a (1970): 74–78.

———. "Nous sommes tous des intellectuels italiens." *Tel Quel* 78 (Winter 1978): 94–96.

———. "Nous vivons une période de régression." *Les Nouvelles Littéraires*, 28 October 1976, 19.

———. "On n'a encore rien vu." *Tel Quel* 85 (Autumn 1980): 9–31.

———. "Où va le roman?" *Le Figaro littéraire*, 22 September 1962, 3.

———. Personal interview. Paris, 5 July 1979.

———. "Philippe Sollers décrit son action." In *Qui sont les contemporains*, edited by Jean Ristat. Paris: Gallimard, 1975.

———. "Picard, cheval de bataille." *Tel Quel* 24 (Winter 1966): 92.

———. "Pourquoi j'ai été chinois." *Tel Quel* 88 (Summer 1981): 11–30.

———. "Préface." In *Théorie d'Ensemble*. Collection Tel Quel. Paris: Seuil, 1968, 1980.

————. "Programme." *Tel Quel* 31 (Autumn 1967): 3–7.

————. "Le réflexe de réduction." In *Théorie d'Ensemble*. Collection Tel Quel. Paris: Seuil, 1968.

————. "Réponses." *Tel Quel* 43 (Autumn 1970): 71–76.

————. "Sept propositions sur Robbe-Grillet," *Tel Quel* 2 (Summer 1960): 49–53.

————. "A Step on the Moon." *Times Literary Supplement*, 25 September 1969, 1085–87.

————. *Théorie des exceptions*. Paris: Gallimard/Folio, 1986.

————. "Thèses générales." *Tel Quel* 44 (Winter 1971): 96–98.

————. "Traité du style." *Le Nouvel Observateur*, 1 January 1983, 50–52.

————. "Untitled Preface." *Le Magazine Littéraire* 215 (February 1985): 15.

————. *Vision à New York*. Paris: Grasset, 1981.

————. "Voir ce qui est, et en jouir." *Art Press International* 102 (April 1986): 44–45.

————. *Writing and the Experience of Limits*. Translated by Philip Barnard and David Hayman. New York: Columbia University Press, 1983.

Sollers, Philippe, and Jean Thibaudeau. "André Breton à la radio." *Tel Quel* 13 (Spring 1963): 61–63.

Suleiman, Susan. "As Is." In *A New History of French Literature*, edited by Denis Hollier. Cambridge: Harvard University Press, 1989.

Tel Quel. "Appel au vote communiste de Sanguineti." *Tel Quel* 33 (Spring 1968): 95.

————. "Chronologie." *Tel Quel* 47 (Autumn 1971): 142–43.

————. "Débat sur la poésie" ("Une littérature nouvelle?" Décade de Cerisy, September 1963). *Tel Quel* 17 (Spring 1964): 69–82.

————. "Débat sur le roman" ("Une littérature nouvelle?" Décade de Cerisy, September 1963). *Tel Quel* 17 (Spring 1964): 12–54.

————. "Déclaration." *Tel Quel* 1 (Spring 1960): 3–4.

————. "Le dogmatisme à la rescousse du révisionnisme." *Tel Quel* 48–49 (Spring 1972): 175–90.

————. "Enquête: Pensez-vous avoir un don d'écrivain?" *Tel Quel* 1 (Spring 1960): 39–43.

————. "Enquête sur la critique," *Tel Quel* 14 (Summer 1963): 68–91.

————. "Groupe d'études théoriques de *Tel Quel* année 1968–1969." *Tel Quel* 38 (Summer 1969): 103.

————. "Mai 1968." *Tel Quel* 34 (Summer 1968): 94–95.

————. "Mise au point." *Tel Quel* 16 (Winter 1964): 95.

————. "Positions du mouvement de Juin 71." *Tel Quel* 47 (Autumn 1971): 135–41.

————. "Remarques." *Tel Quel* 37 (Spring 1969): 103.

————. "Réponses à la 'Nouvelle Critique.'" In *Théorie d'Ensemble*. Collection Tel Quel. Paris: Seuil, 1968.

————. "La Révolution ici maintenant." *Tel Quel* 34 (Summer 1968): 3–4.

————. "Tel Quel." *Tel Quel* 40 (Winter 1970): 100–104.

————. "Tel Quel aujourd'hui." *France Nouvelle* 1128 (31 May 1967): 21–22.

————. *Théorie d'ensemble*. Collection Tel Quel. Paris: Seuil, 1968.

————. "Vérité d'une marchandise: le bluff 'Change.'" *Tel Quel* 43 (Autumn 1970): 77–93.

Teodori, Massimo. *Storia delle nuove sinistre in Europa (1956–1976)*. Bologna: Il Mulino, 1976.

Thibaud, Paul. "Texte de travail: À propos des revues, à propos de l'intelligentsia, à propos de cette revue." *Esprit* 3 (March 1977): 519–28.

Thibaudeau, Jean. *Mes Années "Tel Quel."* Paris: Editions Ecriture, 1994.

———. Personal interview. Paris, 19 May 1979.

Thody, Philip. *Roland Barthes*. Chicago: University of Chicago Press, 1977.

Todorov, Tzvetan. "Formalistes et futuristes." *Tel Quel* 35 (Autumn 1968): 42–45.

———. Personal interview. Paris, 19 June 1987.

———, ed. and trans. *Théorie de la Littérature*. Paris: Editions du Seuil, 1965.

Valente, Mario. *Ideologia e potere: da "Il Politecnico" a "Contropiano."* Turin: Edizioni radiotelevisione italiana, 1978.

Valli, Bernardo. "Tutti uniti in nome del Ciel." *La Repubblica*, 22 June 1978, 14.

Verdès-Leroux, Jeannine. *Le Réveil des Somnambules: le Parti communiste, les intellectuels et la culture, 1956–1985*. Paris: Fayard, 1987.

Vergote, Antoine. Foreword to *Jacques Lacan*, by Anika Lemaire. Translated by David Macey. Boston: Routledge and Kegan Paul, 1977.

Viansson-Ponté, Jacques, ed. *Génération perdue*. Paris: Robert Laffont, 1977.

Vigorelli, Giancarlo. "Il 'Telquellismo' francese." *L'Europa Letteraria* 1, no. 3 (June 1960): 125–27.

Vittorini, Elio. "Una nuova cultura." *Il Politecnico* 1 (29 September 1945): 1.

———. "Politica e cultura: lettera a Togliatti." *Il Politecnico* 35 (January–March 1947): 2–5, 105–6.

Wilkinson, James. *The Intellectual Resistance in Europe*. Cambridge: Harvard University Press, 1981.

Williams, Raymond. *Marxism and Literature*. Oxford: Oxford University Press, 1977.

Winock, Michel. *Chronique des années soixante*. Paris: Seuil, 1987.

Yannakakis, Ilios. "Concilier Sartre et la dissidence." *Libération*, special issue (1980): 39.

INDEX